THE MYSTERY OF THE
LONE
WOLF
KILLER

ANDERS BEHRING BREIVIK AND THE
THREAT OF TERROR IN PLAIN SIGHT

UNNI TURRETTINI

FOREWORD BY KATHLEEN M. PUCKETT, PH.D.

PEGASUS CRIME
NEW YORK LONDON

To the victims of the July 22, 2011 massacre.

∞

THE MYSTERY OF THE LONE WOLF KILLER

Pegasus Crime is an Imprint of
Pegasus Books LLC
80 Broad Street, 5th Floor
New York, NY 10004

Copyright © 2015 by Unni Turrettini

First Pegasus Books cloth edition November 2015

Interior design by Maria Fernandez

Library of Congress Cataloging-in-Publication Data is available.

ISBN: 978-1-60598-910-5

10 9 8 7 6 5 4 3 2 1

Printed in the United States of America
Distributed by W. W. Norton & Company

"A child whose integrity is harmed does not stop loving his parents; he stops loving himself."

—JESPER JUUL

FOREWORD

In September 2001, I was finishing my last assignment as a Special Agent in the FBI. A high-ranking executive in the Counterterrorism Division, Terry D. Turchie, had asked me to conduct a behavioral study of domestic "lone wolf" terrorists. I had earned a Ph.D. in Clinical Psychology during my FBI career, and the Bureau needed to know if social science research could contribute to the identification of lone wolves before they appeared— seemingly out of nowhere—to stage their devastating attacks.

Theodore Kaczynski, the "Unabomber," had single-handedly carried on a bombing campaign for eighteen years before we finally found him in a remote cabin in the Montana wilderness. Timothy McVeigh acted alone in placing a vehicle loaded with explosives outside the Federal Building in Oklahoma City. And Eric Robert Rudolph, the bomber who targeted the Olympic Games in Atlanta, spent five years hiding out in the North Carolina forests without talking to another living soul until his arrest in 2003 for his solitary attack on a birth-control facility in Birmingham, Alabama, that killed a policeman and maimed a nurse.

What made them tick, these American lone wolves who were overlooked by everyone who might have noticed them? They all ended up on "Bomber's

Row" in the federal maximum-security prison in Florence, Colorado, for the rest of their lives. Each of them had acted alone, and none of them had a criminal background. They had not been members of any extremist group—at least not for long, but they were all firm believers in extremist ideologies, and they all killed horrifically in their service.

Kaczynski believed that modern industry and technology were destroying the human race. McVeigh considered himself a patriot but believed that the U.S. government needed to be overthrown. Rudolph believed that support from the "godless" bureaucrats in Washington for abortion and gay rights was destroying America.

As I formed my conclusions, the international terrorist attacks of 9/11 occurred. My report was noted and shelved. At the time, the imminent danger from a vast al Qaeda terrorist network trumped any other concern, and my findings about what makes lone wolf terrorists tick were largely ignored by those in law enforcement charged with what was regarded as a larger international "war on terror."

By 2008, Terry and I observed in our first book that the merging of lone wolf terrorism with international terrorist ideology would endanger communities all over the world with mysterious attacks by their own citizens that seemed to come out of nowhere.

In 2011, when Anders Behring Breivik stunned Norway and the world by savagely killing seventy-seven of his fellow Norwegians—most of them teens—in a sequential bombing and mass shooting, I watched the news coverage with a kind of weary despair. Here was another lone wolf, determined to make his mark on the world. Terry and I were interviewed by media in the U.S. as well as Norway, and we provided answers to the same questions we'd been asked for years.

Yes, it was likely that Breivik was the latest incarnation of the lone wolf terrorist. No, he was most certainly not likely to be a member of any terrorist group. Yes, his objective was to call attention to his own version of an extremist ideology. No, he likely had not targeted any specific individuals and did not know any of his victims. No, he was unlikely to have any history of violent criminal offenses, and law-enforcement and counterterrorism officials had not known of his intent to kill his fellow citizens. Until July 22, 2011, his preparation and planning for his attacks had been carefully hidden by the fact that he was isolated and had no close associates of any sort. And so he appeared to have come out of nowhere, alone, to wage war on his government by killing his fellow citizens.

Billions of dollars have been spent in the "war on terror," on weapons, training, intelligence operations, and task forces. In the case of lone wolves, however, Terry and I had said for years that the key to recognizing lone wolves before they act is citizen awareness and involvement. It was not in a criminal underworld or a prison—or in a terrorist group—that lone wolves are formed and primed to attack, and so they are virtually invisible to law enforcement. Their own communities are where they grow into lone wolves.

Unni Turrettini contacted me through her editor in June 2013. Born in Norway and living in Switzerland, she trained as a lawyer and had been transfixed by the depredations of Anders Breivik since the attacks two summers before. How could this have happened in her peaceful homeland? She wanted to know how and why, and she conducted her own investigation to find out.

Unni has a unique perspective on the country she left to conduct her life with her family elsewhere. Prosperous and peaceful as they appear to the rest of the world, Unni regards her former countrymen as "sleepwalking" through life. From an early age, she says, Norwegians are discouraged from standing out in a crowd and asserting their individuality.

When she began interviews and research for this book, Unni intended to conduct a sociological study of the attacks of July 22, 2011. But there is a subset of psychology that focuses on the development of an individual within society: social psychology.

This expansive and keenly reasoned social-psychology study is a model of concerned citizen involvement in understanding and combating one of the most critical dilemmas of our age: the lone wolf terrorist.

Unni became fascinated with, and focused on, how Anders Breivik developed into a solitary warrior for his twisted cause within the context of Norwegian society. She and I had many discussions of exactly what makes a lone wolf tick and what makes him try over and over again to connect with other extremists who share his ideology but are distracted by the normal social world they inhabit.

Breivik and other lone wolves have no position in the social world. Because of a specific inability to develop meaningful relationships with other people, they are driven instead to intense relationships with extremist ideologies. Being human, they are hardwired to connect; a group was the primeval avenue of survival for a species, like humans, without fangs and claws. Being unsuccessful in connecting with other people would have earned a solitary individual a swift death early in human evolution.

Today, different strategies are possible. What do you connect to when you can't connect meaningfully to other people? In the industrialized Western world, you have a number of opportunities. If you're intelligent, you might connect to the world of art or one of the sciences. You might become a naturalist, most comfortable in the natural world and largely uninvolved with people. Many people prefer their own company to that of others, and a solitary life is their choice.

But what if it isn't your choice? What if, no matter how many opportunities exist for you in the world, you are utterly unable to have the connections you most crave?

Because you are unable to establish the kinds of social connections that preoccupy most human beings, you can't be satisfied by gathering with friends in a park, going on dates, marrying, and having children. And in the absence of such social distractions, you are free to develop grandiose plans to grab attention for yourself and your grand ideas. You are free to live in the basement of your mother's house, or on a remote farm, and make your preparations, unnoticed, as Breivik did.

Throughout history, thousands—if not millions—of violent criminals have placed or sent bombs, shot, or otherwise killed their victims. Many committed their crimes alone; however, there are two things I found in my study that differentiate the lone wolves from other solitary criminals. First, their crimes had to be big, at a societal level. Second, they were shaped and motivated by ideology. They didn't know their victims, and they weren't out for money or any personal gain outside the notoriety of their acts.

Lone wolves like Breivik need to matter in the world. They are repeatedly thwarted in this by the fact that no one recognizes their true genius. They have the answers to the issues that bedevil society, if only they were recognized. Very well, then. The world will be forced to recognize them.

Too bad that people have to die to make that happen. Nothing personal. As Timothy McVeigh said of the children he murdered in Oklahoma City, there is always collateral damage in accomplishing a goal.

Police and counterterrorism officials, limited in number, look primarily at extremist groups and the people who socialize in them. They miss the hidden development of lone wolves because they aren't in those groups.

The only way to uncover and intervene in the development of a lone wolf is to enlist the help of the community he comes from in recognizing the repeated attempts he makes to connect with those groups.

Unni Turrettini does a magnificent job of illustrating the evolution of Anders Breivik in the context of modern Norway, a world she knows is fertile ground for the development of a lone wolf terrorist. She recognizes what Norwegian authorities have preferred to ignore: that privilege and comfort in a society do not eliminate the likelihood of a terrorist blooming in its midst. She is adamant that viewing Breivik as an aberration or as insane only serves to reassure Norway that sleepwalking is the best way to proceed in life.

In doing so, she represents a level of citizen involvement unparalleled by anyone else in the examination of how and why Norway grew a lone wolf like Breivik, and what can be done to prevent the savagery lone wolves inflict on the population in any country.

Kathleen M. Puckett, Ph.D.
Hunting the American Terrorist—
The FBI's War on Homegrown Terror

INTRODUCTION

THE KILLINGS

*This is the big day you have been looking forward to for so long.
Equip yourself and arm up, for today you will become immortal. . . .*

—ANDERS BREIVIK MANIFESTO

189 MINUTES OF TERROR

This is my last day, he thinks as he wakes that morning. Eight A.M. He
needs to hurry. Convinced that he'll be killed, Anders Behring Breivik
struggles to send the e-mail manifesto he's compiled. Too many addresses
slow down his computer and make him late. That won't do. Last night,
he'd put the bomb in his minivan, which he parked a short walk from his
house. Fertilizer and fuel oil, like McVeigh's.

He's exhausted, and he doesn't want to die. For three months, he's been
taking anabolic steroids. He drinks a cocktail of ephedrine, caffeine, and

aspirin. The e-mail goes through. Now, from this manifesto, more than eight thousand people will know who he is. And soon, many more. By the time they read this, it will be over. And he may be dead.

168 VICTIMS

Today the world will know his power. Twenty-seven-year-old Timothy James McVeigh sees himself as a warrior and hero who must defend the Constitution. In the early morning of April 19, 1995, McVeigh drives into downtown Oklahoma City in a rented Ryder truck containing a lethal fertilizer bomb that he and his friend Terry Nichols have made. After arriving at the Alfred P. Murrah Federal Building, he parks in a handicapped zone, jumps out of the truck, and disappears into a maze of streets and alleys. At 9:02 A.M., the bomb demolishes a third of the building, killing a total of 168, including nineteen infants. More than five hundred are wounded. McVeigh, wearing earplugs, is so far away that he cannot hear the emergency sirens clearly. Near the site, his explosion is so powerful that it lifts pedestrians from the ground.

A 102-HOUR MANHUNT

Although Tamerlan Tsarnaev is on multiple U.S. and Russian watch lists prior to 2013, neither the FBI nor the CIA can justify investigating him further. Dzhokhar (Jahar), his brother, manages to fly under everyone's radar. On one occasion, Jahar does tell a friend that the September 11 attacks on the United States may have been justified; but, true to form in the case of lone wolf killers, the friend does not recall this statement until it is too late for Tamerlan, Jahar, or their victims.

On Patriots' Day, April 15, 2013, the annual Boston Marathon begins with sun, cheer, goodwill, and—thanks to two checks by officials—no signs of bombs. Few notice the two young men, one in a black baseball cap, the other in a white cap turned backward, as they round the corner from Gloucester Street onto Boylston Street at 2:38 P.M. Each carries a bulky backpack. They stride toward the finish line, where, just a short time earlier, the governor has hugged race organizers.

No one is sure when Tamerlan and Jahar put down their bags, but they do. They then pause several minutes and leave the scene, moving calmly.

Then, at 2:49 P.M., about two hours after the winner crosses the finish line, and with more than 5,700 runners yet to finish, the worst happens on Boylston Street near Copley Square: about 200 yards from the finish line, two bombs detonate.

The blasts blow out windows on adjacent buildings but do not cause any structural damage. Some runners continue crossing the line until eight minutes after the explosions. The bombings kill three people—including an eight-year-old boy—and reportedly injure as many as 264 others, many losing limbs.

Shortly later, the FBI announces that the Tsarnaev brothers are suspects in the bombings and releases images of them. As the manhunt ensues, the brothers kill an MIT police officer, carjack an SUV, and engage in a shootout with the police in the Boston suburb of Watertown, during which Tamerlan is killed and an MBTA police officer is critically injured. Jahar Tsarnaev, although injured, escapes.

Three mass killings. Four killers who could have been detected before they struck but who were free to go about planning and carrying out their crimes—because they left no paper trail. These are the lone wolf killers, who operate outside of any particular affiliation with a terrorist group, and who must be identified before they strike again. Anders Breivik is the key to finding them.

WHY BREIVIK MATTERS

Anders Breivik is the only one of these lone wolves who is still alive and willing to discuss his crimes. Although Theodore Kaczynski entered into a plea bargain, and McVeigh and Jahar, the surviving Tsarnaev brother, pleaded not guilty, Breivik made his trial a verbal manifesto, an explanation of why he did what he did.

Understanding how this man in a presumably peaceful country committed crimes as terrifying as other lone wolves in the United States and other countries is the only way law enforcement can figure out how to prevent the next massacre. Contrary to a common belief, Breivik is not a Scandinavian nut case or freak that will never again reproduce itself. Few realize that his story is just like, or extremely similar to, those of the American mass murderers. Until now, FBI experts and psychologists have been guessing and speculating as to these killers' profiles. Breivik's case finally sheds the necessary light on a devastating problem, not only in the United States but also in the rest of the world.

COLLATERAL DAMAGE

When investigators finally gained access to the boat where Jahar was hiding, they discovered a jihadist rant on its walls. In it, according to a thirty-count indictment handed down in late June 2013, Jahar appeared to take responsibility for the bombing, although he insisted that he did not like killing innocent people. But "the U.S. government is killing our innocent civilians," he wrote, presumably referring to Muslims in Iraq and Afghanistan. "I can't stand to see such evil go unpunished.... We Muslims are one body, you hurt one, you hurt us all." With this, he echoed the cliché sentiment of Islamic militants. Then, according to *Rolling Stone*, he wrote a final "Fuck America."

In the note in the boat, he also wrote that he didn't mourn the death of his brother, that Tamerlan was a martyr in paradise now, and that he expected to follow his brother there soon. His victims were "collateral damage," he wrote, a statement eerily similar to the way McVeigh and Breivik described their victims.

HOMEGROWN TERRORISM

Inside the building McVeigh had destroyed, many of those who were not out for coffee or other tasks were lost in the explosion (an estimated 168 out of 646). Demolition was even more horrible in the children's day-care center directly above the bomb. Floors crushed those beneath them and set up a chain reaction of destruction. Rescue workers rushed to the scene almost immediately, employing listening devices in search of the living. Professionals and volunteers clawed through the rubble to help dig out the wounded and remove the dead.

One twenty-year-old woman lay bleeding in a foot of water. She had lost her mother and her two children, and for five hours her leg had been pinned under a pile of cement. The massive pile could not be shifted, so the rescue team's only hope of getting her out alive was to amputate her leg without anesthetic, which could send her into a fatal coma. Following the operation, she was finally dragged from the ruins and hospitalized, her life and body shattered.

With McVeigh's acts of violence, terrorism took on a new face—not the crazy killer on every police record. Not the predictable ones. Writing in a crime blog, Ted Ottley (www.crimelibrary.com) summarized the growing danger McVeigh's crimes represented: "Homegrown terrorism had arrived with a vengeance, and the terrorist was the kid next door. And he was cruising away from the carnage—down Interstate 35."

Homegrown terrorism has spread out its roots in these days when we don't know when and where the next killer will strike—only that he will. That day in Boston, the area had already been swept twice for bombs. The last sweep took place only one hour before the explosions. So relaxed was the area that anyone, including the killers, could freely carry bags in and out.

Disbelief spread with the news of the bombing. "I felt like a bullet went through my heart," Jahar's old wrestling coach, Peter Payack, told *Rolling Stone* magazine about Jahar. "To think that a kid we mentored and loved like a son could have been responsible for all this death. It was beyond shocking. It was like an alternative reality." And later, "There are kids we don't catch who just fall through the cracks, but this guy was seamless, like a billiard ball. No cracks at all."

But there were cracks. They just weren't visible. Beneath the surface, Jahar was tormented by his family's broken dreams. And as was the case with other lone wolf killers, his torment turned to deadly fury, searching for an outlet and a focus. The eventual cause Jahar found became radical Islam.

Killing for a cause was McVeigh's mantra as well. The day of the bombing, he wore what was said to be his favorite T-shirt. On the front was a picture of Abraham Lincoln and the words "*sic semper tyrannis*," which is what John Wilkes Booth was said to have shouted either before, as, or right after he shot Lincoln. *Thus ever to tyrants.* The entire statement is "Thus always I eradicate tyrants' lives."

On the back of the T-shirt, a tree with blood dripping from the branches illustrated the statement "The tree of liberty must be refreshed from time to time with the blood of patriots and tyrants." This quote, which originated in a letter Thomas Jefferson wrote to William Smith in 1787 in reference to an uprising in Massachusetts after the American Revolution, is frequently taken out of context. The rest of the letter suggests that we must accept a certain amount of violence to keep freedom free, but it is not intended to incite violence. Both McVeigh and Breivik, however, used that quote to explain their acts. Jefferson could never have imagined that his eloquent statement would be used to justify the bloodshed in Oklahoma and Norway.

KILLING THE GOVERNMENT

When I heard the news in the afternoon on July 22, 2011, I was driving up to our mountain chalet in Switzerland, with my young son and daughter in the car. A friend called and told me about the killings, her voice breathless and panicked on the phone. I immediately turned on the radio. A bomb at the government building. The gunning down of young people on an island, many of whom jumped into the icy water only to drown or be shot.

Paralyzed with shock and disbelief, I felt an even greater blow when I learned that the terrorist was Norwegian, one of us. *How could something like this happen in my native country?*

Soon, the world knew the details. Yet no one has answered the question I asked myself that day.

That summer afternoon in southern Norway was rainy and cold. Until that day, the only thing in the country that wasn't predictable was the weather. Anders Breivik had dressed for it in the uniform of a private security guard, a move to distract attention from himself. He pulled into the parking lot in front of the Justice Department building, despite the no-entry sign. Having been raised there, Breivik knew that people in Norwegian society are basically sleepwalking, the citizens going about their daily lives as if in a daze. No one would be focused on guarding the gate. He would have had a more difficult time carrying out his plans in most other countries, where security is always a cause for focus and diligence. But here, where even the king and the prime minister are accessible to the public, no one responded fast enough to remove the van that should not have been there.

The parking spot Breivik wanted was occupied. He had planned to place his white Volkswagen Crafter so that the explosion would destroy the support structure and collapse the whole building as McVeigh's bomb had done in Oklahoma City. Instead, frustrated, he parked in the next space over.

Due to the public holidays, the offices weren't well guarded. A silver-gray Fiat waited at Hammersborg Square, and Breivik hurried in its direction, away from what he knew would happen next.

At 3:25 P.M., the Volkswagen exploded near the offices of the prime minister. Chaos ensued. Phone lines were jammed. Norway was not used to dealing with a disaster of this magnitude. Witnesses managed to get the license plate number of the Fiat; but in the confusion, the police couldn't act fast enough, and Breivik was able to flee the city.

News of the bombing spread to the tiny island of Utøya, which is only about 600 yards into Tyrifjorden Lake, about twenty-five miles northwest of Oslo, where participants of the Labor Party's Youth League summer camp annually come together in the camp's main house. The island is only 26 acres in size, 1600 yards in circumference.

At approximately 4:55 P.M., Breivik arrived at the landing, where he boarded the ferry to his next target—Utøya and the young people gathered there. Still in uniform, wearing an ID card around his neck, and carrying a handgun and rifle, he introduced himself to his victims as Martin Nilsen from the Police Intelligence Service and asked if they would help him carry his large black suitcase onto the ferry. Trusting of the police and unaware that the suitcase was full of weapons and ammunition, they agreed.

At 5:18 P.M., Breivik arrived at Utøya. Four minutes later, he began shooting.

∞

When I finally went to sleep that Friday night, ten people were reported dead on Utøya, and no number of victims had yet been confirmed from the bombing in Oslo. When I awoke the next morning and immediately turned on the news, eighty-four people were reported dead. Chaos and disorganization hindered the job of identifying victims. By Monday, it was confirmed that seventy-seven people had died, and hundreds more, most of them teenagers, had been injured. The entire country was in mourning; in my home in Switzerland, so was I.

Although no one knew it then, Breivik would inspire copycat killers, including Adam Lanza, the Connecticut school gunman, who imitated him in much the same way Breivik had borrowed from Kaczynski and McVeigh. But in the wake of the aftermath, before the copycats, Breivik would go through a trial where Norwegian experts would deem him sane. He would be sentenced to Norway's maximum penalty of twenty-one years in prison.

As the drama and debates played out, I continued reflecting on my original question. How could this happen? How could the Norwegian society create a monster who would attack his own government and young teenagers? How, in Norway, the second wealthiest nation in the world in monetary value, with the second highest gross domestic product per capita? How, in Norway, with its 2.6 percent unemployment rate and its Nobel Peace Prize?

Any country can produce madmen, one might argue. But Breivik's story is more than pure coincidence. Some of the books published in Norway look at his life, blaming his childhood and parents. Many blame capitalistic influences in the country, while others target anti-Muslim Internet blogs and contra-jihadists. No one, least of all the Norwegian authors, is examining the psychological and sociological issues that help form similar killers in our societies. And perhaps most incredibly, none have brought up the issues raised by Breivik himself in his manifesto.

Maybe they're afraid or in denial. And maybe I would be too, if I hadn't left Norway when I did. But I did leave. I do understand the issues; I have lived them. And although I could never justify his crimes, let alone empathize with such a killer, I can relate to a great deal of the suffering Breivik endured.

That is how this book began, as a sociological study. I believed it would confirm my theories about how Norway facilitated the personality disorders that led to Breivik's killing spree. I wanted to understand how a country could be so stunned and unprepared that the killer himself had to call the police to come out and arrest him.

Writing this book became an act of discovery for me, as I began researching and interviewing experts. I began to discover information I'd never dreamed of when I was originally shocked into writing about Breivik in the context of Norwegian society.

An attorney by profession, I began researching the book by speaking to psychologists. This led me to Kathleen M. Puckett, Ph.D., FBI Behavioral Analyst (ret.). In her work as an FBI profiler, Dr. Puckett wrote her Ph.D. dissertation on what she calls lone wolf killers. Her co-authored book on Theodore Kaczynski, the Unabomber, examines the psychological development of these killers, and she is considered one of the leading experts in the United States on this rare type of mass murderer who symbolically "kills his government" for reasons we will examine shortly.

Although her dissertation belongs to the FBI, Dr. Puckett spoke candidly with me in great detail and explained why she believes Breivik, like Kaczynski and McVeigh before him, is indeed a lone wolf killer. What I learned from her was confirmed by my own research, but Dr. Puckett was the expert who first changed my thinking and greatly altered my plans for a book regarding the Norwegian massacre. As a result, this book is no longer just a sociological study.

Instead, the information I present here will show how countries such as Norway and the United States facilitate lone wolf killers. It will also describe how to separate and identify the lone wolf—the murderer who plans for a major event, as Kaczynski, McVeigh, and Breivik did—though he leaves no paper trail to lead authorities to him.

The lone wolf doesn't murder for fun, for profit, or as a shortcut to suicide. This killer is so shut off and shut down from humanity that the only way for him to matter is to connect so completely with a cause that he is compelled to kill for it.

When she studied the psychological profile of Timothy McVeigh, Dr. Puckett was surprised to find that his personality echoed Kaczynski's. "He didn't write down every thought he'd had as Kaczynski did," she said, "but there were persistent and compelling similarities in the way they saw themselves and their places in the world."

The same is true of Breivik. And though he didn't write down every thought, his manifesto is both an unparalleled glimpse into his psychology and a key to the psychology of others like him.

The lone wolves of the world can be stopped before they strike. We don't have to wait for the next attack at a marathon in Boston, in an outwardly peaceful country such as Norway, or anywhere else. We can take aggressive, positive steps toward stopping these killings.

According to Dr. Puckett, we first need to understand the mental state of these killers—before they strike. By analyzing Breivik, we will also be able to shed light on other mass murderers like Eric Harris and Dylan Klebold of the Columbine massacre. The Columbine killers and other school shooters are not lone wolves in the strictest sense of the term. They are often suicidal and leave a paper trail that can lead authorities to them, and can be easier to stop—if we know what to look for.

Because of Breivik, we now know what that is.

CHAPTER ONE

PLANNING THE ATTACK: TRAINING FOR CARNAGE

I have been storing three bottles of Château Kirwan 1979 (French red wine), which I purchased at an auction 10 years ago with the intention of enjoying them at a very special occasion. Considering the fact that my martyrdom operation draws ever closer, I decided to bring one to enjoy with my extended family at our annual Christmas party. . . .

—ANDERS BREIVIK MANIFESTO

Once the lone wolf decides on a plan, he still goes undetected by family and friends. These killers may have already been perceived as "weird" by those who know them, so even bizarre behavior is frequently overlooked. Yet the signs are clearly there.

McVeigh had been buying and reselling guns to those who didn't want those weapons traced to them. On September 13, 1994, he learned that laws were being passed to halt manufacturing of handguns, semiautomatic rifles, and other weapons. Not only did this threaten his ability to make a living, but it stirred his feelings of paranoia, and he knew he could no longer wait. He wrote to Michael Fortier, with whom he had briefly stayed in the Fortiers' mobile home in Kingman. He, Fortier, and Terry Nichols planned to blow up a federal building. Even though Fortier refused to join them in the end, McVeigh and Nichols, using bomb-building manuals as their guides, began stockpiling materials—such as blasting caps and liquid nitromethane—to make a bomb, just as Breivik did on his façade of a farm.

In May 2009, Breivik founded a farming company he named Breivik Geofarm. Registered to his mother's address in Oslo, the enterprise's functions were listed as the purchase, sale, and management of stocks and project development, including the acquisition and development of real estate. He tried to be as vague as possible, because he wanted to have options regarding what he did with this company. His primary goal was creating the best cover with which to build his bomb, and possibly even a hiding place for after the attacks. By pretending to be a farmer, he could order fertilizer without arousing suspicion.

His descriptions, buying and selling shares and real estate, weren't exactly functions one would associate with the name Geofarm, but his plan worked. Even after he had failed to change the registered purpose of his company, nothing prevented him from ordering the fertilizers, chemicals, and other products needed for building a bomb. When ordering the fertilizer, he said that his farm was set up to cultivate vegetables, melons, roots, and tubers, and again the changes in the list of functions drew no suspicion.

Breivik sought isolation on his phony farm, just as Kaczynski also sought isolation. Once Kaczynski left Berkeley, he moved in with his parents for two years in Lombard, Illinois. Just outside Lincoln, Montana, he built a cabin with no running water or electricity, where he hoped to live without interference from society. Kaczynski being jobless, his parents supported him financially. But even in this self-enforced isolation, society invaded. He wrote about how developers were ruining the land around him, and he planned retaliation.

Much about how Breivik was preparing for his massacre is divulged in the final pages of his manifesto, which he wrote at the farm. He referred to this section as his "Knights Templar Log—Personal reflections and experiences during the preparation phases." Although his matter-of-fact tone remained constant during this several-thousand-word essay, there is something ominous in its totality.

"This log," Breivik wrote after his day's work, "contains a lot of what can appear as 'wining' [sic], but it serves to reflect my mental state during the stay, a relatively detailed list of events, and how I overcame the obstacles that arose. It can also serve as an educational guide or a blueprint for which the goal is to create a more efficient time budget. Learning from other people's mistakes is always preferable to making them all yourself. It should be possible to drastically reduce the time spent on preparation, assembly and manufacturing based on the experiences shared in this log."

Within this detailed account, one can picture how consumed he had become with his project. His transformation was complete. In 2006, at the age of twenty-seven, without a job and in an effort to save money and drop out of the daily social mingling, Breivik moved back in with his mother. The first set of psychiatrists who evaluated him before the trial said in their report that his mental health had deteriorated at this stage, and he had gone into a state of withdrawal and isolation.

"Sure," Breivik stated at the end of his manifesto, three years after moving in with his mother, "some people will think you are a freak for living with your parents at the age of thirty-one but this is irrelevant to a Justiciar Knight." He lived with his mother because he was unable to connect with others. It was a way of removing himself further from society, into isolation, in order to refine his ideology, become one with it, and carefully plan the attacks.

A RETREAT INTO GAMES

After settling into his mother's basement, Breivik spent hours playing games on the Internet, on some days as many as sixteen hours at a time. Yet no one was aware that he was also working on his manifesto. His friends from this time stated that they were frustrated with him for withdrawing himself and avoiding them. His mother and sister were also worried and frustrated by the way he had apparently retreated from all social activity to stay inside, brood, and play computer games. Although he had shut the door on Norway, he was very active in his own way. And in that strange world, he had friends under any number of identities.

In *World of Warcraft*, the biggest and most well-known of the so-called Massive Multiplayer Role-Playing Games or MMO (Massive Multiplayer Online), he logged in using three different avatars. They were *Anders-nordic* (a part-man, part-magical creature), and, later, *Conservatism* and *Conservative*. These last two avatars were attractive, blond females, just like his mother and sister. In various places throughout the manifesto, he expresses his attraction to blond women. However, his motive for using them as avatars was probably to gain cooperation from the other male players.

Other players liked Breivik under any number of his fictional selves. When he announced that he was considering leaving to play *Age of Conan* instead, many wanted to follow him. One even wrote him this e-mail on May 17, 2008: ". . . Things are going ok in the guild but new mage sucks compared to you and xxxxx's missing you so much he's losing hair even faster than before! . . . Anyway, we miss you a lot in the guild and i [*sic*] hope you're (not :P) having fun in AoC and that you'll come back to us soon :("

He communicated with about forty preferred websites and blogs, using approximately twenty different e-mail addresses and thirty different nicknames and aliases.

The last couple of years, Breivik spent a considerable amount of time on a Call of Duty series, called *Modern Warfare 2*. In his manifesto, he wrote that the game was excellent target practice. He also played other war-strategy games and watched *Dexter*, the American TV series about a forensic specialist who has a secret life as a serial killer. For Breivik, the TV series must have also been inspiring, for here was a hero who every week committed murder for the most honorable of reasons—and got away with it.

In his manifesto, Breivik claimed that the games were a cover for his real activity, namely organizing his plan of attack into "phases," as well as writing his masterpiece. The games also allowed him to escape from his old life and to feel part of something, a feeling that he had failed to achieve for very long in school or politics. After dropping out of high school, Breivik had attempted to have a career as a politician for the Progressive Party; however, despite all the efforts he made, the party rejected him.

This new world of games changed the way he communicated. The language in his manifesto is inspired by the language used in the games: strategizing, speaking of tasks, primary and secondary weapons, using percentages.

For example, he wrote: "I know there is a[n] 80%+ chance I am going to die during the operation as I have no intention to surrender to them until I have completed all three primary objectives AND the bonus mission. When I initiate (providing I haven't been apprehended before then), there is a 70% chance that I will complete the first objective, 40% for the second, 20% for the third and less than 5% chance that I will be able to complete the bonus mission." This is game talk.

However, Dr. Kathleen Puckett believes that games alone cannot take the blame for Breivik's—or any other mass murderer's—actions. "Games were his way of having a social life," she said. "It does facilitate an artificial connection. He had to be the leader—it's a matter of needing to get to the place where he thinks he needs to get in the world. Nobody knows how great and grand he is. All of these people who live online are dissatisfied with their person-to-person contact in real life." Gaming does not create lone wolves, but they are drawn to that world.

Breivik's reality was now based on cover stories, fake identities, avatars, secret bank accounts, and lies. But the relationships he made via his computer would not keep him satisfied for long. And underlying all this, he had a wish to become someone, to be famous, to be free from anonymity.

IN SEARCH OF WEAPONS

In 2009, Breivik visited Prague in an attempt to purchase illegal weapons. In his manifesto, he speaks of being "fit as hell" during this time but says he was trying to avoid any sexual involvement with girls, as this would complicate his plans. No one-night stands for him.

"I'm not that person any more. I did screw two girls in Prague, though," he admits. "But that was mainly because there was a realistic chance that I would end up dead during establishing a weapons connection."

Biological needs were evidently his rationalization for sex outside of marriage, a small sin, he claimed, when compared to the "huge amount of grace I am about to generate with my martyrdom." He referred later to how he must keep his morals and motivation at a high level. "A week prior to the execution of my mission," he wrote, "I intend to spend a portion of my funds on a high quality escort girl." But first he would attend his final martyr's mass at Frogner Church in Oslo, hoping to ease his mind. "I will get tense and very nervous," he predicted. "It is easier to face death if you know if you are biologically, mentally, and spiritually at ease." At this point, Breivik had given up on having a meaningful intimate relationship, and he had replaced a connection with humans with a connection to his ideology.

The only gun he had was a Benelli that he had obtained in 2005 after his hunting-license application had been approved. His friends, who were also shopping for hunting rifles at this time, found his choice strange, as it was not the best hunting rifle. But then again, Breivik wasn't planning on using it for deer hunting. Nor was he planning to hunt animals when he purchased the €800 silencer, created specifically for automatic rifles, in 2011. He had other game in mind.

Unable to obtain the weapons he had deemed necessary during his trip to Prague in 2010, he decided to purchase a semiautomatic Ruger rifle and a semiautomatic 9-mm Glock 17 pistol through legal channels back in Norway, using his hunting license and his affiliation with a pistol club as justification.

So far, he had managed to hide various items he had collected for these phases in waterproof Pelican cases that he buried in a remote area of the forest. He also hid equipment and materials in his mother's apartment, as well as the basement storage room. In the police investigation following the attacks, they discovered 112 relevant purchases, from ninety sellers in ten different countries between September 2009 and July 2011, of effects that could have been connected to the planning and execution of the massacre. Most of these sales took place via the Internet, especially eBay. The police weren't able to find any relevant purchases before the autumn of 2009, which led them to believe that that was when Breivik had started planning his mayhem. (However, this turns out not to be correct. That may have been the time that he decided to go through with the killings, but his planning had begun much earlier.)

After having kept busy in front of his computer for almost three years, and content that he needn't worry about his mother or friends discovering his motives, Breivik returned to working out in 2009, trying to replace the body mass he had lost while writing his masterpiece and playing computer games. At this time, he also began "another steroid cycle." In the gym, he made a special effort to keep to himself.

The few people he did interact with said that he spoke about a book project, and that he soon would be traveling to market his book, which was why he needed to be in good shape. The book he referred to in these conversations evidently was his grand creation, his manifesto. Realizing that no publishing house would want to buy his masterpiece, he started gathering (farming) e-mail addresses of people on Facebook who would be interested in his cause and who would also likely spread the information to others. The massacre was his "marketing plan" for his vision, the largest-scale advertising he could think of, just as their bombings were for Kaczynski and McVeigh.

While still in Oslo, he noted that his funds were running low. He decided to sell his dear Breitling Crosswind watch and his Montblanc Meisterstück pen, along with other luxury items, in order to strengthen his operational budget. He sold the Crosswind for €1,800 and the pen for €200. This left him with €3,750 in the bank, and the same amount in cash, along with a car he valued at €4,500. The Montblanc was one he had purchased on the way back from Liberia in 2002, a symbol, at that time, of the successful businessperson he hoped to be.

A QUIET, ISOLATED PLACE

In 2010, he began looking for a remote hiding place in Sweden, not far away from Oslo. During July of that year, he contacted several real estate agents, explaining that he was in the process of writing a book about investing in stocks and that he needed a quiet and isolated place. Agents responded to his polite, eloquently written e-mails and personal inquiries, but he changed his mind and decided to remain in Norway.

Only in the spring of 2011 did he sign a rental agreement for a farm located in the rural town of Åmot. Why did he stall? Maybe he wanted to gather more material. He might have been trying to save money. Perhaps he was just putting off the inevitable.

As he was now pressed for time, he moved all the materials he had been storing at his mother's home to this new residence, and not a moment too soon. Seeking a property had taken him more time than he had planned—which is curious, considering how well organized he was. Perhaps, at that last minute, he was unconsciously sabotaging his own efforts. After all, the lone wolf killer does not necessarily take any pleasure in the actual killing. It is, as they themselves say, "collateral damage." However, his ideology got the best of him, and he continued with his plan.

Norwegian law requires that anyone leasing farmland must cultivate it according to the public listing. Breivik was permitted to use a specific farming ID number, mandatory for the ordering of large amounts of fertilizer from the national supplier. His scheme, justifying his order, ran ten pages and stated his purpose as testing the production of sugar beets. Following him along through his obsessive planning, trying to get into his head and read his thoughts, one can't help but imagine what this clever and focused young man might have accomplished if he had not been so twisted.

With limited time and limited capital, there was little opportunity for introspection. He had made his bed, so to speak. Now he would check the list of items still essential for a successful mission and what capital he would have to lay out for their purchase:

1. Plastic sheeting: 30 Euro.
2. Aluminum/wood ramp for loading and unloading truck: 30 Euro.
3. Fertilizer—large 500 kg bag: 1 × CAN, 1 × N34, 1 × 0-5-17 (for show), repeat after a couple of weeks: 2,000 Euro.
4. Cement mixer—rent or buy: 100 Euro.
5. Ethanol 96%, × 6L: 30 Euro.
6. Blue Police flashing LED light—for one of the trucks: 150 Euro.
7. Splash proof face mask: 30 Euro.
8. Fork jack—for 600 kg sacks: 200 Euro.
9. Plastic base for 600 kg sacks (used with above): 200 Euro.
10. Refrigerator: 100 Euro.

11. Freezer: 100 Euro.
12. Fume hood: 1,000 Euro (not yet decided).
13. Micro balloons, 20 kg. Glock 17: 700 Euro.
14. More ammo: 1,000 Euro.
15. Dunnage air-bag for securing transport load, bought from eBay: 100 Euro.
16. Straps/net for securing large load in truck, may use aluminum/metal profiles with screws to support them.

The chemicals proved to be a hellish mixture, much like the one used by McVeigh, and it is unnerving to learn how readily available they were at nearly any agricultural wholesaler. Breivik must have been concerned about how ordering these dangerous ingredients went unquestioned. Surely the chemicals, along with the various mechanisms needed for ignition, would cause a stir somewhere along the line.

"If I messed up by being flagged," he wrote, "I would be neutralized before I finalized my operation."

On Monday, July 11, 2011, Breivik had to transfer €2,000 to his credit card in order to reserve a second vehicle from Avis. The vehicles were to be used on that deadly day of the attacks, July 22. He also consumed "a lot of exquisite food and candy" in order to "recharge" his batteries and increase his morale. He had to take care of more dangerous chemical mixing that required wearing his protective suit. As was his habit, he drank a Red Bull and swallowed one of his dangerous ECA stacks (a combination of ephedrine, caffeine, and aspirin) as rewards for the difficult tasks and to give him the extra energy he needed.

So far, his cover had been effective. The farmer working the land adjacent to his later described Breivik as a city-slicker type who seemed to know nothing about actual farming. Moreover, his neighbor must have thought it strange that this young man, wearing fancy clothes, had covered up all his windows. Yet, this suspicion did not amount to anything further. The owner of a bar not far away, who had once worked as a body-language profiler for the airport in Oslo, later informed the police that there was nothing unusual about this young man who would order an occasional drink in his establishment.

Now living on the farm, Breivik was extremely isolated, working on his manifesto and his bomb, occasionally watching a little television. Although he had been working as covertly as possible, he did break his pattern once to visit his three best friends since childhood.

On June 30, 2011, his log noted: "I guess I have been somewhat reckless in regards to maintaining my social network. Choosing complete isolation and asocial behavior would probably have better ensured my secrecy. However, complete isolation and asocial behavior can also defeat the whole purpose if you end up losing the love for the people you have sworn to protect. Because, why would you bless your people with the ultimate gift of love if every single person hates you?"

It is not clear in his log whether or not he actually spent much time with his friends. However, he worried that he would appear suspicious if he didn't visit them. He may have even, in a brief moment of loneliness, wanted to say good-bye. In their eyes, he was probably improving his life by moving away from his mother's house, to the farm, and breaking free from his obsession with computer war games.

Claiming to be the "glue/social administrator" of this group of pals, he wrote how, in his absence, a particular member had been stepping up to fill his shoes. Whether or not Breivik actually was the metaphorical glue of his small circle is unclear. His narcissistic thoughts seemed to increase the closer he got to his mission, almost as if he were developing a bravado to propel himself through the final days of preparation. If he were to carry out his actions, he needed to justify them to himself. In short, he needed to convince himself that he was a savior.

The last two or three months before the massacre, he estimated, using the language of his beloved games again, that he had a thirty-percent chance of being reported to the system protectors at the National Intelligence Agency in the middle of his pursuit.

Was there ever a time that he paused to reflect on the carnage he was striving desperately to commit? Here, in his own words, written in the spring of 2011, he explains how he evaluated what his actions could mean to the innocent people whose lives would be in jeopardy should his efforts not be stopped.

"My concerns and angst relating to this phase impacted my motivation to a point where I had to initiate specific counter-measures to reverse the loss of morale and motivation. I decided that the correct approach to reversing it was to initiate another DBOL steroid cycle and intensify my strength training. I also spent some time locating and downloading new music. A lot of new vocal trance tracks and some inspirational music by Helene Bøksle. In addition, I decided I would allow myself to play the newly launched expansion, *World of Warcraft—Cataclysm*. The combination of these three counter measures, in addition to my 3 weekly indoctrination/meditation walks, resulted in my morale and motivation again peaking."

So, there would be no searching his soul at this point.

THE COUNTDOWN

On Day 8, in his log, he continued his online search for the correct way to purify salicylic acid. After many hours of searching the Net, using various search phrases, he managed to locate a single YouTube clip, with very few hits (views), which explained in detail an unconventional method for synthesizing acetylsalicylic acid from aspirin. Breivik, not one to settle for the first method he found, figured out a way to substitute an air-drying method of his own for the more expensive laboratory pumps in the illustration. Confident that his method was viable, he set out to create this material that most people can't even pronounce.

The following day, he decided to form an evacuation plan, in case his neighbor, or anyone else, decided to stop by and see what he was up to. The potential scenarios must have been chilling, as he began to mentally sketch out an emergency plan in his head. He wrote later that day: "I would have to pack my largest backpack with survival gear and relating [sic] equipment, including survival rations, 10L of water, weapons, ammo and suitable clothing. I started to prepare the above."

When Day 14 of his log rolled around, he seemed to be in a lighter mood. Evidently, he had been following the Eurovision song contest with a passion. "Crap music," he admitted, "but a great TV show, all in all." He had been following the semifinals and would watch it online after a day's work. Norway had entered with—what he considered a crappy, politically correct contribution—an asylum-seeking Kenyan who performed a bongo song.

"Very representative of Europe," he said, obviously aiming his sarcasm at Norway. "In any case," he added, "I hope Germany wins."

"BOOM"

In the middle of June, Breivik was ready to test his first bomb. He prepared his test device and drove off to an isolated site he had picked out for the event. He lit the fuse, sprinted out of range, and waited. It was probably the longest ten seconds he had ever endured. Here is his description of what happened. Breivik's written language and the smiley face he added makes one think he was sending an e-mail to a friend, instead of rehearsing for mass murder:

"BOOM! The detonation was successful!!! :-) I quickly drove away to avoid any potential unwanted attention from people in the vicinity. I would have to come back a few hours later to investigate the blast hole, to see if both compounds had detonated."

After returning from a restaurant, where he had celebrated his success, he went back to the blast site and evaluated the explosion. His primary compound had detonated successfully, but the dry picric acid booster had not detonated at all. He felt that he could solve the problem, commenting in his log that "Today was a very good day as I really needed this success."

There was no turning back for him. Yet was he moving forward with purpose, or putting off the inevitable? Because of his indecision about finding the right property for his pseudo-farm, he was already behind schedule. His mishaps, if that was what they were, would continue.

His Day 52 log entry speaks of how much he had been relying on the Internet, both for his continual flow of journaling his thoughts, and the functions he would be counting on to promote his book (his manifesto) when the time came for him to publish it electronically. His day included an attempt to reinstall Windows 7 on his computer, to no avail. Something was wrong, either the network card or the phone line itself.

He drove into town to get it fixed by a computer expert. Told the machine would be ready for him the next day, he returned to prepare the chemistry equipment required to manufacture more batches of a chemical called DDNP, which, when triggered by a detonator, acts as a primary charge that then ignites the main secondary charge. When finished with that task, he purified the last batch—yes, the last and final batch—of picric acid, yielding several liters that had to be chilled. Drawing closer and closer to the day he had been working toward for years, he then drove to town and bought three portions of Chinese takeout. "Beef with noodles and fried rice, yummy!" he wrote. "I took an early night as I didn't have any PC."

After a full day's work, Anders Behring Breivik went to bed early, exactly one month prior to the day he would commit the most reviled act that his nation would ever experience, an act that would forever brand him as the most evil and hated man in the world.

On Day 73 of his log entries, he wrote:

"Wednesday July 13—Day 73: I cleaned my 3M gas mask today. It was full of AL powder/smearing and the multifilter were [sic] full of AL dust. Unfortunately; these are my last multifilters (particle and vapor filter combined) so I can't replace them. I do have a couple of sets of particle filters but I believe they won't be of much use to filter the diesel fumes when mixing ANALFO.

"Continued to evaporate RC fuel outside and mixed 2 bags of ANALFO. After mixing the second bag I began to experience dizziness, blood pressure elevation and nausea, classical symptoms of excessive short-term exposure of [sic; if it isn't already obvious to the reader, Breivik wrote his manifesto in English, which is not his native language] diesel. Diesel is a vicious substance as it is absorbed even through most glove material. Nitrile gloves are best, neoprene somewhat good, but vinyl gloves provide little or no protection. At this point in time, the clothing I am using to mix ANALFO are more or less soaked in diesel, and I knew it was not healthy. But the problem is that using a hazmat suit for mixing is problematic as it will be very hard to labor while wearing it. I have another chemical suit that are more comfortable than the hazmat suit so I will try using that for the last batch. Diesel poisoning isn't lethal, but will weaken your body over time. However, excessive exposure over a long period of time can shut down your kidneys, which will obviously be lethal. To somewhat counter all the crap I've been exposed to the last two months I'm using anti-toxin tabs (herbal supplements strengthening the liver and kidneys), protein supplements, creatine and a multitude of mineral/vitamin supplements."

This passage gives us an understanding of the mind of a lone wolf killer, and how self-preservation and taking care of himself were important for him. This wasn't the writing of a suicidal rampage killer: it was the writing of a man who wanted to survive.

On July 14, Day 74, he wrote: "I'm not feeling so hot today. I'm in a weakened state . . . most likely due to diesel poisoning. It shouldn't take more than 24 hours before my immune system has defeated the negative effects of this exposure. I hope I haven't been overexposed as it may lead to acute kidney shutdown. Needless to say, I'm going to use my protective suit to mix the last 4 bags today. Finished the last 4 bags. Using the protective suit (fertilizer sprayer suit, used by farmers) proved to be better than expected, except the fact that I completely soaked my t-shirt and boxer with sweat by the time I was done."

Now it was time to take care of all the small things that would ensure his project's success, including a short YouTube movie to promote his manifesto. He had notified a few close friends that he was still in the final phase of his book, which he had hoped to conclude with a coinciding publishing tour, visiting cultural conservative organizations in western Europe.

On Friday, he took an early morning train to Oslo, where he completed a few final errands and picked up the Avis van (carrying capacity, 1340 kg). He then went back to the farm. His preparation had come to an end. He now had a van in which he could load the bomb. He needed only to make final preparations before he drove the van down to Oslo to spend the last night at his mother's apartment. That was where he would write the final entry in his manifesto.

In that entry, he included a couple of age-old platitudes that he had heard during his upbringing. This is all he offered the reader.

"The old saying, 'If you want something done, then do it yourself' is as relevant now as it was then. And more than one chef does not mean that you will do tasks twice as fast. In many cases, you could do it all yourself. It will just take a little more time. AND, without taking unacceptable risks, the conclusion is undeniable."

He signed off in this manner:

"I believe this will be my last entry. It is now Friday, July 22nd, 12.51.

"Sincere regards,

"Andrew Berwick

"Justiciar Knight Commander Knights Templar

"Europe Knights Templar Norway"

Breivik's manifesto was an obsession that allowed him to write himself into the mental state he needed if he was to follow through with the massacre without any hesitation. He was without any other source of hope. He was convinced that he would be forever powerless and invisible if he did not go ahead with his plan—what appeared to be the only way forward for him. And go ahead he did. Not even his own unconscious attempts at self-sabotage, like putting off finding a farm to create his bomb or waking up late on the day of the massacre, could prevent what years of oppression and lack of meaningful relationships had put in motion.

CHAPTER TWO

TROUBLED CHILDHOODS

I didn't really have any negative experiences in my childhood in any way. I had way too much freedom, though, if anything.

—ANDERS BREIVIK MANIFESTO

Breivik's quote mirrors McVeigh's childhood. "I have very few memories of my childhood, or the interaction with my parents," McVeigh said in an interview with the authors Lou Michel and Dan Herbeck. "I can't blame them for anything that happened to me. I was often by myself or with neighbors. Most of my memories focus on that."

Like Breivik's, McVeigh's upbringing appears unremarkable at first glance. His father was a factory worker, and his parents divorced when he was a teen. Young McVeigh grew up in a middle-class American family, in love with TV, movies, and the outdoors. Like so many other kids, Breivik included, he loved sports and superhero comic books.

Born April 23, 1968, McVeigh was the middle child of three, and the only boy. He grew up in Pendleton, New York—a small town near the Canadian border—a white, blue-collar, mostly Christian town where children could run into a neighbor's house without knocking. "Timmy" did just that, and he was always welcome. As a child, Timothy McVeigh was likable and full of fun.

Conversely, Theodore Kaczynski grew up in a working-class neighborhood in Chicago. He remembered his mother focusing on his dialect, encouraging him not to talk like the kids in the street, and he responded by speaking one way at home and another way when interacting with his young peers.

By the age of eight or nine, according to Dr. Sally C. Johnson, who wrote a psychological report in connection with his trial, Kaczynski no longer felt accepted in the neighborhood or at school. The children "bordered on delinquency," Kaczynski said, and he was neither willing nor interested in being involved in their debased activities. The family moved several times and eventually landed in Evergreen Park, Illinois—a middle-class suburb of Chicago—when he was ten.

"He was the smartest kid in the class," Russel Mosny, a classmate in math club, told a *New York Times* reporter. "He was just quiet and shy until you got to know him. Once he knew you, he could talk and talk." But when the others began attending dances and dating, Kaczynski stayed home. "I'd try to get him to go to the sock hops," Mosny said, "but he always said he'd rather play chess or read a book."

While studious, Kaczynski was remembered by an aunt as affectionate. But the aunt, who asked the *New York Times* to let her remain anonymous, said she saw a change after his younger brother David was born on October 3, 1949. Kaczynski was seven then, and the aunt said he seemed crestfallen at having to share his parents' attention.

"Before David was born, Teddy was different," the aunt said. "When they'd visit, he'd snuggle up to me. Then, when David was born, something must have happened. He changed immediately. Maybe we paid too much attention to the new baby."

McVeigh was also remembered with affection. In *One of Ours: Timothy McVeigh and the Oklahoma City Bombing*, Richard A. Sorrano quoted a neighbor who described McVeigh as "a clown, always a happy person." He was clever and always found a way to make a little money. Some Halloweens, he could charge admission to a nearby haunted house. "The kids in the neighborhood thought it was great," the neighbor said.

His father, Bill McVeigh, worked long hours in a local car-radiator plant to support the family, and his mother Mildred ("Mickey") liked to socialize and stay out late. Torn between fun and family, McVeigh and his sisters experienced turbulence and were often left on their own.

When McVeigh was nine years old, a major blizzard hit town. Out for drinks at a local hotel, his mother phoned to say they were snowbound and that she wouldn't make it home that night. The deadly blizzard claimed lives. Victims were buried in their cars. By the time it let up, days had passed, and many had run out of basic supplies. Always helpful, McVeigh shoveled neighbors' driveways and learned about survival. The family began stockpiling food, water, and other necessities to cope with the enemy, which in this case was the weather.

His grandfather, Eddie McVeigh, had a great influence on the boy and taught him about the outdoors and hunting, which included Timmy's introduction to guns at age thirteen. That was when Grandpa Eddie presented Timmy with a .22-caliber rifle, the first of many guns he would own. He was so passionate about firearms that he answered the question "What do you want to be when you grow up?" with "Gun-shop owner." McVeigh sometimes took one of his guns to school to impress the other boys. It worked.

Kaczynski, as a teenager, had a passion for explosives, and—according to Patrick Morris, a member of the high school math club, in an interview with the *New York Times*—Kaczynski once showed a school wrestler how to make a powerful mini-bomb. It went off one day in a chemistry class, blew out two windows, and inflicted temporary hearing damage on a female student. Everyone was reprimanded, the *New York Times* reported, but Kaczynski was unfazed. He later set off blasts that echoed across the neighborhood and sent garbage cans flying.

When the FBI visited his mother Wanda Kaczynski's home in Schenectady, New York, to gather enough evidence to arrest him, they discovered a fictional story written by Kaczynski as a teenager titled *How I Blew*

Up Harold Snilly, by Apios Tuberosa, a pseudonym he used back then. Like McVeigh, young Kaczynski developed an interest in survivalism soon after becoming interested in guns or explosives, respectively.

When Timmy was in his teens, Mildred left for good, and in 1986 she and Bill finally divorced. Young McVeigh, who stayed with his father and resented his mother, became captivated by computers and turned his bedroom into a computer lab. Although his parents' divorce marked him, it didn't affect his performance in school. Always a good student, he continued his excellent grades and graduated from high school with honors. Tim was "... a nice kid," his Spanish teacher Deborah Carballo said in an interview with Sorrano. "You'll never find a person at Starpoint who can say a bad thing about him."

Kaczynski far surpassed his classmates in high school—able to solve advanced mathematical equations before his senior year—and through the years he skipped several grades. Although he was placed in a more advanced mathematics class, he still felt intellectually restricted.

"Ted was technically very bright, but emotionally deficient," according to Morris. "While the math club would sit around talking about the big issues of the day, Ted would be waiting for someone to fart. He had a fascination with body sounds more akin to a five-year-old than a fifteen-year-old." Once, Morris said, they were talking seriously about their futures. "Ted seemed more interested in smearing cake frosting on this guy's nose."

So how do McVeigh's and Kaczynski's childhoods compare to Breivik's? Breivik was described on Norway's state television channel shortly after his apprehension as a "normal Norwegian boy," yet he became the worst killer in the history of a country where such a thing was not supposed to happen. Not ever. How could anyone fathom such cruelty as this? How could a seemingly normal boy turn out to be a monster?

Breivik's childhood could match that of anyone growing up in Norway in the 1980s. He was born in 1979 to economist Jens Breivik, the Norwegian embassy's diplomatic attaché to London and Paris, and Wenche Behring, a nurse from southern Norway. Jens Breivik had two sons and one daughter from a previous marriage, while Wenche, his new wife, also had a daughter from a past relationship.

Soon after Anders's birth, the marriage fell apart, and Wenche decided to return to Norway, taking both her six-year-old daughter and one-year-old son with her. With monetary assistance from Anders's father to add to her modest nurse's salary, she settled in Skøyen, an area within Oslo's affluent West End. Not far from the grand neoclassical villas that the area features, the family of three made their home in an outlying district of glass-fronted warehouses and apartment blocks.

Breivik grew up in a social-democratic society, one where both fathers and mothers were employed. Rarely did any parent stay at home during the day. Childcare was available for the very young, and grade school followed. The kids went to class while the adults worked. In this accepted, orderly equation, children learned early on to function on their own without becoming exceptionally independent.

Norway prides itself in having employed the United School of compulsory education. A model based on equal opportunity for all students, it has remained free of charge for anyone hoping to study in Norway, regardless of their nation of origin or their economic status. Beginning in 1889, seven years of education were available in the cities and in small scattered schools across the country. After World War II, various industries offered employment for a wave of displaced agricultural workers, and a distinctive type of working class began to populate the larger cities. In 1967, nine years of free education were offered to students; then in 1997, that number was raised to ten years.

This uncomplicated model for schooling children, aged six or seven years until they reach the age of sixteen or seventeen years, has enjoyed a 150-year reign. On paper, this type of agenda looks solid, and there are years of history to back its ability to rank among the world's most successful educational systems.

If one were to follow the system as it was laid out when Breivik was a child, one might pause at the different school reforms. Under the Labor Party's directive, the system must adhere to the rules of the Norwegian Association of Local and Regional Authorities, the teachers' unions, and the Ministry of Education and Research, and it must follow a Strategy for Competence and Development in Primary and Secondary Education.

The overriding principle for Norwegian compulsory education is that all children—regardless of where they live, their gender, social background, ethnic affiliation, or aptitudes and abilities—shall have the same right to education, and shall receive this education in the local school. This means that a child cannot be removed from one school and placed in another (whether this be another school in the ordinary system of education or one of the few special schools), except on the initiative of either the parents or the school. And no child can be removed from the local school against the wishes of the parents.

Primary and lower secondary schools are founded on the principle of a unified educational system with equal and adaptable education for all in a coordinated school system based on a single general curriculum. All children and youth are to share in a common pool of knowledge, culture, and basic values.

"We see it as important to exploit the school as a community of work for the development of social skills," according to Sissel Anderson, adviser to the Norwegian Board of Education. "It must be structured in such a way that the learners' activities have consequences for others, and so that they can learn from the impact of their decisions. The school must find the difficult balance between stimulating and exploiting the culture the young themselves create, and forming a counterweight to it."

The aim of this type of training is to develop empathy and sensitivity toward others, provide practice in assessing social situations, and promote responsibility for others' well-being. Those who have been insufficiently stimulated at home or in their neighborhood, according to the Norwegian Board of Education, must be given the opportunity for maturing in a learning environment where the students take responsibility for one another's development. Students are therefore encouraged to enlist in practical work, both as providers and recipients of services, where they get into the habit of taking responsibility in their own current society.

With the reform in 1976, upper secondary education also became one single, nationwide system to ensure that all young people have the same opportunities for education and training at this level. Reform in 1997 changed the school-starting age from seven to six years old and made ten years of schooling compulsory (instead of the previous nine).

"The Knowledge Promotion," or *Kunnskapsløftet*, is the most recent reform and was introduced in all Norwegian primary and secondary schools

(Grades 1 through 10) in 2006. By changing the substance, structure, and organization, the overall goal of this reform was to increase the basic level of knowledge among students, including reading, writing, and mathematics. A study made by Norwegian Social Research (NOVA), initiated by the Ministry of Education and Research, concluded that the reform may have failed to attain its goal. According to NOVA, the Knowledge Promotion has led to increased social inequalities between girls and boys, and between students from families of "low" and "high" socioeconomic status. A particularly worrisome trend in the first period of the reform is that more students leave school without a full diploma. Nevertheless, students from major immigrant groups have approached the level of students with non-immigrant backgrounds.

A QUESTION OF HOME LIFE

The first-born child to second-generation Polish-American Wanda and Theodore Richard Kaczynski, Kaczynski experienced intense isolation at nine months of age when, due to an allergic reaction, he was placed in a hospital for eight months.

"Baby home from hospital and is healthy but quite unresponsive after his experience," his mother wrote in his baby book in March 1943.

Johnson's psychological report that was created in connection with his trial fifty-five years later indicates that Kaczynski's mother perceived his hospitalization—and especially the separation from her at so young an age—as a significant and traumatic event for her son. "She describes him as having changed after the hospitalization in that he was withdrawn, less responsive, and more fearful of separation from her after that point in time," Dr. Johnson stated.

Despite his brilliance, Kaczynski's mother described him as uncomfortable around other children and "displaying fears of people and buildings." She noted that he played *beside* other children rather than *with* them, and she considered enrolling him in a study conducted by Bruno Bettelheim regarding autistic children. Instead of pursuing this opportunity, Wanda Kaczynski utilized advice published by Dr. Benjamin Spock in attempting to rear her son, according to Johnson's report.

Spock was the first pediatrician to study psychoanalysis to try to understand children's needs and family dynamics. His ideas about childcare influenced several generations of parents to be more flexible and affectionate with their children, and to treat them as individuals. His message to mothers in his book *Baby and Child Care*, published in 1946, was that "you know more than you think you do." Instead of using discipline and confrontation with a misbehaving child, Spock wrote, the parent should rather divert the child's attention to something else. In Spock's opinion, complaining or scolding a child was counterproductive.

Breivik's mother also maintained that she used Dr. Spock's advice when raising young Breivik.

McVeigh's home life seemed fine until his parents divorced in 1986. McVeigh, then a teen, isolated himself in his room with his computers and became skilled at programming and hacking. Anders Breivik chose similar isolation.

Before entering grammar school, Breivik had some serious adjustment problems. It is questionable whether he was close to his sister, Elisabeth, and doubtful that she, being several grades ahead of him in school, had much to do with him. He was three years old, possibly younger, when his mother began showing signs of erratic behavior in her parenting style. Neighbors watched and gossiped about her smothering her son with inappropriate affection, having him sleep in her bed with her, and then suddenly turning on him with a mix of anger and fear, as if she were frightened for her own safety.

With this unusual social structure of a single mother and son demonstrating such behavior that was almost unheard of in Norway at this time, Anders's home became an object of discussion. Due to exhaustion, his mother contacted the State Center for Child and Youth Psychiatry (SSBU), and the family spent three weeks there when Anders was about four years old. Child Protective Services, upon hearing reports of Wenche Behring's fear of her small son, and of her own general instability as a mother, stepped in to recommend that the boy be sent to a foster home. His mother was clearly too immature to handle her sporadic workload and the two children she had failed to raise in a controlled and settled environment. And the fact that she felt threatened by the small boy was also unsettling to the authorities.

"Even when [I was] breastfeeding him," she would say later, "he was a terrible child."

At SSBU, it quickly became clear that young Anders was a quiet and docile child, showing no signs of violent behavior. One of the many psychiatrists involved in studying Breivik's boyhood concluded about Wenche that "She projected all of the anger she felt for her former husband onto her son."

Neighbors expressed shock at the mother's "sexual language" with her children, and the Center for Child and Youth Psychiatry referred to her as "a woman with an extremely difficult upbringing . . . [who] projects her primitive aggression and sexual fantasies onto her son." The fear she felt of Anders was a subject of her imagination. If anything, the psychiatrists concluded, Anders needed protection from his mother.

Breivik himself told authorities he remembered nothing of all this. Despite his statement, he also said "I probably would have been better off had I been raised with my father and stepmother."

The Psychiatric Center (SSBU) considered Wenche Behring too unstable to care for Anders. His father had remarried, and along with Tove, his new wife, he came from Paris to pursue custody of his son. Although there seemed to be a case for Jens and Tove—a woman whom Anders seemed to dote upon immediately—to take custody of Anders, a special court ruling allowed Anders to remain at home in Oslo with his mother.

Had his family life stabilized? Inspecting these years, an educated answer would have to be *no*. It had, in fact, gotten worse. The conclusion of the Center for Children, after it studied the boy for three weeks, might not have been illuminating at the time, but now we can appreciate their findings. The Center wrote: "Anders has become a withdrawn and passive child, a little afraid. He responds mechanically, with restless activity."

Those observing the case concluded that Anders had difficulty communicating. Although his language was well developed, he seemed unable to express his emotions. Something else they noticed had the tone of what could have been a warning. The report stated that "He almost completely lacks spontaneity and elements of joy and happiness."

As a preschooler, did Anders's brooding and the manner in which he projected his role as a loner suggest that he lacked empathy? Or was the instability at home, along with the fraught relationship with his mother, starting to take its toll? Or was he merely one of hundreds, perhaps thousands, of youngsters who were facing a culture where becoming invisible in a crowd seemed a better choice than standing out?

Anders's parents grew up in post–World War II Norway, a country in ruins which was slowly being rebuilt after the war. The Labor Party came into power and, except for a few years in the 1980s, it stayed there until September 2013. The social-democratic state focuses on groups and institutions, making the individual no longer responsible for social problems, education, charity, unemployment, or poverty. Norwegians drift from home to work like sleepwalkers. Nobody seems passionate about their jobs. It's just the thing they spend their days doing. No one is even openly critical of anything, including the government. Because Norwegians are not mindful of their lives—because they are not allowed to question—they don't take care of one another either. In this small country, very few know their neighbors. The fact that the neighbors even noticed the bizarre behavior of Anders's mother toward him as a toddler speaks to how remarkable her behavior must have been. This was the Norway into which Breivik was born and educated.

Almost all children in Norway are mentored to some extent by state caregivers, most of whom have completed little more than a high school education. Anders, from age two until he was six, had been exposed to the collective ethics that did little more than keep him under control. Mediocrity was the standard he would be judged by.

Anders's early behavior is similar to the definition of "orchid children," those who are highly sensitive to context, making them more susceptible to both positive and negative environments. This coincides with Swedish folk wisdom that asserts that most children are like dandelions and grow despite their circumstances, but others are more like orchids and are highly susceptible to changes. Both terms appeared in a 2005 research paper by human development specialists Bruce Ellis of the University of Arizona and Thomas Boyce of the University of California, Berkeley, who borrowed a Swedish idiom to name a new concept in genetics and child development. *Orkidebarn*, or "orchid child," contrasts to *maskrosbarn*, or "dandelion child." As Ellis and Boyce explained, dandelion children seem to have the capacity to survive—even thrive—in whatever circumstances they encounter. They are psychologically resilient, but at the same time they are less sensitive to nourishing stimuli. Orchid children, on the other hand, are highly sensitive to their environments, especially to the quality of the parenting they receive. If neglected, orchid children promptly wither; but if they are nurtured, they not only survive, but flourish.

James Fallon, professor at the University of California, Irvine, is known for his work examining psychopathic murderers and other personality disorders. In studying their genes and brains, Fallon compared the killers' tests with his own, and the result stunned him. According to his findings, Fallon himself should have ended up with a personality close to Breivik's.

"My case fits well with the theory of orchid children," he said to *A-magasinet*, a weekly segment of the newspaper *Aftenposten*. Fallon has the genes of an individual prone to violence and crime. In his family, there have been several killers on his father's side. However, Fallon turned out to be a non-violent famous researcher. He confirms that people with the "warrior gene," as researchers call the MAO-A gene, are not only more prone to destructive behavior, but also to greatness if raised in a nourishing environment that helps them funnel their inner "warrior" to a constructive outlet.

Had Anders shriveled under his adverse home conditions? Could he have bloomed under the right mentors in an environment where his intellect was allowed to roam and be free? Although the folk wisdom is old, the genetic research is still in its infancy, and the *what* and *why* of Anders Breivik is still at large. It is the eternal question of "nature" versus "nurture."

After the court chose to allow Anders to remain with his mother in October 1983, Child Protective Services kept the family under supervision another seven months. Eventually, authorities decided that things had stabilized, and the little family was left alone, off the radar.

His father, although distant in his attitude toward his ex-wife and Anders himself, arranged for the boy to visit him in Paris. According to Anders, he got on well with his stepmother, Tove, but his relationship with his half-siblings never seemed to develop any closeness. Later, his written words would castigate Elisabeth, the half-sister with whom he was raised in Oslo, who was six years older. He also reproached his mother. It seemed, in the long run, the only one who would escape his wrathful pen was his father.

If by magic we could visit Anders at the age of seven, beginning school at Smestad Grammar School, Class 1C, what sort of little fellow would we find? He would be joining about five hundred other students in this yellow, fundamentally designed, multi-story building that, in the winter with its outdoor playing courts covered in snow, could be a setting for a Christmas card. This was the same school the royal family of Norway attended. He would be taught reading, writing, and arithmetic. He would learn how his homeland had originated, how it had grown from the Viking Age to the present and was ruled by a king who was really just an ambassador. The power, he would be told, rested with the prime minister and Parliament, and no longer with the state Lutheran Church, of which he was a born member. The world, he would learn as a grown man, was a place of many ideas, most of them contrary to what he had been taught.

"You're asking too many questions," a typical teacher might tell him on a typical day. "Be quiet and let somebody else speak." What they meant was "Don't rock the boat. Don't challenge the fundaments of our system."

His mentors looked at the world through a socialistic lens. "The capitalistic United States is the worst of the countries we will be studying," one would point out, following the national curriculum. "They spend their wealth invading other countries."

Breivik's experiences mirrored those of all students growing up in Norway, most of whom lived in a middle ground where there was no passionate viewpoint. No strong right. No strong wrong. The child's goal? Stay in that jelly-like center where you will not cause the teachers—or yourself—any discomfort.

How could anyone possibly predict that Anders would become a killer, especially one capable of such slaughter? If we had been able to observe Anders during his first couple of years at Smestad, we would have had a difficult time determining what would happen twenty-some years later when he armed himself to the teeth and marched off to commit mayhem and murder. It is difficult to find much said about the boy until he reached the fifth and sixth grades. Perhaps he blended in with his classmates and found a level of mediocrity that would enable him to remain unnoticed.

How about his teachers? Had they, in their own inadequacy or desire to herd the students at an easily workable level, numbed him into a type of nonentity? Could he have been posing as an average student with no desire to stand out?

A child wishing to excel and achieve would be considered a misfit by his teachers and told that he was "too noisy" and "too loud." Anders's hunger to succeed and be recognized would find little nourishment in this environment. A misbehaving or openly ambitious child would quickly be put in its place by the teachers and even by fellow students. Sticking out, even if in a positive way, was unaccepted in Norwegian schools. Perhaps it still is.

In the sixth grade, he, considering his undeveloped physicality, took on an unlikely project. He persuaded a few classmates to join him in founding a boy-only gang he'd named the Skøyen Killers. The members listened to hip-hop and made versions of Shako weapons, large boomerangs they fashioned after the weapon of choice in *InuYasha*, manga artist Rumiko Takahashi's fictional series based on Japan's ancient Warring States period. Trying to appear threatening, Anders and his mates chose to wear headbands as a trademark of their legion. However, the group proved to be dangerous in name only. Although failing in his first try at being menacing, he was considered a good student.

Skinny and self-conscious, Anders still lacked a stable base. He didn't fit the expectations of Norwegian society of that era. He wasn't among the first wave of disenchanted children to rebel, but his generation, with social media exploding in the center of its existence, was different from any before it. Maybe it was the difference people didn't see coming. Maybe such changes were so subtle, this nation couldn't measure the slow metamorphosis. After all, in a culture that rewarded sameness, they might have become blind to difference.

In his manifesto, Breivik claimed that his mother had been infected with genital herpes by her boyfriend, Tore Tollefsen, when Breivik was a child. He blamed the infection for causing her to take an early retirement and said that she then had the intellectual capacity of a ten-year-old.

"Both my sister and my mother have not only shamed me but they have shamed themselves and our family. A family that was broken in the first place due to secondary effects of the feministic/sexual revolution," he writes. "I can only imagine how many people are suffering from STDs as a result of the current lack of sexual moral [*sic*]."

Breivik certainly didn't have a stable family situation and parents who were there for him. In order to survive, he had to make his teachers and everyone else believe that he accepted what he was being taught. As soon as he was placed behind a small desk, and a teacher acknowledged his presence, he was required to fit in with the majority of his schoolmates. Being a good student meant blending in. A normal student soon realized that making noise of any kind would get him or her nowhere. Anyone too ambitious, trying to excel a bit too hard, was denigrated.

"Who do you think you are?" every Norwegian child who tries to stand out is asked while growing up. "Do not think you are any better than the rest of us."

Anders Breivik was told that many times during his grammar-school years. Was he a bad student? Not really. Was he entering puberty without any supervision or guidelines? Was he having trouble with his mother? The few who bothered to notice him at that time would, no doubt, agree. The history of their troubles at home when he was a small child would no doubt be exacerbated by Anders's maturation into puberty. Were these signs of a young boy becoming the most malicious man in Norway's recent history? Certainly not. Other young people manifested criminal behavior far beyond anything young Breivik had exhibited as he approached his teens. Before entering the seventh grade at Ris Junior High School, however, he definitely could be described as a kid who had run into a turbulent phase.

Dr. Puckett said that Breivik's social pattern as a young man is typical of a lone wolf. "What really struck me the most was, despite the fact that these killers were drawn to the ideology of extremist groups, and that they were angry, they lacked the ability to connect with other people meaningfully," she said. "Humans are hardwired to connect with each other to survive. It's really hard to be alone. They can't make the connections they crave with other people, although they try over and over to make those connections." So, like McVeigh and Kaczynski, although their behavior started to become more odd and menacing, none of them necessarily fell in with a "bad crowd" or gang, because they lacked the social ability to connect with these people, despite their misfit status.

The theory of attachment was originally developed by British psychoanalyst John Bowlby as he was trying to understand the immense distress experienced by infants who were separated from their parents. The attachment behavior system is, according to Bowlby, important because it provides the conceptual linkage between the study of human behavior and development and modern theories on emotional regulation and personality. Basically, the attachment theory states that if the attachment figure, in most cases a parent, has been nearby, accessible, and attentive, the child will feel loved and secure. These children, as discovered by psychoanalyst Mary Ainsworth, will act in a playful manner, be easily comforted after being separated from their parents, and have the necessary confidence to easily develop relationships with others, as children and as adults. But when a child hasn't had his attachment needs fulfilled by his parents, he may develop, among other disorders, anxiety, difficulties in connecting with others, and, in some cases, depression.

Researchers only began taking seriously the processes of attachment and its influences on adult relationships in the mid-1980s. Psychologists Cindy Hazan and Phillip R. Shaver were two of the first to conclude that adult attachment is guided by the same motivational system that makes a child have a close emotional bond with his or her parents. This system is also responsible for the bond between adults in emotionally intimate relationships, or the lack thereof, which is often the case with lone wolves.

UNABLE TO CONNECT

Because the lone wolf cannot connect with others—not even in "extremist" groups—these individuals connect with just the ideology of the group, as Breivik ultimately did. With their intelligence ranging from high to genius levels, as was the case with Kaczynski, they have the mental capacity to connect with an idea as a substitute for human relationships. They convince themselves that they are killing for a cause, and they plan carefully. And the lack of social interaction to dilute or distract from their connection to this idea makes the possibility of extreme violence that much more likely. Group dynamics, while they often function in a negative way by pushing teens toward alcohol, drugs, or sex, can also mitigate extreme behavior. Most people who are attracted to violent groups do not commit violent acts: they get together to hate together, and that feeling of belonging meets their social needs.

But this is not the case for a lone wolf. Dr. Puckett believes that being unable to connect is not a situation that anyone chooses, and that the lone wolf suffers before taking action. Being alone is not easy. Humans are social animals. Even Kaczynski, isolated as he was, wrote of wanting to be with a woman and have a family. Yet evidence suggests that he was never able to establish a sexual relationship with even one woman.

"If you can't connect to others, and you're intelligent, you're able to connect with an idea," Dr. Puckett said. "You don't have the social distractions other people have."

Breivik could not connect with others. The attachment issues he experienced as a young boy, with an unstable mother and a distant father, no doubt contributed to his difficulty in developing meaningful relationships and to his rejection from every group with which he tried to connect. He embraced the ideology of a group that, as we will soon see, wanted nothing to do with him. Furthermore, he knew that, in Norway, he would probably live to see himself vindicated as the grand person he believed he was.

"All [the] lone offenders I studied wanted to take care of themselves," Dr. Puckett explained. The lone wolf is, according to her, not suicidal. "He [Breivik] was self-protective, and he planned very, very well for the violence he unleashed. It had to be at a societal level. He had to be seen as mattering, as being doing something more important than anyone else."

A few days at Ris Junior High School passed. Anders had been absent for most of them, and his mother was beginning to show signs of a breakdown. She had already received the first of twenty-two letters from the school's principal. Student Breivik was causing trouble.

CHAPTER THREE

BULLYING AND REPRESSION

The fact that hundreds of kids our own age all over Oslo West, and even Oslo East, looked up to us was one of the driving forces, I guess. At that time, it felt very rewarding to us. . . . The more reckless you were, the more respect and admiration you gained.

—ANDERS BREIVIK MANIFESTO

Isolation doesn't happen overnight. Bullying, especially when it happens at a young age, makes one retreat even farther. Kaczynski and McVeigh both experienced some form of bullying, Kaczynski because of his intellect and for being so much younger than his peers; McVeigh, highly sensitive, was so affected by the bullying he experienced that he transferred those feelings of anger to the government.

Everybody in Norway, even the king, goes to public school. There's no motivation to get better grades until secondary school, and then only if one wants to attend medical school or civil engineering studies, both of which are also subsidized by the government. Only a few private schools and even fewer educational opportunities exist for the gifted. A young person goes into the system and can't really get around it. Regardless of which school one attends, it is the same system, through and through.

After six years of primary school, Breivik entered Ris Junior High School at a turbulent time in his life. At his previous school, his attendance had been fairly consistent, and although the teachers at this level didn't issue him grades, Breivik, like the other students, was given progress reports to take home. His evaluations would be recorded in the school archives and, for many years, school still presented no problem.

Although he often skipped school, he still performed well. But now, as a junior high student, his primary ambition was to be "cool." Joining a gang might be the safest way to assimilate into the mainstream, but Breivik had something to prove. He had made it plain that he wouldn't back down if threatened and expected his friends to have his back and not "sissy out" when called upon for help when he was being picked on or bullied.

He thought a particular Muslim friend, also an outsider, shared this type of pride under fire. But before long he, too, disappointed Anders. He was already taking on the personality of a lone wolf, unable to connect with others, even in fringe groups. Faced with becoming just an anonymous student as he fell out with his "gang," and again at a new school, he thought he might be good at a form of vandalism called "tagging." Considering the spraying of paint onto public structures and buildings to be an art rather than an act of defacing property, he decided to give the practice his best effort.

The first thing he learned after a few tries was that he'd need a lot more paint than he could afford. Finances were tight at home. His mother wasn't working, and he wasn't sure when he would see Tove, his stepmother, again. When he was about twelve, Tove divorced his father, and, as part of her job as a diplomat, she was sent to different countries far away from Norway. Although they did keep in touch, they didn't see each other often, so Tove couldn't be the presence in his life that either of them might have liked her to be. Early on, Breivik took on odd jobs before and after school in order to make his own pocket money and to keep up with the other students. His father did assist with child support, but still finances were tight, and his mother depended on social welfare to make ends meet.

In 1994, Breivik, in the midst of carrying out a tagging adventure, was picked up by the police at Oslo Central Station. He had been to Denmark, where he had obtained forty-three aerosol paint cans at a taggers' black market. Child Protective Services found that his mother had no knowledge of his trip to Denmark, nor was she aware that he had already had two charges against him for tagging. CPS resumed its observation of his home environment.

Although Norway had legislated all unauthorized street art to be considered disgraceful graffiti, the police took no further action. Breivik never acknowledged his guilt in any way. This seemed to be his mantra: *Never admit you were doing anything wrong, and never confess to a crime.*

Tagging gave Breivik a taste for underground activity. It also taught him the importance of planning his acts. He had learned to be secretive about the cache of tagging gear and spray paint he hoarded at home. The more strategic planning he put behind his illegal moves, the more he felt that he would never again be apprehended. Not a talented tagger, he began to execute a plan he hoped would make him notorious: he began to paint over other taggers' masterworks. For him, it was more about the illicitness of the ventures—and being noticed—than it was creating pieces of art.

His signature while tagging, *Morg*, would become his alias, his first "other self." Most likely, Breivik had thought his new alter ego, lifted from the evil Marvel Comics character, would bring him notoriety, since the alias sounded like "morgue," and in the popular comic, Morg's weapon was an ax which he used on his own people.

Although showing signs of unwillingness to follow the rules of society, Breivik did not lack empathy or emotion. At around fourteen years old, his stepmother Tove took him on a vacation to one of the Greek islands. In an interview, she recalled Breivik as a gentle and caring boy. He was fascinated by the history and culture of the place and eager to try new types of food. One night, young Breivik discovered some newborn kittens under his bed at their hotel. According to his stepmother, Breivik cared for them for the rest of their stay and was in tears when he wasn't allowed to take them with him back to Norway. "What's going to happen to them when I'm gone?" he wondered.

The lone wolf is no sociopath, someone who is completely devoid of empathy for others. When a lone wolf commits his gruesome acts, he takes no pleasure in harming others. As a child, McVeigh had a strong sense of what was right and wrong, and he couldn't stand injustice or cruelty. One incident—one that in many ways echoes Breivik's story—marked him. Tim watched a neighbor drowning small kittens in a pond near where they lived. When he asked what was happening, the neighborhood boy said "Those are kittens my cat had. We had to get rid of them." Young McVeigh loved animals and especially kittens, and the realization of what he was witnessing hit him hard. He ran home and cried for days.

Kaczynski's outlook also conforms to the précis that lone wolves are not psychopaths or bloodthirsty killers. The killings for him were a necessity, the point of his ideology, but it was not killing for killing's sake. It was also a way to release some of his built-up rage.

"Since committing these crimes reported elsewhere in my notes I feel better," Kaczynski wrote. "I am still plenty angry, you understand, but the difference is that I am now able to strike back, to a degree. . . . My first thought was to kill somebody I hated and then kill myself before the cops could get me. (I've always considered death preferable to life imprisonment.)"

Traditionally, Ris Junior High was a school attended by wealthy Norwegian students. The Labor Party and the 1968 generation did get rid of most of the stigmas of the different classes, yet some of the students who went to Ris later said that they applied to go to a different high school than those available in that district because they wanted more diversity, more differences in opinion, and, basically, more freedom. Instead of being defined by traditions and old habits, they said they wanted to discover new things, to take part in more socialistic political discussions, or be involved in activities such as theater. In speaking of Breivik's early education and specifically of Ris Junior High School, author Aage Storm Borchgrevink wrote "Freedom flourishes best in an open, egalitarian, and inclusive society."

What he and so many other Norwegians haven't considered is that they went from the tyranny of a class-divided society to a different kind of tyranny, but a tyranny all the same. The ultimate personification of Norwegian society—the Labor Party and its followers—were less open and honest about their tactics. Using brainwashing and the Law of Jante, which is a traditional mantra utilized to disparage a positive attitude toward individuality, they have suppressed the right of the individual to be just that: a unique person. The result is an uneasiness: a collective feeling of guilt for not wanting to be like everyone else—even if, on the surface, people appear to be part of the group.

Norway is now one of the wealthiest nations in the world and gives away billions to developing countries. The professed sentiment is that all wealth should be redistributed, that it is evil for an individual to make too much money, and that people with money are somewhat unethical or immoral. Yet, secretly, everyone wants to have more for themselves, and they don't want their income redistributed.

Maybe an entitlement state is the right thing for society, and maybe it isn't. But that's not the point. The population has been bullied into espousing social-democratic ways, and there is no room for anything else. "Just look at the capitalistic United States and all its problems," they say.

This is not freedom. This is mind control. Yes, the United States has problems; but by focusing only on what is wrong with others, Norway was missing things that were still wrong with Norway. The Law of Jante is ingrained in Norwegian society; and by the time children start attending primary school, it is so familiar to them that the young students don't even ask any questions. A lot in Norwegian society doesn't feel right; but at the same time, people have been taught not to speak up about certain matters, taught to accept whatever the group decides to do, no matter how wrong it might feel. It has gotten to the point where the citizens are so numb that the conformity probably doesn't even feel bad to them any longer. The group has become the government, and its truth is the only truth. Norway's young people have been persuaded into a pattern of group behavior that opposes individual self-aggrandizement as unworthy and inappropriate.

Omnipresent throughout a Norwegian's life, the Law of Jante originated as a concept at the beginning of the twentieth century by Danish-Norwegian author Aksel Sandemose. In his novel *A Fugitive Crosses His Tracks* (*En flyktning krysser sitt spor*, 1933, English translation published in the United

States in 1936), the notion was identified by ten rules, all beginning with the word *Don't*, as in Rule One: *Don't think you're anything special.*

Children become aware of the Law of Jante before starting primary school, and the law is constantly reinforced later in school where students are told not to stick out. Very quickly, a child learns to hide his or her academic success or creativity so as not to be punished.

Don't think. . . . Don't think. . . . Don't think. . . . Long before a child has heard of the Law of Jante, the ten rules are already burned in his or her brain.

1. Don't think you are anything special.
2. Don't think you are as good as we are.
3. Don't think you are smarter than we are.
4. Don't think you are better than we are.
5. Don't think you know more than we do.
6. Don't think you are more important than we are.
7. Don't think you are good at anything.
8. Don't laugh at us.
9. Don't think anyone cares about you.
10. Don't think you can teach us anything.

Sandemose's book containing those ten stifling rules that govern Scandinavian culture is taught to students in junior high school. The novel is a classic, much as *1984* and *Brave New World* are. Jante, a fictional Danish city, could be any Scandinavian town. Sandemose, back in the 1930s, captured current Norwegian culture. Yet, although the book—which is taught in the schools as a warning—shows how pack mentality brings out the evil in a person, nothing in the schoolroom or anywhere else moves past a basic discussion. Debates may ensue; however, nothing changes.

Breivik must have felt like an outsider, someone to whom rules and the law of the land did not apply. Perhaps he didn't have an earnest desire to adhere to what was expected of him in Norwegian society.

In his manifesto, he later described himself this way. "I was able to function socially when I set my mind to it. I was good at putting on the game face." This manipulation of the self is indicative of the Norwegian mindset. One must hide one's true identity and put on a "game face" if one is to survive in society. That is what Breivik did. He felt he had no choice, in order to be accepted. But he was never able to keep that "game face" on for very long, either with regard to school or socially, amongst his peers.

When a few Muslim students had begun to enter his school, a public institution that had, for years, been "all white," his Lutheran classmates, though not overly religious, balked at welcoming the new students. "Just too different," some said openly. "And they have no intention of changing, either."

But Breivik befriended a Pakistani classmate. Both were considered outside the circle: his new friend, because he was a Muslim, and Breivik, because he hadn't yet come to fit in with any group, at least none that accepted him for long. Perhaps he couldn't quite bring himself to adhere to a gang mentality born from the Jante law's rules against individual success, given his ambition to be somehow exceptional. But his need to connect made him try in different environments. In his manifesto, he claims that his Muslim acquaintances from his youth were tactical alliances, most probably to justify his earlier friendships to his current anti-Muslim audience.

He writes: "In Oslo, as an ethnic Norwegian youth aged [fourteen to eighteen], you were restricted. If you didn't have affiliations to the Muslim gangs, [y]our travel was restricted to your own neighborhoods in Oslo West and certain central points in the city. Unless you had Muslim contacts you could easily be subject to harassment, beatings and robbery. Our alliances with the Muslim gangs were strictly seen as a necessity for us. At least for me. . . ."

Since the Muslim integration had been gradually increasing for a decade, the two boys would be exposed to classes teaching tolerance and respect for other ethnic beliefs and customs. Muslims were accepted by most citizens because they had no choice. Yet many of these new citizens didn't adhere to their new country's customs, and certainly not the Laws of Jante.

At the age of thirteen, Breivik, still underdeveloped physically, was persuaded by his sister, Elisabeth, to spend more time in the gym. She was the one who had brought him there for the first time. With Elisabeth getting ready to move to California, Breivik had a new workout mate in his Muslim friend. The two of them started going to the gym regularly in an effort to build their muscles. As was true with many boys his age and older, he began experimenting with anabolic steroids. For one this young and underdeveloped, we can only guess how these drugs, containing hormones, would affect him, if he indeed continued using them.

Around this time, other boys in his class began "mobbing" him, catching him off guard and belittling him in front of girls. Breivik had disciplined himself to weather the attacks with little outward emotion. Teachers would remark years later that he had become invisible. One of his teachers from this period of his life, when contacted by the police after the attacks in 2011, vaguely remembered him. "Just another unremarkable kid," was all she recalled.

Maybe, in his own way, he had learned to hide his loneliness and alienation from the remaining few people with whom he had tried to connect. Maybe he was already beginning to disconnect from the pack. The people around him marched to a law that seemed part of their DNA. Perhaps Breivik began to regard the idea of having an all-knowing set of rules as paradoxical to success.

Even in junior high, hip-hop music had begun to work its way into the students' awareness. Movies, television, and video games tended to rely on violence for their success in gaining a foothold in the culture. And drug and alcohol abuse were no strangers to this generation of teens (nor are they today).

This age group is always the first to feel the slack caused by unprepared or unqualified teachers. A faculty that begins to lose control of its students seems at its worst when faced with junior high students who realize they'll never be punished for deeds that deter not only their own education, but the education of others. It's as if they have an acute sense of smell, one that enables them to sense the fear emanating from their new teachers' failure to discipline them. They also pick up fear and weakness from someone who is alone and vulnerable, as both Breivik and Kaczynski were.

After it was determined that Kaczynski had an IQ of 167 in the fifth grade, and his parents were told he was a genius, he skipped a grade and enrolled in the seventh grade. In his journals, Kaczynski described this as a critical event in his life, and in high school he would skip another grade.

He recalled not fitting in with the older students and being subjected to bullying.

"Mr. Kaczynski denies any history of physical abuse in his family," Dr. Johnson reported. "He does admit to receiving occasional spankings, but felt that this was not excessive or cruel. He does specifically describe extreme verbal and emotional abuse during his upbringing, although he did not identify this as a problem until he was in his 20s."

McVeigh was also exposed to bullying, beginning at age ten at Little League baseball practice. He was small and skinny for his age, and a bigger kid grabbed his baseball cap in front of the other children. When McVeigh tried to retrieve it, the bully punched him. Stunned and humiliated, Tim ran to his father's car and hid in the back seat, crying.

Over the course of her study on McVeigh, Dr. Puckett realized that he was not the steely-eyed, cold-hearted young man pictured by the media, but someone who needed to protect himself from harm and who needed to believe that he mattered in the world despite his discomfort with a life inside it. Like Breivik, he was seeking recognition and accomplishment.

Between May 28 and 30, 2002, Breivik posted on the Progressive Party's Youth Unit's blog. He was writing about liberals, which in Europe, unlike the United States, are those with right-wing political beliefs. The Progressive Party is even farther to the right than the Conservative Party in Norway. On the blog, Breivik wrote: "Liberals are in many ways individualists and should feel disgust for the principles founding the Law of Jante. I have been a member of the [Progressive Party/Progressive Party's Youth Unit] for several years, and I've noticed that the Law of Jante is, unfortunately, quite at the core in this fantastic organization."

He continued: "One should not be ashamed of being ambitious! One should not be ashamed to have goals and then reach them! One should not be ashamed to break with established norms to obtain something better!"

To that, he added: "I have seen quite a few good people be sabotaged or frozen out just because they are too good, too ambitious—a threat, maybe, to others who have been part of the organization longer but who have not climbed as well. This is a sad development, especially in an organization that should take the high road above this loser mentality that, unfortunately, is deeply rooted in the Norwegian culture. The myth about the timid Norwegian who stands holding his hat in his hand is very real. It is still not politically correct to stand out, to be different, or to show that one has succeeded, but one should follow a pattern set by our ancestors."

Norway's particular culture was a facilitator in Breivik's process to becoming a killer, but other countries—including the United States—can contribute to one's sense of isolation in similar ways, like that government's use of massive covert surveillance programs and by covering up civilian casualties at war. Having seen what really happened in the Persian Gulf in 1991, McVeigh couldn't stomach his government's manipulations of the American people during Operation Desert Storm. Because of the lone wolf's fragile and sensitive personality, he sees his government as the ultimate bully that is stifling him.

"The government is continually growing bigger and more powerful, and the people need to prepare to defend themselves against government control," McVeigh said in an interview at the Waco siege, where he went to lend support to people's rights to bear arms.

"Politicians are further eroding the 'American Dream' by passing laws which are supposed to be a 'quick fix,' when all they are really designed for is to get the official re-elected," McVeigh wrote in a letter to the Lockport *Union Sun & Journal*, published on February 11, 1992. He gushed about issues from government and its leaders to crime, taxes, and racism. "America is in serious decline," he wrote. "We have no proverbial tea to dump. Should we instead sink a ship full of Japanese imports? Is a civil war imminent? Do we have to shed blood to reform the current system? I hope it doesn't come to that, but it might."

Kaczynski's war on technology was founded from the same rage as Breivik's and McVeigh's rage against their respective governments.

"The system needs scientists, mathematicians and engineers," he wrote in his journal. "It can't function without them. So heavy pressure is put on children to excel in these fields. It isn't natural for an adolescent human being to spend the bulk of his time sitting at a desk absorbed in study. A normal adolescent wants to spend his time in active contact with the real world."

In 1959, as a sophomore at Harvard University, Kaczynski was recruited to participate in a personality assessment study conducted by psychologist

Henry A. Murray. Students in Murray's study were told they would be debating personal philosophy with a fellow student. Instead, they were subjected to a "purposely brutalizing psychological experiment" stress test, which, according to author Alston Chase, was a personal and prolonged psychological attack. During the test, students were taken into a room and connected to electrodes that monitored their physiological reactions, while facing bright lights and a one-way mirror. Each student had previously written an essay detailing their personal beliefs and aspirations. The essays were turned over to an anonymous attorney, who then entered the room and individually belittled each student based in part on the disclosures they had made. Students' expressions of rage were filmed and later played back to them several times.

According to Chase, Kaczynski's records from that period suggest that he was emotionally stable when the study began. The stress tests would likely be more harmful to a lone wolf's particular psyche than to someone less vulnerable. Kaczynski's lawyers attributed some of his emotional instability and dislike of mind-control techniques to his unwitting participation in this study, which lasted three years. Indeed, some have suggested that this experience may have been instrumental in Kaczynski's future actions.

In 1995, at the age of sixteen, Breivik began at Hartvig Nissen High School. At Hartvig, he was elected student representative for his class and finally seemed to fit in. But for some reason, he decided to change high schools after his first year at Nissen and began attending Oslo Handels-gymnasium (Oslo Commerce School).

Also in 1995, his mother had surgery. Never a stable parent, she grew more mentally fragile and seemed unable to care for herself after the procedure, let alone be responsible for Breivik's needs. Slowly, he and she began to change roles. Eventually, he brought in money from a morning job of delivering newspapers; and before he left for school, he took care of his mother as if she were his ward.

Staying focused on school while taking care of her, spending time at the gym, and multitasking with all of his odd jobs could not have been easy. Still, he shopped, did much of the cooking, and earned excellent grades.

In Norway, mandatory military service begins after high school. In his last year at Oslo Commerce School, he applied for an exemption from military duty, citing his mother's almost complete dependence on him. A board of civic officials, after reviewing his situation with his ill and jobless mother, granted the deferment. The reluctance he showed toward military service might have been the kindling his classmates needed to classify him as "weird" once and for all, and to consider him "feminine," too, as some have admitted to these many years later. His effort to counter such opinions of him no doubt led to his hanging out with a gang from Tåsen in the northern part of Oslo. This band of strictly Norwegian boys in their late teens protested the influx of Pakistanis. Claiming that their motive wasn't racist, they pledged to fight back against the Pakistani gangs who were causing a scare in the Oslo community.

Breivik was only partially accepted by the group. These Norwegian boys were a rough bunch. They felt that violence would be needed to defend their territory from other gangs. Breivik, who had been picked for his daredevil days as a tagger, didn't quite fit into this violent organization. He would be found among those holding a "Go home, Pakistani!" sign, but little evidence exists that he participated in any physical rumbles. Other members of the Tåsen group admired his intelligence, but soon they, too, no longer desired his membership. Falling short of the gang's social code, Breivik once again failed to make his mark. When he began dating a girl unpopular with the rest of the boys, they expelled him from the gang for good.

This latest try at coming in from the outskirts to join in the center of an organized activity, but being rejected again, must have affected him deeply. Due to his past failures at joining the mainstream functions at school, and now being cast away from the more macho types who were springing up in his realm, Breivik started to withdraw and disappear. Unfortunately, his experience was not exceptional. The tyranny of the pack had just claimed another victim.

Before Christmas in his final year of high school, Breivik decided to quit school. He wrote a very polite—and humorous—letter to the principal:

> *To Oslo Commerce School,*
> *I hereby notify you that I, after thorough consideration, have decided to quit in my last year of high school. I would like to thank*

*you for having me and for everything I have learned during my
time at school.*
Kind regards,
Anders Behring Breivik
(Only a joke)
PS: Had I not been forced to take French, I would not have left. D.S.

Living in his mother's basement, he envisioned himself not as a soldier
against immigration, but as a budding businessman. He was smart, well
organized, and a great planner. Why, he must have been asking himself,
couldn't he prove to the world that he could excel in business or politics?
He must have wanted to prove the Law of Jante wrong, and dropping out
of high school was his way of extricating himself from the system so that
he could finally achieve his goals of success.

In a repression-based culture, respect is not based on trust and reci-
procity, but on fear and power. People are aware of the problem, but
somehow the awareness is not internalized. Somehow, an individual—a
teacher, for instance—can understand and communicate the danger of
a society of suppression, yet continue to suppress themselves even in their
conscious attempts to teach and nurture.

Nobel Prize nominee philosopher George Santayana wrote: "Those who
cannot remember the past are condemned to repeat it." This is the case in
so many places around the world, and Norway is no exception. Norway
today has not forgotten the danger inherent in the Law of Jante, yet it has
not necessarily changed. Has Norwegian culture learned its lesson from
the massacre of 2011? Has it learned what happens when it ignores the
individual, however ambitious or troubled, in favor of the group? And if it
has not learned, what then will be the price of ignorance?

CHAPTER FOUR

THE TURNING POINT

If you see the ship is burning, you don't ignore it and start cooking noodles, do you?

—ANDERS BREIVIK MANIFESTO

After he dropped out of Bryant & Stratton College and as part of his quest to become a survivalist, Timothy McVeigh read everything he could get his hands on about firearms and self-defense. On May 24, 1988, the month after he turned twenty, he joined the Army. McVeigh had finally found his calling. The Army was everything he wanted in life and more. When he joined, he was not a leader but an eager follower.

"McVeigh had never really felt like he fit in back home in Pendleton, but he felt comfortable here," Lou Michel and Dan Herbeck wrote in *American Terrorist* about McVeigh joining the military. "He threw himself into Army life with everything he had. Military life gave him structure—a code of honor, a sense of purpose—that he'd never felt before. He enjoyed it all—the frantic 5 A.M. wake-ups, the rushed meals in the chow hall, the crass jokes, even the uniform inspections. He thrived in the outdoors, the smell of sweat mingling with the scent of Georgia pine. Most of all, he loved everything to do with firearms."

McVeigh dreamed of becoming a part of the U.S. Army's elite Special Forces. The Green Berets are given the toughest and most dangerous jobs, and the Army calls its prototype Special Forces soldier "a breed apart, a cut above the rest . . . mature, highly skilled, superbly trained . . . a fighter of uncommon physical and mental caliber, ready to serve anywhere at any time." As a star soldier, McVeigh had a chance of making it.

"Some at Fort Riley did consider Tim McVeigh an oddball," Michel and Herbeck wrote. "Some were put off by his political views [he railed against gun control, the government's abuse of power, and conspiracy theories including drugs and UFOs]. But even the harshest critics were impressed by McVeigh's dedication to Army life. He was devoted—fanatically, some would say—to becoming the best soldier on the entire base."

When, at 5:30 every morning, the soldiers had to get up for uniform inspection, McVeigh would be up by 4 A.M., his roommate William Dilly recalled, "not only getting himself ready, but cleaning up the barracks." He would keep an extra uniform, boots, and set of equipment in immaculate condition, just for inspections. "The man was a perfectionist," Dilly said, according to Michel and Herbeck.

Instead of going out on his free time, McVeigh preferred to stay at the barracks, cleaning his weapons or reading books. At night, he would often receive calls from fellow soldiers asking him to pick them up from the bars nearby, which McVeigh was happy to do—for a fee. McVeigh had a superb business sense and his taxi service paid off. He also made a profit as the army lender and, as an excellent card player, he made money on the poker games he always won. He was so successful, in fact, that he stopped out of guilt. "It's too easy," he said.

Before he had the chance to be evaluated for the Special Forces, the Gulf War erupted in 1991, and McVeigh's First Infantry Division was dispatched to the Persian Gulf to serve in Operation Desert Storm. Again, McVeigh served with distinction, was promoted to sergeant, and became lead gunner on the Bradley Fighting Vehicle in the first platoon.

Although he was an outstanding soldier, the war changed McVeigh, as it did many other young people. But perhaps this traumatizing experience was more harmful to McVeigh than most, given his fragile psyche. It troubled him that the Army would lie to the soldiers and the press about what was really going on, shattering his illusions about the Army and forcing him to question his near-blind devotion to the military lifestyle. Later on, McVeigh cited as an example an incident on February 13, 1991, when the U.S. Air Force bombed a shelter in Baghdad and more than three hundred, mostly women and children, were killed. The Army kept the incident hidden from the public.

"McVeigh hated to hear the Army lie, to soldiers or the public," Michel and Herbeck wrote. "He saw a reporter after the news briefing, and for a moment he thought about telling him what [had] really happened. But he didn't. He was still a soldier."

And a decorated soldier, at that. He earned the Army Commendation Medal for fighting in Iraq, as well as the Bronze Star. Now he renewed his attempt to gain acceptance into the Special Forces. But McVeigh was emotionally exhausted and had lost the physical stamina he'd built up during his training before the war. A commander recognized the difficulty facing McVeigh and the others returning from Desert Storm, and gave them a chance to defer the Special Forces tryouts. But peer pressure was strong, and McVeigh, afraid he would appear weak if he waited, refused to postpone. McVeigh was simply not fit enough and, on his second day of the assessment program, told the commander he was giving up. Disillusioned and shattered, McVeigh quit the Army shortly after.

Returning home to a civilian life, he felt nobody was interested in welcoming a war hero back into the workforce. McVeigh, having lost faith in the Army and his country, started giving way to bitterness, anger, and an increasing desire for isolation. He had reached his turning point.

Breivik's turning point came after high school as well. He had given up his chance to graduate and continue his studies. With his ability to organize his time, his innate curiosity, and his strong desire to become a businessman, he was ripe for further schooling in a facility where he could graduate with a bachelor's degree in business; but instead, he had chosen to quit. One might argue that in no other land could this free education be accomplished with such ease as in Norway. Why then would such a young man, who had exhibited himself capable of achieving a degree of excellence in his high school classes, leave all this bright opportunity that lay within his reach?

Breivik put it this way. "Formalizing your education is all about prestige and the possibility of working for various organizations. I care little about prestige and even less for the opportunities to work for 'publicly approved' politically correct entities. It was therefore no incentive whatsoever for me to invest so many of my resources in formalizing my education in any of the fields that interested me."

A true lone wolf, McVeigh did not pursue further schooling, although he had graduated from high school with honors and was named the school's "Most Promising Computer Programmer." At Bryant & Stratton business college, he had wanted to devote himself to programming and not delve into old subjects that had bored him in high school. The college required all new students to take a lengthy math aptitude exam, according to Michel and Herbeck. McVeigh breezed through the test in twenty minutes, to the teacher's amazement, and scored 99 percent. None of the other students scored more than 80. Thinking he didn't need a piece of paper telling him how smart he was, he quit. Unlike Breivik, however, McVeigh dropped out of college also because of the steep tuition and because he didn't want to add on to his father's financial burden. His days of formal education were over.

Instead of seeking a career in the Army like McVeigh, Anders Breivik decided that he was going to go into politics, and that he was going to be an entrepreneur, something he felt he could succeed at, even without finishing school. Surely this was yet another attempt at connecting with others.

Ted Kaczynski graduated from college with an undergraduate degree in mathematics in June 1962, at the age of twenty. He began his first year of graduate study at the University of Michigan at Ann Arbor in the fall of 1962, and had completed his master's and Ph.D. by the time he was twenty-five. Following graduation, he accepted a position as assistant professor in the mathematics department at the University of California at Berkeley in 1967.

Kaczynski's position there was short-lived. He seemed uncomfortable in a teaching environment, often stuttering and mumbling during lectures, becoming excessively nervous in front of a class, and ignoring students during designated office hours. After having received numerous complaints and low ratings from the students, he resigned from his position at age twenty-six.

Disillusioned and angered, he moved home to his parents for a time, before finally settling as far as possible from civilization. He had given up on people; he too had reached his turning point.

A CULTURAL CLASH

Norway's social revolution came about when mining and timber entrepreneurs, along with the recently formed textile industries, needed funding in order to compete in the global marketplace in the mid-19th century. Banks were founded to serve these new requests for venture capital. Industries began to hire a relatively large number of workers, thus reducing those who had been scratching out their livings on small farms. This phenomenon led to a clash between rural and city development, between traditional culture and politics. Industrial conditions were hazardous. Unions were formed, and the workers demanded collective bargaining. Soon, socialism grew stronger, and eventually it became a way of life, a part of the political discourse.

How did this movement fit into a society traditionally ruled by a monarch? Economic situations just before and during the early years of this revolution had relied on an economy supported by agriculture, fishing, and timber. Several kings, in succession, had been rewarding loyal constituents of their choice with land. As the land became more depleted from years and years of cultivation, many farmers started going broke and this practice stopped. Soon the monarchy was reduced to the nation's ceremonial figurehead, and its political power diminished. Land-owning farmers were the main source of Norway's political bloc until the beginning of the 19th century.

Then after World War II, the Labor Party became the major political faction. Its left-wing agenda imposed state control over the rationing of dairy products until 1949 and the rationing and price control of housing and automobiles until 1960. Under the leadership of Prime Minister Einar Gerhardsen, many reforms were accomplished through state-financed organizations, including the flattening of income distribution, lessening poverty, and ensuring retirement programs, medical care, and disability payments for all citizens. These reforms resulted in public-sector growth, and the divide between liberals and conservatives began to decrease. This was a peaceful, non-conflicted time in Norwegian history. The socialist speeches about solidarity, equality, and distribution of whatever wealth could be found were welcomed by a people who had lived in scarcity and terror throughout the five-year Nazi occupation.

The Marshall Plan (European Recovery Program), named after United States Secretary of State George Marshall, consisted of monetary aid given to European countries after World War II to rebuild those countries' economies and to prevent the spread of communism. Beginning in 1948, it was in effect for four years and had much to do with Norway's becoming a mixed economy.

The rising cost of living over the course of several decades has spawned the question about Norway's capability to stabilize an economy threatened in a post-petroleum era. A signatory to the European Free Trade Agreement since 1994, a trend has developed toward making Norwegian industries more open to competition. Information technology has led to small and medium-sized companies specializing in technology solutions. Successive political parties in control have reduced government ownership over companies that require the benefit of private capital, and since the late 1990s there has been increased entrepreneurship and less government funding.

FROM ENTREPRENEUR TO POLITICIAN

In 1998, the year he dropped out of high school, Anders Breivik must have been wondering how he would start his own business. He was facing an economy in transition, where the means to business production in Norway primarily existed under private ownership for the first time. Profit-seeking enterprises currently dominated the economic activity in which he hoped to compete. The nineteen-year-old could not have been fully aware of the obstacles presented by a government that used to dominate the economy, top marginal taxes, strong regulatory oversight, and various unpredictable economic downturns.

On the plus side, Norway had a rather predictable business climate overall. As one of the richest countries per capita according to the United Nations' Human Development Index, Norway has since the 1990s enjoyed the best standard of living, education, and life expectancy combined. A stable political environment and a respected judicial system ensure well-functioning markets and a top-ten ranking in the World Bank's Ease of Doing Business Ranking. Norwegian monetary policy successfully maintains a stable inflation and exchange rate. The Ministry of Government Administration would be there to guide him. The Norwegian Ministry of Trade and Industry would offer him access to its website. The Brønnøysund Register Center would be providing practical information for both companies and individuals who wished to open a business. How could an eager candidate for business success such as Mr. Breivik lose?

To Breivik, it was all about finally being able to act upon some ideas he had been thinking about for months, like using his computer skills to start up an Internet-based telecommunications business. In his later writing, he reflected on this period in his life. He was willing to work full-time in a customer-service company to gain some financial independence while he focused on his ideas for a startup.

"I was not rich at the time," he admitted. Here was his chance to free himself from the constant pressure of the Law of Jante and finally become the success he always felt he should be. His goal was to become rich enough to break away from his peers, who had already ensconced themselves in mainstream society and who had rejected him throughout his youth. He had already started to plant some seeds toward his dream before dropping out of school, by setting up meetings for a company called Acta Dialogue Marketing. Then in 1997, before he formally dropped out, he was hired as a salesperson by the telemarketing company Direkte Respons-Senteret (DRS). In fewer than three years, he had moved up to team leader of the company's customer-service department. He was making money, but he wanted to be more than just another employee.

With a friend from high school, he opened his first business. His idea was aimed at immigrants in Norway who needed a cheap way to phone their home countries. He and his associate began selling cheap telecom minutes for long-distance phone calls.

In Oslo, after just starting this telecom business, Breivik began to think seriously about entering politics. He was from the affluent area commonly referred to as Oslo West, and he was an entrepreneur who believed in less distribution of wealth and more restrictions on immigration, despite the fact that his telecom business specifically targeted the immigrant population; so, naturally, the Progressive Party (FrP) appealed to him. He spent time attending the party's school of politics, became active in debates, and contributed more than two hundred articles to the party's blog. He wrote mostly about financial policies and immigration, but nothing aimed specifically against Muslims. On the contrary, some of his blog posts were Muslim-friendly.

In a July 11, 2002 post, he wrote:

> *First of all, it is important to stress that Islam is a great religion (as is Christianity) and that Muslims in general are good people (as are Christians). This is not a battle against Islam but generally a battle against undemocratic habitual opinions, prejudice, and unfairness existing in Norway. The immigration, asylum, and integration politics of FrP have in principle nothing to do with Islam. There are of course some Muslims involved, but Islam as a religion should be held separate.*
>
> *There are many who get burned when they criticize Islam directly when they in principle should be criticizing certain aspects of cultures (non-cultures). There is an essential difference.*

Breivik's telecom business was a brilliant idea, but the potential clients were reluctant to leave the more-established Telia for a startup. Although the company might have succeeded over time, as in his past close relationships, Breivik failed to keep a satisfactory connection with his partner. They quarreled over almost everything, and Breivik called his friend incompetent. A few months later, he stood alone in his mother's basement, the small company he'd originated now dissolved. He decided to never again go into business with someone without sales experience. Again, Breivik's attachment issues prevented him from keeping any meaningful relationships for long.

Bruised but not beaten, he must have realized that his ideas were timely, for he began planning another enterprise. Founding Media Group, an outdoor advertising company, he began leasing billboard space. Coincidentally, his office was in the building that housed defense attorney Geir Lippestad and his colleagues. In fact, the two occasionally shared the building's canteen. Later, Breivik would remark how Lippestad's impressive defense of Ole Nicolai Kvisler, a member of the neo-Nazi group BootBoys accused of murdering Benjamin Hermansen, a Jewish man, in 2001 had drawn his admiration.

The billboard business never really got off the ground, certainly not well enough for Breivik to reach the high ambitions he had set for himself. Bowing to his mighty ambitions, Breivik wasn't above straying from the truth. Claiming that he held a degree from a Florida University, he soon began selling fake diplomas to individuals seeking counterfeit degrees from U.S. universities. At the same time, Breivik decided to blog on the Conservative Party's website.

During these attempts at building a big-time career for himself, he was trying to be more socially active. There is evidence that he also frequented Oslo's nightclub scene. During one such outing, he met a young woman from the Progressive Party Youth Organization and dated her for a few months. Although he appeared to lead a more normal social life during this period, none of the relationships would last.

His mother's boyfriend, Tore Tollefsen, a former major in the Norwegian Navy, who became Wenche Behring's partner when Breivik was twelve years old, has testified that Breivik had occasional girlfriends come around. "And they were all cute," he told an interviewer, as if that justified or explained his stepson's choices, or at least justified why Tore thought Breivik was normal enough and that there was no real cause for concern.

Tollefsen, then a pilot on active duty, saw Breivik mostly on weekends. Although he was generous in terms of gifts, the couple kept their separate homes and he never helped Wenche and her children financially. When Wenche had surgery and had to stop working, Breivik was the one who cared for her.

"He was a good guy," Tollefsen said of young Breivik, "sympathetic, a soft person, not a tough guy." He described how he had given up trying to teach the boy how to drive. "Anders failed his first driving exam because he was driving too slow and too careful." One can only imagine how Breivik reacted to failing to live up to his mother's boyfriend's macho image.

Just as his fake-diploma business was taking off in 2002, Breivik was rejected by his political party. His primary goal had been to create a common youth platform for the more independent-minded younger voters, who were more right-wing in their beliefs. Despite his ambitious efforts, the Progressive Party demoted him to a choice of lesser positions, and he was crestfallen.

This follows what Dr. Kathleen Puckett believes about lone wolves being unable to connect with anyone, even those who seem to share their ideas, and thus only instead to an ideology itself. It was not Breivik's first rejection, but it appears to have been a breaking point for him, just as failing at Special Forces in the U.S. Army had been for McVeigh and leaving academia had been for Kaczynski.

Not all radicals or fundamentalists will actually turn to violence. In fact, there is a big difference between a person with radical beliefs and a true lone wolf. "Even in violent extremist groups, the likelihood that they will act out is rare," she said. "The extremists get together in groups to hate together." Dr. Puckett believes the social interaction is what holds the group together, rather than going off and actually creating an agenda to plan and carry out terrorist acts. "They hate everyone together. They socialize and become part of each other's lives. But for the lone wolves the social connection is unachievable, so the extremist ideology of the radical group is their companion. They don't fit in, but they still have that need for connection." And so they try again and again, as we shall see Breivik do, even after he went into his state of isolation at his mother's home.

In 2002, a few months after September 11, 2001, Breivik embarked for Liberia in an attempt to break into the blood-diamond trade. He left a letter with one of his few remaining friends to be given to his mother in case he didn't return. This male companion, as it turned out, couldn't refuse the temptation to open the envelope and later testified as to its message.

Breivik had written that his mother was not to feel sorry for him, that he had left to seek happiness and success elsewhere.

In Liberia, Breivik reinvented himself. Using the name Henry Benson as his new alias, he entered a war-torn country and plunged into a dangerous business. The United States government had prohibited the import of diamonds from Liberia, as Liberian president Charles Taylor had been using the diamond trade to finance wars against his neighboring countries. Was Henry Benson the transitional avatar between Morg and another identity, Andrew Berwick, the Judiciary Knight that he would later use?

While in Liberia, he didn't buy any diamonds, but he did invest a considerable amount of money before returning to Norway. He was likely swindled by financial schemers in Liberia, who were targeting men just like Breivik who were naïvely attempting to break in to an incredibly sophisticated and corrupt black market. The police investigation after the 2011 massacre uncovered the fact that Breivik had sent thousands of dollars to Liberia while he was there, but never discovered what Breivik had invested in. He had also met with a Serbian war veteran known as "The Dragon" in Monrovia. According to Breivik, this man introduced him to the Knights Templar network; however, no proof exists that this was true. Breivik asserted that the Serb directed him to London to attend a Knights Templar meeting there. On his way, he purchased an expensive Montblanc pen, a symbol of the success that he felt sure was imminent, and stayed at the Saint Georges Hotel in London before finally returning to Oslo. (This is the pen he later sold.)

In his manifesto, he speaks of his burgeoning business career. Many who have studied his investments have found that he had reason to brag about his prowess in building a fortune. Others, content to settle for the accounts most publicized about him, point to the aforementioned failures and the more modest profits. Perhaps his amassed wealth at that time was somewhere between those extremes.

Breivik put it this way:

> The next three years I worked an average of twelve hours per day with my company, E-Commerce Group. At one point I had six employees, two in Norway, two in Russia, one in Romania, and

one in Indonesia. I registered an off shore company and several off shore bank accounts in order to avoid excessive taxation (anonymous debit cards and ATMs). This way, I could build up funds faster.

His desire was (and is) to start a pan-European conservative movement. Indeed, he is still trying to direct that movement from his prison cell today. As of the fall of 2014, he was still attempting to establish a new political party.

Funding for E-Commerce Group must have been coming in at a reasonably steady rate, for Breivik claimed it had started out with a bang, and he made his first million (NOK) at the age of twenty-four. This goal, he said, peaked at four million just a year later. At this time, in 2006, a recession lowered the income margins, and he decided to dump the company, but not before salvaging most of the funds.

He writes:

The most cost-efficient way of doing this in my country is to file for bankruptcy, which I did. I now had completed my goal and I had enough funding to proceed with the planning of an assault operation.

During the trial, Breivik claimed that he hid his radical opinions during this time in order to avoid drawing negative attention that could later ruin his ulterior plans.

The following, condensed, transcribed, and edited, is from one of his blogs after the party agreed to keep him on its board. It is as close as possible to his exact text:

June 8, 2002. I have founded and have run two companies, and am working on a third right now. I sold my last company eight years ago to a competitor. In order not to consume my saved capital, I work part-time at a bank.

Am I a Capitalist [sic]? According to the definition, I appear to be. Moreover, I react to the Socialists' prejudice and delusions about so-called capitalists. I am an entrepreneur/capitalist and I work my ass off, and must therefore sacrifice a lot of prime time and resources on a project that might go to hell. This is a risk that I'm taking, and like all entrepreneurs I'm risking going bankrupt, having a nervous breakdown, losing contact with friends, etc. Now chances are that I can create income for the state welfare system and that I can live the rest of my life without financial worries.

I will never accept that certain people (after looking at my future Ferrari) will label me a cynical asshole of a Capitalist (who must have stolen money from the poor) driving around laughing at the homeless. Capitalism is the force behind advancing!

Kind regards,
Anders Behring
Oslo West FpU
Board Member FpU Majorstuen

∞

If Breivik is to be believed, this was a time of great change in his life. Though stretching the law at times, he had proven his capability to succeed financially. And with this came his renewed hope of entering the political arena in some way.

His rules to himself read like a pamphlet titled "How to Become a Rock Star in the Progressive Party." These axioms appear later in his manifesto, and are listed here in a template he surely had been planning since the time he quit high school. Mainly, they apply to preparing himself to face the minions and deal with the photo hounds. The list is eloquent testimony to his grandiosity. After all, his every moment, he was sure, would be examined and measured by and for history.

Whenever he became lax about his appearance, he would scold himself:

As a Justiciar Knight you will go into history as one of the most influential individuals of your time. So you need to look your absolute best and ensure that you produce quality marketing material prior to operation.

Take a few hours in a solarium [that would be a sun-tanning parlor in the United States] to look fresher.

Train hard [work out] at least seven days prior to photo session.

Cut your hair [and] shave. Visit a male [hair] salon if possible and apply light makeup. Yes, I know that this sounds repulsive to big badass warriors like us, but we must look our best for our [photo] shoot.

[Wear] your best clothing. For example, bring . . . different sets of clothing to the shoot. (1) Suit and tie (2) Casual wear (3) Sportswear (4) Military wear.

Additional notes:

Obviously you can't bring guns or anything that might indicate you are a resistance fighter. Carefully consider the use of symbols as it might backfire. Cross of the martyrs is fine (St. George) but avoid any symbol associated with Nazism.

Advice:

Don't let friends dig into your background, or ask too many questions while you are planning a secret military operation.

Say you play World of Warcraft or another MMO and have developed an addiction for it.

Say you're going hardcore for the year and no one can convince you otherwise.

Say you think you are gay and in the process of discovering your new self and you don't want to talk about it. And make them swear not to tell anyone.

Warning:

[No] buying wine and hiring whores.

Also, a choice of proper wording:

"Martyrdom operation"

"Demographical genocide and the reverse of the Islamization of Europe."

∞

STRUGGLE AND CHANGE

So, here was Anders Behring Breivik, a couple of years before his crimes, jotting down notes as to how he should approach the society he lived in. While other young people, a few he lived among as a neutral companion, were in the process of settling down in their jobs, choosing friends, dating, and perhaps making plans to marry, live their lives together, and raise a family, he was writing notes to himself on how to become the great political and historic figure he knew he would be.

Of all his strict advice—much of it toned to a fictional group of people he thought might care about him—this, above all, appears especially pitiful in print. In the axioms, however, there is a tone of warning, so ulterior that it is difficult to read without feeling a chill, without asking oneself: "Is this the chart of a man interested in advancing a right-wing agenda in order to better steer his home country away from what he, and many other Norwegians, young and old, felt was an invasion upon their beloved homeland? Or is this the markings of a man planning something extreme, something so unworldly vicious that it would shock their nation's very soul?"

For Breivik, this was a time of struggle and change. He wasn't accepted in the political roles he had envisioned for himself. The Progressive Party he seemed to adore so much kept him at arm's length. And many Norwegians frowned upon his rapid accumulation of money, something he apparently did well.

In *A Norwegian Tragedy*, Aage Storm Borchgrevink writes: "In the compendium—his 'master-work'—Breivik appears as consumer society's lost son, the loser in the capitalistic war-zone, the player who could not separate reality from fantasies created on the web. The compendium describes two different persons: one awake and political . . . , and one sleeping, passive and unconscious consumer—almost like the plot in *Matrix*, a movie he refers to often."

Borchgrevink compares Breivik to a character "walking right out of the novels by Michel Houellebecq, Bret Easton Ellis, and Chuck Palahniuk." In Ellis's novel, *American Psycho*, Patrick Bateman spends his days working on Wall Street and his nights involved in torture and murder. He is a metaphor for American corporate life gone bad. Borchgrevink calls Breivik the Norwegian Psycho, ". . . the human who is almost completely superficial and empty, whose best friends are not people, but brands. Breitling Crosswind, Chanel Platinum, Egoïste."

It is not surprising that this Norwegian author can blame capitalism for Breivik's killing spree or compare him to a fictional character as metaphorically evil as Bateman. Breivik was obsessed with being successful in business, with succeeding in general. He wanted to prove everyone wrong, and he wanted to emerge from the Law-of-Jante state as the premier example of someone who didn't follow the group.

In "The Norwegian Psycho," an article by Shabana Rehman Gaarder, published in August 2012 on *NRK* (www.nrk.no), the author attempts to answer the question of whether the threat to society lies more in a state of mind without inhibitions, such as Breivik's. "Breivik was not only an extreme rightist. He acquiesced to a culture where many are willing to do almost anything for money and success, to succeed, and to compare themselves with their neighbors.

"He also represents a culture that collects its view of the world from *World of Warcraft* and other utopias created by the Internet. Maybe the threat is more in a state of mind without inhibitions?

"Maybe this is also a signal of a generation. When Bret Easton Ellis wrote *American Psycho*, he diagnosed the modern, extreme materialism in the USA. What does The Norwegian Psycho symbolize?"

Breivik saw his life, which had spiraled out of control, grow from "a so-called arrogant self-centered fuck" who didn't care about anything outside his family and friends, to what he described as "something better." He writes that, in seeking a more responsible level, he became a better man, but he had to pay a high price for that transformation.

"I left several aspects of my old life behind and had to completely reestablish myself on an existential level," he writes. "It was hard because everyone I used to know felt I had abandoned them. I never burned any bridges though which might explain why many of them are still pressuring me to come back. Obviously, I do not intend to. If they knew my real intentions, my cover would be blown, and I would risk being exposed. I cannot allow that to happen."

Breivik's cover was not blown, and he was not exposed. Instead, he was pushed down by the political system, which would not accept him, and by the anti-capitalistic Norwegian society, which was not responding as he had hoped to his self-perceived business acumen. His options were disappearing, not because of immigration, and not because of the Muslims. He had attempted to break away from a restrictive, repressive, and bullying society, yet he had a need to connect to someone or something, and he was still treading water in this regard. Even he must have known he had failed. He had reached his turning point.

CHAPTER FIVE

MANIFESTO:
INDEPENDENCE FROM ANONYMITY

We are sick and tired of feeling like strangers in our own lands, of being mugged, raped, stabbed, harassed, and even killed by violent gangs of Muslim thugs, yet being accused of "racism and xenophobia" by our media. . . .

—ANDERS BREIVIK MANIFESTO

No one knows the moment that Anders Breivik decided to focus on murder and violence, but we can guess. His future, in his own perception, went from visions of grandeur to something quite bleak, with limited opportunities. In 2005, after he quit actively participating in the Progressive Party, he was wealthy. According to the police, who investigated his funds six years later, he had fourteen bank accounts in seven different countries, ranging from the Caribbean to the Baltics. Slowly and systematically, he began to bring this money back to Norway through his mother's account, making her an accessory to the sale of illegal diplomas and the laundering of hundreds of thousands of dollars. After getting away with his fraudulent schemes, he ended it a year later, afraid that if he pushed his luck, his new plans would be shattered. At this time, he moved back into his mother's home and began writing his manifesto. This overwhelming and depressing document is essential to understanding Breivik's mind at that time in his life. No other book on the topic has attempted to break down and explain the manifesto in detail—perhaps because of the enormity of the job, or maybe due to the fear that paying close attention to Breivik's writing will validate him further. And perhaps it does.

However, this manifesto provides a unique understanding of what Breivik was thinking before he committed the killings. Furthermore, if we refuse to even consider what motivates such a killer, we leave ourselves vulnerable to others like him.

∞

One might speculate how Breivik started to collect information for his document, and how radical his viewpoint was at the time he began. Almost certainly, the document was written by a man who planned to kill. When Breivik started writing his manifesto, he had already retreated from the world of politics, from his attempts to lead a professional life, and from most social activity. He was a castaway from society, had failed to make any sound connection with any group, and likely felt like a stranger in his own country. Something wasn't right, but he didn't know what had gone wrong in his life or how he could change it.

Peter Svaar, a journalist for the Norwegian Broadcasting Corporation (NRK), which is state-owned, told how, during these years, he had seen Breivik occasionally in the nightclubs. A former high school classmate of Breivik's, Svaar would remark, after the massacre, how devastated he was that Breivik had been the one apprehended, declaring that his boyhood pal just didn't fit the stereotypical role of a mass murderer. But wasn't that what everybody had been saying?

"He was not a complete loner," Svaar said, "or a person you couldn't hang out with." He describes Breivik as kind, loyal to his friends, strong-headed, and intelligent. Basically, he did not seem that much out of the ordinary to the casual observer, like Svaar. To him, the manifesto didn't appear to be the work of a madman. "Rather," Svaar went on, in what could be described as a measured, contradictory tone, "[Breivik] is cold, intelligent, and calculating. What keeps me up at night is the fact that he is not a monster. He is a normal Norwegian boy. He has buried himself in an incredible political analysis, and unfortunately, was resourceful enough to execute his plan."

Other reports about Breivik during his self-imposed exile aren't plentiful. Breivik admits in his writings that he had dropped out of society. This was no short sabbatical he had decided to indulge himself in for a few days, weeks, or even months. No, this timeout would amount to years, devoted to what would eventually be his last words to the world as a free man, his final credo. Not isolated from the world completely, he actively blogged on sites critical of current immigration politics, but he rarely physically interacted with the outside world anymore. Alone and secluded, Breivik continued to make attempts to connect with others sympathetic to his cause. His all-time hero in this social-media environment was the Norwegian Fjordman, which was the pseudonym of Peder Are Nøstvold Jensen, a critic of immigration and, in particular, Muslim immigrants. Unknown in Norway before the attacks, he had, and still has, a large international following.

Breivik's manuscript would eventually run to 777,724 words, 1,516 pages. There must have been times he felt imprisoned, shackled to his chair in front of his computer. He admits to playing assault computer games as much as sixteen hours a day when not detailing his ideology and goals. How, one must wonder, was he able to endure such a hermitage? Many metaphors must have been traveling through his brain, like how he had to eventually get out of his favorite chair, leave his mother's basement, and dive back into the wave of life. But he remained devoted to his new "cause."

The massive manuscript would go out to his hand-picked audience under the title *2083: A European Declaration of Independence*, by Andrew Berwick. Again, this shadow of a man chose to use an alias for no apparent reason. Maybe he was worried that he might be apprehended before he'd be able to set off the bomb and murder the teenagers on the island of Utøya. Maybe grabbing for a fake name was just a habit. Breivik had used so many aliases throughout the years that perhaps he felt as if, through these killings, his old self would disappear and he would finally become his avatar. One thing is certain: his narcissistic side wanted him to take credit for his acts, to become infamous, to matter.

When Breivik's manifesto was examined later, *Time* magazine described it as a template for right-wing terrorists. Terror experts wrote that it was little more than a mirror image of a Jihadist/al Qaeda manifesto.

The first two sections of the manifesto, Book 1 and Book 2, are mostly cut-and-paste mosaics of Breivik's favorite authors, whose work he felt underscored his own philosophies. A great deal of it makes sense and has nothing to do with violence, probably because it's not Breivik who wrote it. Breivik also copied Kaczynski the Unabomber's manifesto, without giving him credit. He must have been inspired by Kaczynski's eloquent writing and arguments about what was wrong with society, and he adapted the speech to his own cause by replacing the word *left* with *politically correct*. He also must have felt kinship with Kaczynski and his disillusionment with the world.

There is a difference in Book 3, where the language seems to be less eloquent and the text more disorganized. He himself claims that he was running out of time. One might speculate that when he started collecting information, he was more moderate in his choices of reference, and that through the years he became more and more radical and militant in his views. In this final book, Breivik takes the writings of others and twists their message into motivation for his violence. This part of the manifesto shows how he was able to plan and ultimately carry out his attacks. As discussed, it was a guide to those who followed him, regardless of his own fate, but it was also a way for Breivik to reassure himself and justify his actions.

His title refers to the American Declaration of Independence of 1776—and the essay by the blogger, Fjordman, contained in the manifesto. It is no accident that Breivik compares Norway's situation to the citizens who broke away from British reign and formed the United States of America. He writes that it is necessary for Europe to break free from Islamic reign, which he believes is taking over the continent. The American Declaration of Independence is also the symbol of the free world, of protection of the basic human rights, such as freedom of property, speech, and the sovereign rights of a country, all of which Breivik felt were being threatened in Norway and Europe.

In Norway, a signatory state to the Universal Declaration of Human Rights, everyone is allowed to speak freely, provided they get police approval *in advance*. Most European countries have hate-speech laws, prohibiting citizens from making statements in public that threaten or ridicule a person or a group of people, or statements that incite hatred for someone due to their skin color, ethnic origin, sexual orientation, religion, or philosophy of life. However, statistics show that hate-speech laws do not reduce hate crimes. The United States, unlike Europe, has protected individual rights and freedom of speech in its constitution. Even there, freedom of speech is limited by hate-speech laws. Becoming more "European" by limiting freedom of speech will not prevent more killings, because these killers want to be heard and will do whatever it takes to do so.

This is an example of how Breivik used facts to color and justify his actions. Yet it wasn't fact that drove Breivik, and it isn't fact that drives other lone wolves. Revenge and rage are part of it. So is repression and a need to matter.

BOOK 1

The exhaustive, multi-footnoted document begins with an introduction about political correctness, which Breivik calls "cultural Marxism." He also presents theories on "radical feminism" through the lens of political correctness. Book 1 is titled "What you need to know, our falsified history and other forms of cultural Marxist/multiculturalist propaganda." It is a historic description of the crisis in Europe today and what led to it. He begins by quoting George Orwell: "Who controls the future controls the past."

"I must admit," Breivik writes, "when I first started the study on Islamic history and Islamic atrocities more than 3 years ago, I really had my doubts about the 'politically correct' information available. I started to scratch the surface and I was shocked as I uncovered the vast amount of 'ugly, unknown' truths concerning Islamic atrocities. There is a common misconception regarding Islam and Christianity. A lot of people believe today that Christianity still is and was as evil as Islam?! [*sic*] I can attest to the fact that this is absolutely incorrect. Jihadi-motivated killings, torture, and enslavement count for more than 10 times as [many as] Christian-motivated killings. However, the politically correct Western establishments want us to think otherwise."

QUOTING FJORDMAN

Fjordman, Peder Are Nøstvold Jensen, was forced to reveal his identity in 2011 after the attacks and has since tried to distance himself from Breivik. Like Breivik, Fjordman fills his writing with lengthy quotations from others. It was suggested by Norwegian media during the trial that Fjordman and some right-wing American bloggers such as Pamela Geller and Robert Spencer were somehow responsible for Breivik's acts. These accusations are ludicrous. Breivik would have taken any idea or ideology to heart. His fight against multiculturalism was really a fight and, ultimately, an attack on his own government.

Fjordman concludes one essay by pointing out that at the same time universities in China, India, Korea, and other Asian countries graduate millions of "motivated engineers and scientists" annually, Western universities ". . . have been reduced to little hippie factories, teaching about the wickedness of the West and the blessings of barbarism." He goes on to say that there is a strong tendency in Europe to vilify the United States and capitalism; that in school, we were taught about the evil consumer society and the socialistic propaganda focusing on solidarity, redistribution of wealth, and that it was good to sacrifice oneself for the "common good." He says one might ask if the Marshall Plan for rebuilding Europe after World War II somehow created a simmering resentment toward the United States.

"This represents a serious challenge to the long-term economic competitiveness of Western nations," Fjordman writes. "That's bad, but it is the least of our worries. Far worse than failing to compete with non-Muslim Asians is failing to identify the threat from Islamic nations who want to subdue us and wipe out our entire civilization. That is a failure we quite simply cannot live with. And we probably won't, unless we manage to deal with it."

Breivik, of course, has a plan to "deal with it," if we are to believe the manifesto. That plan is violence, murder, and the eradication of Islam from Europe.

ISLAM AND JIHAD

Breivik includes, in the first section of Book 1, something titled "Islam 101," which he has plagiarized from Gregory M. Davis, as an attempt to help the public understand the truth about Islam and also to provide information for those who want to share the truth with others.

He explains that the term *jihad* translates as "struggle" and says that it does not mean holy war. He questions if struggle means "an inner, spiritual *struggle* against the passions, or an outward, physical struggle." He then says that one must refer to the Koran and the Sunnah, which he has included references to.

"From those sources (see above) it is evident that a Muslim is required to struggle against a variety of things: laziness in prayer, neglecting to give zakat (alms), etc. But it is also plain that a Muslim is commanded to struggle in physical combat against the infidel as well. Muhammad's impressive military career attests to the central role that military action plays in Islam."

In a section of frequently asked questions about Islam, Breivik responds to the question of why Muslims are peaceful people if Islam is violent, by pointing out that many Christians do not practice what Christianity teaches either. "Just as it is often easier for a Christian to sit back, play holier-than-thou, or disdain others, so it is often easier for a Muslim to stay at home rather than embark on jihad. Hypocrites are everywhere."

He further states that some people who don't understand their own faith act outside of its prescribed boundaries. Because the Koran is frequently recited in Arabic, many Muslims did not understand it. He suggests that Muslims in Norway are more likely to be attracted by Western ways and less likely to act violently against the society to which they may have fled.

However, he warns, ". . . in any given social context, as Islam takes greater root—increasing numbers of followers, the construction of more mosques and 'cultural centers,' etc.—the greater the likelihood that some number of its adherents will take its violent precepts seriously. This is the problem that the West faces today." He says many immigrants to Norway, Muslims included, have a hard time integrating. The new generation that is born in Norway, or the United States for that matter, find themselves torn between wanting to fit in with their wider group of peers and their families' cultures and norms. Often, their parents win this struggle. As an example, many first-generation Muslim girls are not allowed to date Western men and are forced to marry within the Muslim community. Many are also sent back to their homeland to marry there.

Breivik concludes Book 1 by focusing on the Knights Templar. "I would strongly advice [*sic*] all Justiciar Knights to visit Valletta, Malta, and Jerusalem, Israel and to visit all the Knights Templar historical sites. There are various Templar buildings in several European countries; France, the UK, Portugal, Spain, Italy, etc."

Breivik was fascinated with secret societies, and he still longed to be part of a group, of something important. In 2007, he managed, with the help of a relative, to become a member of Saint Olaf Lodge, a part of the Norwegian Order of Freemasons. He went through the numerous interviews and tests before finally being accepted with ease. He was good at "putting on the game face," as he wrote, and making people believe he could fit in at first. Although he was still a member of this secret society when he went through with his massacre, he never managed to make any close connections in this group either. He never showed any interest in participating in the organization's activities, nor did he hold any functions within the lodge, according to Ivar A. Skaar, Grand Master of the Norwegian Order. When Breivik distributed his manifesto on July 22, 2011, he issued photographs of himself wearing Masonic costumes and regalia.

Knights are common in the world of computer games, a world with which he is all too familiar. At the time he was writing this, Breivik appeared to be living partly in an imaginary world of war, online killings, secret societies, and medieval heroes.

BOOK 2

Book 2 in the manifesto is called "Europe Burning." Breivik promises his readers that they will review and analyze the current problems Europe faces, as well as possible solutions for those problems.

"You shall know the truth and the truth shall make you mad."—Aldous Huxley.

With this quote, he begins the section, describing the different parts of the ongoing civil war from 1950 to 2083, when he believes the war will come to an end and a new Europe will rise. The years 1950 to 1999 were the preface to the war—"the years of the dialogue," as Breivik calls them. Phase I of the war started in 1999, when NATO attacked Serbia and invaded Kosovo. In his manifesto, Breivik claims that this was his turning point. But it is more likely that he borrowed this idea from the Serb called "The Dragon," after listening to his stories in Liberia in 2002. According to Breivik, we'll be in this phase until 2030. Phase I is, as explained in Book 2, the time for small attacks, such as what we experienced on July 22, 2011. Phase II, from 2030 to 2070, will be characterized by more resistance to the Islamization of Europe and, at the same time, more colonization of Europe by Muslims. Phase III of the war is the period in which the culturally conservative will stage a coup of Europe, execute all traitors, and deport all Muslims. This is where it becomes clear that Breivik wrote himself into becoming a murderer. He is no longer the "normal Norwegian boy."

FJORDMAN LISTS "BIG LIES"

Another Fjordman piece discusses steps taken in schools, resulting in ". . . completely rewriting European history books to make them more Islam-friendly, and gradually silencing 'Islamophobia' as racism."

As a solution, Fjordman proposed three possible approaches to teaching religion in schools. "1. Teach the traditional religions within a particular country, which in Europe means Christianity and Judaism. 2. Teach all the major world religions. 3. Leave religion out of the curriculum."

He goes on to say that the European Union treats Islam as a traditional European religion, on a par with Christianity and Judaism. "This is a crucial component of Eurabian thinking and practice," he writes. "Notice how EU authorities in this case directly interfered to force a once-independent nation state to include more teachings of Islam in its school curriculum in order to instill their children with a proper dose of Eurabian indoctrination. Notice also that they didn't ask for more teaching of Buddhism or Hinduism. Only Islam is being pushed."

Fjordman may have a point here. Germany and France have a large number of Muslim immigrants, and that has influenced their countries' changing demographic, in the ways of culture and education. France, especially, has taken in many Muslims from the former French colonies. Because Germany and France are the two most powerful countries in the European Union, they also have the most influence in this organization. Other authors, such as Bat Ye'or, have also written extensively about this.

In studying Fjordman's articles, one can imagine Breivik, consciously or not, adopting the same structure. Both include long quotations and multiple sources, like college students writing their first research papers. Breivik's role model, Kaczynski, was even more lengthy. It is difficult not to think of Kaczynski when reading Breivik's manifesto.

In the piece on Eurabian indoctrination, Fjordman lists "some Big Lies." They are:

"Diversity is always good;

"Multiculturalism is inevitable, as is continued EU integration;

"Those opposing it are ignorant racists standing against the tide of history;

"Muslim immigration is 'good for the economy' and is necessary for funding the welfare state in the future, despite the fact that it drains away enormous resources."

We can sense the anger that lies behind these statements in Fjordman, as well as in Breivik. The Law of Jante and the government's social-democratic politics have silenced the non-believers and made it almost impossible to express their views without being ridiculed and rejected, sometimes even violently. Fjordman goes on, calling Eurabia "one of the greatest betrayals in the history of Western civilization. But that does not mean that all EU federalists are evil." And then he quotes Hugh Fitzgerald: "A whole class of people has gotten rich from Arab money and bribes; lawyers, public relations men, and diplomats, journalists, university teachers, and assorted officials."

Yet others, Fjordman believes, "must have convinced themselves that what they were doing was for a just cause, if for no other reason than because human vanity demands that we justify our actions by covering them with a veneer of goodness."

In yet another piece in this section, Fjordman explains, as his title clearly states, "Why the EU Needs to be Destroyed, and Soon."

"I'm really worried about a complete collapse of the democratic system here," he writes. "It has already been weakened by the EU, the UN, etc. for a long time, and now we also have direct physical threats by Muslims to freedom of speech. Ordinary Europeans are no longer in control of our own fates. Sweden has for instance in reality ceased being a democratic country, in my view. We need to recapture this, or Europe is finished."

Fjordman's frustrations against the EU, UN, and intergovernmental treaties that give up on our sovereign rights are shared by many, especially in the United States, because the treaties take precedence over local law, even the Constitution, in case of conflict.

Fjordman and Breivik aren't the only ones sharing their frustrations and anger toward immigration and integration policies on the Internet. A great many writers, bloggers, and followers, not only in Europe but everywhere, share the same thoughts. Some of the Americans cited numerous times in Breivik's manifesto are Robert Spencer, best-selling author and founder of *Jihad Watch*, as well as Pamela Geller and Bruce Bawer, who are also part of the contra-jihadist environment.

The manner in which multiculturalism is practiced in most countries assumes that all cultures are equal, when in fact they have very different beliefs regarding the value of human life. As Fjordman puts it: "Multiculturalism serves as a tool for ruling elites to fool people, to keep them from knowing that they have lost, or deliberately vacated, control over national borders. Leftists who dislike Western civilization use multiculturalism to undermine it, a hate ideology disguised as tolerance. Multiculturalism equals the unilateral destruction of Western culture, the only unilateral action the West is allowed to take, according to some."

Multiculturalism and affirmative action actually create more discrimination because they make race an issue. If someone is given privileges for some reason other than merit, for example, anger and feelings of injustice can lead to racism.

Breivik's Fjordman-fest continues with "The Failure of Western Feminism": "As a Western man, I would be tempted to say that Western women have to some extent brought this upon themselves. They have been waging an ideological, psychological and economic war against European men for several generations now, believing that this would make you 'free.' The actual result is that you have less freedom of movement and security than ever, as a direct result of the immigrant policies supported by you and your buddies."

Fjordman attacks everything from low birth rates to what he calls the "fatherless civilization," and Breivik faithfully includes essay after rambling essay. Breivik must have felt at home in Fjordman's writing, connected to someone he felt was of like mind and intelligence. After all, he had grown up fatherless, with a mother who could not take proper care of him and in a society that he felt had bullied him into a corner. He reached out to Fjordman numerous times via e-mail, attempting to connect with his hero.

An attempt in 2009 actually got a response, although certainly not the one Breivik was hoping for. He began his outreach with a compliment: *"LOL@ your tourettes comment, insanely good :O"*. Then he added an invitation and finished with a comment that probably earned him a response— that he was coming too close to disclosing Fjordman's identity. *"Hoping you come on Thursday (you should jump in your car from trondheimi:D) By the way, I chatted a lot with a FB [Facebook] friend, xxxxx, it turns out she was dating your best friend, xxxxx. Small world. . . . Add me on FB you slacker:D"*

Although Breivik would not learn Fjordman's name until the trial, he was reckless with the information he obtained, and his message in 2009 obviously hit a little too close to home and was enough to draw Fjordman's attention. Fjordman responded with this: *"I would appreciate if you say as little as possible about me publicly. I might go public one day with my full name, but I would like to wait a bit until I have finished what I'm writing on now. F."*

Then, in February 2010, one of Breivik's messages again got Fjordman's attention.

"Hey again Fjordman:-)

"Thought I would send you a couple of suggestions. I have approximately 5000 contacts on Facebook now, absolutely all the best (well connected) patriotically oriented in Europe (East/West), US, Canada, New Zealand, and Aussie, etc. (even South Africa). You will lose terrain if you do not use FB as all other European intellectuals do. I will happily share my two networks with you (I have two profiles). I could, for instance, give you the 200 absolutely best connected FB patriots in Europe and in the US. Many of these would, by the way, let you post

your articles on their pages, myself included. You would hence reach up to 30,000 to 50,000 by simply posting on a few high quality profiles. In addition there are twenty-something FB groups that are worth mentioning. Many of the contacts I know reasonably well are running many of these groups and would with pleasure let you contribute. Just let me know :-)"

He follows the offer with a further attempt at bonding: *"My compendium will be finished within a couple of weeks after three years of work. Will send you an electronic version when it's done. You are going to like it;-) Have given up on dokument.no. Hans is censoring even the most moderate contributions that share your ideology :P Anders."* (Dokument.no is a Norwegian website and blog. At this time, Breivik had stopped posting on it.)

Fjordman wrote back almost within the hour, and again his message was one of rejection: "Thanks for the offer. But I am not planning on using FB directly at the moment. I will be writing on dokument.no for now, but so many of my comments have been censored that I might not bother for long. F."

Once more, all that was left for Breivik to connect with was not the man, but the increasingly radical ideology.

ISLAM

Throughout the second book of the manifesto, we are warned about the dangers of Islamization.

Under the heading "Modern Jihad," Breivik begins with these quotations:

Sura 9 Verse 29
Fight against those who believe not in Allah, nor in the Last Day, nor forbid that which has been forbidden by Allah and His Messenger.

. . . and fight against those who acknowledge not the religion of truth (i.e., Islam) among the People of the Scripture (Jews and Christians), until they pay the Jizyah (Tax for Jews/Christians) with willing submission and feel themselves subdued.

Sura 9 Verse 5
Kill the unbelievers wherever you find them. . . .But if they repent and accept Islam . . . then leave their way free.

He lists a website that presents an overview of Jihadi terror acts since 2001. "Unfortunately, this is only the top [sic] of the iceberg," he writes. "There are hundreds more attacks occurring every single day, across the world, which are not documented. This includes Europeans slain by Muslims living in Europe. There is no website as far as we know who catalogue these atrocities."

Steven M. Kleinman is the Director of Strategic Research at The Soufan Group. Kleinman, a career intelligence officer, a colonel in the U.S. Air Force, and a recognized subject-matter expert on human intelligence, counterterrorism, special operations, and strategic interrogation, with thirty years of operational and leadership experience across the globe, had this to say about Brcivik's claims:

"I suggest—based on my observation and interaction with both terrorists and counter terrorists—that there is no such thing as a 'peaceful' religion (or, for that matter, one that is not a peaceful religion). There are, however, both nonviolent and violent individuals who claim an affiliation with (or a faith in) a given religion. Certainly, contemporary terrorism is filled with examples of violent extremist groups with Islamic roots. Then again, the Ku Klux Klan is still active (on a very small scale) in the United States. Many of its followers are members of Christian congregations led by clergymen who offer extreme views of Christian theology that promote the eradication of certain ethnic groups (notably African Americans and Jews) as allowed (even required) by God."

Of the major religions, he said, it seems that Buddhism was the only belief system that not only promoted peace, but whose adherents dutifully followed this creed with great discipline. He goes on to say:

"Now, one need only examine the escalating violence between Muslim and Buddhist groups in Myanmar to see that Buddhism can no longer be considered as belonging in a separate category. Have the tenets of Buddhism changed? Not at all. Given the violence perpetrated by Buddhists, should we now consider Buddhism as 'not a peaceful religion'? I don't think so.

"Thus, I would submit that however we characterize Islam—as a peaceful religion or as one that promotes violence—we would, to be fair, objective, and mindful of history, need to perceive every other major religion in the same light."

Breivik, so disconnected with his own pain, transferred his frustrations with Norway's culture and, via proxy, the government to fear and hatred of Muslims.

It is clear that Breivik agrees with George Orwell's quote "In a time of universal deceit, telling the truth is a revolutionary act." Breivik's idea of truth is repeated over and over and examined from every angle and source and related fact, as if the very redundancy of it will convince the reader and perhaps himself of its validity. Breivik writes:

"Approximately 70 percent of Western European males would sacrifice their lives to prevent Europe from being conquered by Islam while less than 10 percent would sacrifice their life for their race. As such, it isn't exactly rocket science to foresee which ideology (with given rhetorical strategies) will win over the 'modern patriot.' Waking up enough of our fellow Europeans will take several decades. Do not expect him to accept and embrace the light immediately; especially when we are fully aware of [the fact] that he has been taught to avoid the light."

Again, we see the influences of computer games in Breivik's writing. And throughout his entire manifesto, he is convinced that there is a conspiracy of the politically correct governments and the Muslim communities against the native European populations. We now begin to understand Breivik's transformation from lonely outsider to murderer.

At the conclusion of his essay "A European Declaration of Independence," Fjordman writes in a voice that might as well be Breivik's:

"If these demands are not fully implemented, if the European Union isn't dismantled, multiculturalism isn't rejected and Muslim immigration isn't stopped, we, the peoples of Europe, are left with no other choice than to conclude that our authorities have abandoned us, and that the taxes they collect are therefore unjust and that the laws that are passed without our consent are illegitimate. We will stop paying taxes and take the appropriate measures to protect our own security and ensure our national survival."

It isn't surprising that Book 2 concludes with "Islamization of Europe and Policies to Prevent It."

Breivik wanted to see European policies on multiculturalism and immigration become more like those of Japan and South Korea. He admires the monoculturalism of Japan and calls on all "nationalists" to join in the struggle against the cultural Marxists or multiculturalists.

He writes, "I believe Europe should strive for: A cultural conservative approach where monoculturalism, moral, the nuclear family, a free market, support for Israel and our Christian cousins of the east, law and order and Christendom itself must be central aspects (unlike now)."

Up until that point, everything reads as fairly consistent with the thoughts and writings of others who support Norway's Progressive Party. But when we look closer at Breivik's solution, we can see that it moves into much more extreme territory and comes very close to a fundamentalist Islamic society—in other words, everything he detests. Breivik's new society is based on hierarchy, patriarchy, and strong authority (totalitarianism). He wants to reinstate the patriarchal model, the nuclear family, and get rid of "the creation and rise of the matriarchal systems, which are now dominating Western European countries."

For instance, he wants to abolish freedom of choice regarding abortion. Although Breivik states that he had a happy childhood and can't remember Child Protective Services' involvement, his ramblings in the manifesto are a clear indication of his own issues growing up, and especially his issues with his mother. In Breivik's ideological construction of society, we find, according to Øystein Sørensen, professor in modern history at the University of Oslo, the following characteristics:

- A great number of supreme laws and principles, with extremely detailed rules on what is allowed and what is not;
- An institutionalized religion that permeates all of society, especially cultural aspects;
- A cultivation of an idealized past, and a cultivation of traditional values;
- Hierarchal and patriarchal reform;
- A strong aversion against Western liberal sexuality and against Western feminism;
- A ruthless hunt for and cleansing of anything or anyone deviating from the detailed laws and principles;
- A parliament with limited authority;

- Strict rules governing public advocacy of political views; and
- A conservative council whose role is to guarantee and protect the political system.

The country whose regime most resembles Breivik's solution is Iran, based on Ayatollah Khomeini's political and cultural ideas and his implementation of a totalitarian state.

Ironically, had Breivik somehow been successful, he would have helped create the type of society he was trying to destroy. By now, his thinking had become so deranged that he believed the arrival of Muslim immigrants in Norway was tantamount to an invasion. He wasn't a racist, and ultimately, despite the words in this section of the manifesto, it really wasn't the Muslims who concerned him: it was the government—his government—that he believed discriminated against Norwegians and gave more privileges and rights to Muslims. These Muslims weren't integrating. They weren't respectful of Norwegian culture. Yet the Norwegian government gave them more attention and care than they did Norwegians like Breivik. At least this is how he saw it. But they were there, and the Norwegian way was to assimilate, always assimilate, with little regard for the individual parts of the whole. The government was not forcing these new immigrants to assimilate, and Breivik could not forgive this.

A DECLARATION OF INDEPENDENCE

That Breivik used *2083: A European Declaration of Independence* as the title for his manifesto brings us right down to the essence of his suffering. As he explains in his manifesto (taken from an essay on political correctness written by the Free Congress Foundation), the United States' founders recognized three primary values in the Declaration of Independence: life, liberty, and the pursuit of happiness. The essay goes on to state that the order of these fundamental rights is crucial, and if they are to be switched— with happiness before liberty or liberty before life—the result is moral chaos and social anarchy. This is Breivik's cause against these conditions, described by Judge Robert Bork as "modern liberalism." The problem with modern liberalism, according to Bork, is "radical egalitarianism," or equality of outcomes rather than of opportunities, and "radical individualism," meaning the drastic reduction of limits to personal gratification. The first is what exists in Scandinavia, and the second is closer to the social climate of the United States.

The "appropriate measures" that Fjordman mentions in his essay are interpreted by Breivik as violence and murder and, in the end, ethnic cleansing. He must have taken Fjordman's writings, as well as others, as justification for what he would ultimately do. In his narcissistic mind, the world depended on him. He would show them. He would finally matter. Again, he was connecting with ideology, making that ideology his sole reason for living.

His conclusion that Muslims want to take over the world, and that the government must be overthrown, is an attempt to find a solution for a problem that no one else knows how to solve—but him. Breivik's reasoning has now degenerated, and he has merged his hatred of Norwegian society and hatred of the Muslims. Once that occurs, he finds himself on an irreversible path of destruction. Soon, he will cease to be another voiceless person who doesn't matter. Soon, the very system that has tried to silence him all these years will hear his message, and everyone will know who Anders Behring Breivik is. He will make sure of that.

CHAPTER SIX

JULY 22, 2011:
FINALLY TAKEN SERIOUSLY

Defending your people and culture from genocide is the most basic and recognized human right and one of few causes actually worth dying for.

—ANDERS BREIVIK MANIFESTO

THE BOMB

The large white-paneled Volkswagen van is caught on the surveillance camera as it drives past a no-entry sign and into the plaza fronting Norway's seventeen-story central government building in downtown Oslo. After coming to a stop for almost two minutes, the driver turns the vehicle in a complete U-turn and drives closer, with its hazard lights blinking, to the

H-block section, where the prime minister's offices are located. The main entrance, with its beautiful lobby, is hidden in this view, but it is just a few meters away.

Seconds later, the driver is seen getting out of the van. The video is a bit grainy, but against the white vehicle it is easy to see that he is wearing a helmet, the kind with a clear face shield, and dark clothing that resembles that of a security or police officer. From certain angles, one can see that he is holding what looks to be a large pistol against his thigh. He seems to pause while two figures hurriedly cross the camera's view on the sidewalk nearest the camera. Then he calmly begins to stroll, left to right on the video, picking up his pace a bit now as he puts distance between himself and the van.

Another surveillance camera shows the side view of the building, with the glass-fronted H-block section on its extreme right profile. The tall trees between the camera and the high-rise move slightly in the silence. Then suddenly, the entire building seems to rock from a horrendous impact. A bright glow emerges along the building's front, and it looks like everything up and down the many stories of offices is being forced from the inside out. Flames, smoke, and a belching cloud of debris, containing objects turned into shards and floating particles, engulf the street. The trees show the force of the shockwave as they move back and forth in a whip-like frenzy.

Cell-phone videos captured at the time later revealed office workers stumbling out of the main entrance. Some quickly fell in pools of their own blood. Others staggered out into the cold afternoon, their faces frozen into masks of pain, shock, and utter confusion. Something terrible had happened. *Never*, victims and witnesses thought and uttered in snatches of disoriented speech. *Not here. Not at home. Not in Norway.*

The debris cloud rained paper, torn strips of draperies, and shrapnel from furniture, cement, glass, and metal. Whole window frames and large sheets of glass were still falling from the height of several stories. Alarms from nearby buildings in the square howled as the shockwave struck their façades, breaking windows and throwing debris. The street began to fill with stunned people, some who had come from blocks away to see what had made the earth shake straight through their vehicles and into their stomachs. Most, though, were afraid there would be a second explosion, and they hurried away from the impacted zone. At the same time, the police arriving at the scene ordered everyone to get as far away as possible.

Ambulances began to arrive, their sirens and blinking lights enabling them to get as close as they dared to the most seriously injured. As moments passed, rescue workers in yellow vests and hardhats began to help in any way they could, their commands to others hesitant in their own ignorant panic.

"Was it a gas main?"

"More like a bomb."

"From a plane?"

"My God! Is it another September 11?"

"How can we help these people?"

"I saw one lady with a piece of steel impaled in her forehead walking about."

"There must be hundreds out here bleeding!"

The crater where the lobby had been slowly became clear through the haze of sulfur-infused smoke. There was little left of the white van that had been right there in that same area just minutes before.

Breivik had spent his last day as a "normal Norwegian boy" at his mother's apartment in Oslo, his white Volkswagen Crafter containing the bomb parked down the road.

McVeigh had slept in his Ryder truck, guarding the bomb, at a gravel lot near a roadside motel in northern Oklahoma. It was past 7 A.M. when he pulled out of the parking lot and started making his way to his target in Oklahoma City. He had planned to be outside the FBI building at 11 A.M. but changed his mind as he woke up that morning. He didn't want to take the risk of causing suspicion waiting at the motel, so he left early. Driving toward his target, McVeigh made sure to take his time, drive cautiously, and stay well within the speed limit. The last thing he needed was a traffic accident with the explosives in the back of his truck. Furthermore, he didn't want to be in front of the Alfred P. Murrah Federal Building before it was filled with people. The whole point of his mission was to be heard, to make a statement that couldn't be ignored. The number of bodies mattered.

A careful planner, much like Breivik, McVeigh had prepared for every aspect of his attack. Apart from constructing the bomb, he had scrutinized the exact route he would take to Oklahoma City, looking at speed limits, highway construction, road hazards, and underpasses too low for his truck.

McVeigh was ready to kill anyone who got in the way of his mission, according to Michel and Herbeck. Not far from Oklahoma City, he noticed a police car behind him. Considering possible scenarios, McVeigh decided that he would run the police car off the road if he had to, or shoot the officer with the loaded Model 21 semiautomatic .45-caliber Glock pistol he was wearing in his shoulder holster. Breivik was armed with the same type of gun. The police car, however, was not planning on stopping McVeigh. After a while, the officer exited the highway and took a different road.

According to Michel and Herbeck, McVeigh had planned to park the car in front of the building, light the two fuses sticking into the cab of the truck just behind his left shoulder, and walk away. "If needed to, I was ready to stay in the truck and protect it with gunfire until the bomb blew up," he said. He was not suicidal but, like Breivik, he was ready to give his life to his cause. He also realized that he might be captured or killed after the bombing, and he had left an envelope with articles in his escape car, hoping they would be made public in the event he could not return.

The date of McVeigh's bombing—April 19—signified the second anniversary of the raid in Waco, Texas, as well as the 220th anniversary of the Battle of Lexington and Concord, the beginning of the war between the American patriots and their British oppressors. "To McVeigh," Michel and Herbeck wrote, "this bombing was in the spirit of the patriots of the American Revolution, the stand of a modern radical patriot against an oppressive government."

No one noticed the Ryder truck on that warm and sunny day as McVeigh reached the downtown area. Ryder trucks were all over the city, which was one of the reasons McVeigh had chosen that vehicle. As he spotted the location he had chosen for his bomb, McVeigh was relieved to see that it was empty.

Walking with a measured speed away from the truck and the government building, McVeigh, wearing earplugs, was about 150 yards away from ground zero when he felt the explosion. Even that far away, it lifted him an inch off the ground. He later said that even with the earplugs, the sound was deafening.

"The brick façade tumbled down from one of the buildings," Michel and Herbeck wrote. "A live power line snapped and whipped toward McVeigh. Some falling bricks struck him in the leg, but he was able to hop out of the way of the power line. Smoke and dust billowed high into the air. Fires erupted."

At ground zero, a massive ball of fire outshone the sun, and the north side of the building disintegrated. Traffic signs and parking meters were ripped from the pavement. Glass shattered and flew like bullets, mutilating pedestrians blocks away. Buildings in a sixteen-block radius surrounding the blast were damaged, many of them so badly that they later had to be demolished.

McVeigh never looked back, not even to admire his work. He kept walking away from the mayhem and toward his escape car with the sign PLEASE DO NOT TOW in the windshield.

Sixteen years later, Anders Breivik appeared equally calm with his helmet on the passenger seat as he drove the silver-gray Fiat he had named *Sleipnir* (The Slipper), after Odin's mythological eight-legged horse, out of Oslo. Anyone, if they were to look across the lane into his face, would have seen a man not all that different from most others driving that afternoon. But behind his calm front, Breivik was listening to the radio, curious as to the ramifications of his bomb and maybe even estimating the number of individuals he had destroyed or maimed for the rest of their lives. The sound of his creativity, the feel of its fruition coming up through the floorboards—finally, he had made his mark for all to witness.

Still, there was more work to be done. From the radio, he learned that the government building had not collapsed, and this disappointed him. He had hoped to top McVeigh's explosion in Oklahoma.

Time to execute Plan B.

His getaway had been clean so far. Unsure of the level of damage caused by his attack, he was encouraged by how many vehicles were on the road. They had to be evacuating Oslo. On the other hand, the last thing he needed was a traffic jam. Would he be able to make it to the island in time to catch his prime target, former prime minister Gro Harlem Brundtland, also referred to as "Mother of Norway"?

As a man who vowed to live by precise planning, he must not panic now.

At approximately 4:20 P.M., he pulled onto a two-lane road that would take him to the ferry dock. Knowing the MS *Thorbjørn* departed on the hour, he slowed the Fiat to a halt. This would give him ample time to take care of a few preparations before meeting with the port's guard. The less time he spent chatting with him, the better. The tricky part that, no doubt, worried Breivik was persuading the man to help him load his heavy Peli case of weaponry and ammunition onto the ferry without any hassle.

THE SHOOTINGS

Monica Bøsei, age forty-five, known as "Mother Norway" for her long-time management of the Labor Party's Youth League summer camp, took a call from a man identifying himself as Martin Nilsen, from the Oslo Police Department, shortly before five P.M. He informed her that, due to the unrest since the bombing of the government building down-town, she was to immediately send the ferry to the mainland's shore to pick him up. The sole purpose of this unplanned trip, the voice on the phone explained, was to see to it that he, Nilsen, an officer trained in dealing with the apprehension of suspects fleeing from the downtown attack scene, would be able to ensure a degree of safety once she got him to the island.

Bøsei must have felt her apprehension lessen. She, along with others on the island, had been feverishly discussing the attack. In fact, for the last hour, the city-center bombing had been the focus of conversation at the Labor Party's summer youth camp. After all, for the six hundred visitors to the camp too young to remember World War II, this was the first major attack on Norwegian soil in their lifetimes.

For the decade she had been running the camp, Bøsei and her partner, Jon Olsen, had watched young enthusiasts meet, make friends, and mix together political discussion and good times at the idyllic retreat. Concerned about a terrorist force still being active, Jon, who was also the boat captain, guided the MS *Thorbjørn* ferry across 600 meters of silent water in the evening's mist. Who was this Officer Nilsen he would be picking up? And what would he tell them about the terrorist or terrorists? Wouldn't the island of Utøya disappearing behind him now, with all its safe buildings among the forest and outcroppings of rocks, be safe from some mad bomber?

At first glance, the man waiting on the dock could have been straight out of a futuristic war film. Dressed in black trousers, a multi-pocketed vest with the word POLITI on its right breast, the man, especially with all his commando-like garb worn over what appeared to be a skin-tight wet suit, was unlike any policeman Jon Olsen had ever seen.

Back on the island, Monica Bøsei noticed how all the youths had been following the news of the Oslo bombing and its immediate aftermath. The bomb had damaged the offices of Prime Minister Jens Stoltenberg, and Bøsei was sure this would prevent the prime minister from making his planned visit to the youth festival the next day.

When Jon and the passenger stepped onto the shore, they were met by Bøsei and Trond Berntsen, an off-duty policeman who worked as a volunteer at the camp. Berntsen was also the stepbrother of Crown Princess Mette-Marit.

Upon noticing the policeman's kit bag and the way in which his assault rifle was equipped with sniper sights and bayonet, Bøsei gasped audibly. She looked closer at the well-built, handsome, blond young man and told him he had better hide his weapon. "It will frighten the children," she said, referring to all the teens and young adults camped on the island.

After the introductions, Jon and Trond placed the passenger's heavy bag into a truck and Jon began driving it up the slope, parking it behind the main house. The newcomer impressed the curious island regulars with his polite and professional demeanor. But soon, Berntsen's police instincts had begun to gnaw at his conscience.

"Why is your dress and kit not standard police issue?" he asked, as he and Bøsei began leading the young man up the incline from the beach. "And what's with the iPod and water pack?"

"I'll brief you thoroughly once we reach the main house," the man assured him.

Evidently still somewhat baffled by this stranger from out of nowhere, Berntsen started to phrase another question but was stopped in his tracks. The man had put a pistol to his temple so calmly, yet so swiftly, that the veteran policeman hadn't been able to react.

Monica Bøsei had caught sight of the pistol. "Don't point it," she said, as if a simple rule of safety had been broken. Certainly this young officer of the law would know better. "Don't point it," she repeated, this time in a shriek.

Then a sound echoed across the island like thunder in the rain-darkened air and she watched Berntsen go down. As his blood spattered the grass at her feet, she instinctively began to run, no doubt hoping that she might have time to warn the "children."

But quickly she too went down.

Pleased, Anders Behring Breivik turned to the fallen Berntsen and fired two more shots into his victim's head at such close range, one could have measured it in inches. Then, as if still doubting his specially crafted hollow-point shells' capability of blowing human faces and bodies into atoms, he walked down the path and repeated his actions upon Bøsei's supine form.

From the camp up above, where many youths had been discussing the news about the bombing and preparing for their involvement in the evening programs, shouts answered the ringing echoes of the shots. Some of them actually saw the man walking unhurriedly up toward the three main buildings and then turning left to where the students had pitched their tents. Many who were witnessing this bizarre scenario wondered if it was all a drill or a sick joke. Who would be pretending to shoot? Was the sound from fireworks? The man looked like a policeman, a savior. Why would he be carrying such weaponry? Why had he been firing, and whom did he want to kill?

Breivik was on the move. He faced a girl, maybe nineteen or twenty, coming out of the shower facility. Perhaps the sound of gunshots and shouts had been lost to her under the spray of the showers and, while she dressed, to the music from her earphones. A few feet away, she calmly slowed her pace. Her half-smile changed to a mask of horror when she saw the gun. Breivik's aim was superb. His head shot produced a plume of blood in the air behind her, and the girl's lifeless form fell, splayed on the ground before him. "Yes!" he said triumphantly. Breivik watched her feet jerk, fired once more for good measure, and then moved on again.

By his own admission later, after his apprehension, his actions were mechanical and inhuman as he proceeded toward the cafeteria building. Near the building, a group of the campers were out in the open, zigzagging in panic. Some bolted upright, some crouched, all hoping not to be spotted and somehow spared. Breivik picked out one boy, shot him eight times and then another boy five times. Through the cafeteria windows, eyewitnesses, frozen in indecision, watched in horror as he murdered five girls with what someone counted as eighteen bullets.

Was Breivik counting his weapon's discharges or how many he had killed? He later admitted to having no feelings of remorse as he killed one helpless victim after another. Always the planner, he was determined to circle the entire island. He knew no one would try to stop him, as no one on the island was armed except him. So, his strategy was straightforward; he would get rid of everyone along the way.

Before hunting down the youths fleeing into the woods, he darted into the buildings and, in an execution-style manner, shot to death the students too paralyzed with fear to move.

As he shot, he shouted "I'm going to kill you all!"

On the southern tip of Utøya, where scattered rocks marked trails toward Tyrifjorden Bay's cold waters, Breivik noticed clothes and personal belongings strewn on the ground: shirts and pants, shoes, phones, watches, and wallets, all left by campers as they stripped down to swim away from his onslaught. Using his pistol, he killed the ones who hadn't yet braved the water and those who hadn't made it far enough from shore, where they hoped to stay clear of the bullets. Laughing at the distance the swimmers had managed to put between themselves and the shore, he began firing at them with his assault rifle.

"Like shooting ducks in a pond," a wounded survivor would later remark.

By this time, many of the students' cell-phone calls had been getting through to family and friends at home, begging them to alert the police and come to their rescue. But because of the chaos in downtown Oslo, the police's emergency lines were saturated. Even after the police had been alerted, it took them almost an hour and a half to get to Utøya. One can only imagine the emotion of the youths and their families during that ninety minutes.

Survivors later spoke of how each moment seemed an eternity as they hid, played dead among the brush and rocks near the beach, or paddled off in the icy water, trying to disappear for just one more click of time, all hoping, praying the man with the gun would cease firing. Parents spoke of the agony they endured, not knowing if their children would be able to hide from the shooter, and their frustration with the police's lack of response.

Later, Breivik granted two males a stay of execution, dropping his weapon after holding them in his sights. The eleven-year-old son of Berntsen, the veteran policeman who had become his first victim an hour or so earlier, had stood up in the water and pleaded for his life. "Don't shoot," he said. "You have killed enough. You have killed my father. Let us be."

Somehow the remark stopped Breivik, and he moved quickly on, focusing on another potential victim, Adrian Pracon, who also survived the massacre. This survivor was also in the water, exhausted and sputtering his plea to be spared. As we will examine later in this book, Breivik saw something in the young man that reminded him of himself. At any rate, Breivik passed him by for some reason.

About an hour into his attack on the island, Breivik dialed 112 (the Norwegian version of 911). But he too experienced saturated phone lines. Afterward, he said he had tried at least ten times before he managed to get through. After finally being routed to the North Buskerud Police Department, he informed the operator that he was willing to surrender. It has been established that he continued to kill after placing this call and kept on even after he made a second call some thirty minutes later. He had completed his mission on behalf of the Knights Templar, Europe, and Norway, he told the operator who answered the call. "It's acceptable to surrender to Delta," he said, referring to the elite police force in Norway.

Both calls were dropped from the record.

The authorities were completely unprepared. Police headquarters couldn't communicate with the cars heading to the scene, and those at various police stations nearby didn't know who was on their way or what they were doing. The first car of Delta officers went to the wrong ferry landing. Although they eventually managed to get a boat, it was so small and so heavily loaded that it had to stop in the middle of the lake, short of the island. The officers aboard were forced to wait until a tourist boat came by. They commandeered the boat and finally managed to get to the island.

The real heroes that day were those in the tourist boats, who risked their lives by rescuing many of the young people from the lake's icy water, who otherwise would have drowned or been shot. Had they not picked up these youngsters, the loss of life would have been even greater.

Two Delta squads arrived on the island at approximately 6:25 P.M., in boats they had commandeered, about ninety minutes after Breivik came ashore on the MS *Thorbjørn* ferry. Having no idea that there was only one killer, they kept searching the island for others even after apprehending Breivik. Yet all the survivors described the same perpetrator. The stories were the same.

"Methodical."

"Like a robot."

"Laughing as he killed."

"Coming back to shoot again and again, as if he didn't want to leave a single soul alive."

"Gleefully firing bullet after bullet into teenagers, both male and female, as if they were armed warriors in a war game instead of young innocent kids."

As he walked around the island, Breivik would call out for everyone to gather around him, luring them from their hiding places, saying he was a police officer, and that he was there to save them. And those who came out were then shot execution-style.

The Delta squads concentrated their search in the areas where they believed the shooter might put up a last stand. One of the spots they suspected turned out to be correct, but there would be no "come and get me" shootout.

Anders Behring Breivik, whom no one in Delta had ever heard of before, was found in a clearing, his assault weapon on the ground before him, his pistol in its holster, and his arms outstretched, not in the usual position of surrender with arms straight over his head but out to his sides, palms up in a pose that suggested religious fervor.

THE REACTION

He had done his best to spread the word, to become known to all. A lesser man, he thought, would not have lasted the course. The physical strength it took to load the bomb would have been too much for any normal man. And on the island, he had shot hundreds of rounds for an hour and a half, his last shots ripping apart the body of a sixteen-year-old boy who could run no longer and plead no further to be forgiven the grown man's wrath.

While the Delta team squared him in their sights, they ordered him down on his knees. Seeing his bulging vest, they thought perhaps he had a bomb strapped around his chest and didn't want him to approach them. At this point, they had no idea how many people he had killed and were totally unprepared for the horror of what had occurred. Breivik didn't respond at first, either unable to hear or, at least, comprehend the command.

"On your knees!" the Delta leader repeated.

"How do you want me?" Breivik finally asked, grinning slightly at the mixed shouts as to how he should surrender to their liking.

Håvard Gåsbakk, a police officer assigned to make the arrest, thought the capture was unreal. How could this man, after what he had done, be so pleasantly compliant? In fact, the man was trying to convince his captors that he had nothing against them personally.

"I look at you as brothers," he said, trying to make a connection. "I am a commander of the Norwegian anti-communist resistance movement."

Cuffed and guarded, Breivik had about an hour of lying on the ground in the clearing to think about how he had been perceived by the men sent to pick him up. Two more boatloads of policemen arrived, and the more curious in the bunch must have further exemplified how far from being his brother they actually were. In their grumbling, Breivik must have been told several times that his "anti-communist resistance movement" was unknown to them and meant nothing against the measure of his crimes. Inspector Gåsbakk listened to Breivik emphasize how there were two more cells still on the move. A statement like that must have sent a chill through him. More terror on that day was the one thing all of Norway feared. How could all that terror be the work of one killer? Others must have been involved.

The inspector checked Breivik's identity and called his headquarters to ask that Anders Behring Breivik's background be researched immediately. Who was he? And what kind of organizations was he tied to? Then they led him, handcuffed, to the second floor of the camp's main building. Gåsbakk's reaction to this man's suggestion that two more cells were on the warpath was to have Breivik stripped to his shorts, inspect his body for a bomb or more weapons, and then interrogate him for the remainder of the night.

It had become darker, the rain still falling. Private craft out on the water were still doing their best to bring in the few survivors. Some had hoisted the dead and near-dead onto their boats. Helicopters had finally reached the island. There had been one hovering over the scene during the killing spree, but it had been one of Norway's state TV channel choppers, able only to send back video of the teenagers running and climbing for their lives. Now, police aircraft were directing the squads of lawmen and volunteer tourists and survivors toward the youths who had climbed the rocks to hide in the small caves the coastline offered. At the bottom of these outcroppings, the young people who hadn't been able to escape the killer's scope in time were being collected, most of them dead or critically wounded.

And here was this man, standing, nearly naked, on the main house's second floor, flexing his muscles in an Atlas pose. Then, while the members of Delta and the Oslo Police Department stared in disbelief, Breivik dropped his hand in front of his face to inspect his finger. In a sincere voice, he asked if someone could provide him with a Band-Aid.

Gåsbakk studied him. This man, with all the death he had caused, some of the corpses still lying within his sight, was worried about a scratch on his finger. "You'll get no Band-Aid from me," he said. "It's not exactly a high priority."

Back in his uniform, Breivik posed for police photographers. He pleaded for water, explaining how the cocktail he had drunk earlier was affecting him. He needed water, or he would die of dehydration. No one hurried to comply with his demand. He must have been going into a slump, perhaps a letdown, wondering if he had accomplished enough to warrant the glory he had hoped for. He had expected hatred, but he must have been wondering why no one of higher authority had been sent out to interrogate him. When Ørjan Tombre arrived, he became more alert.

Tombre was a superintendent with the Special Operations Unit of Oslo's organized crime section. Breivik may have heard of him, but he didn't seem impressed. He felt he deserved someone higher up the chain of command, a member of PST, Norway's Police Security Service. Told that that wasn't going to happen, Breivik simmered in silence.

Tombre's methods seemed standard procedure. They needed an initial interrogation, to establish who this monster was. They needed to learn his motive—and, even more important, whether there were any more killers on the island.

Breivik answered by displaying the Knights Templar symbol he wore around his neck. "My life ended," he said, "when I ordained myself to the Knights Templar of Europe." Pleased to have an audience of some magnitude, he explained how his organization had been established in London. Proudly, he declared that the Knights Templar would take over Europe within sixty years. "We are the crusaders and nationalists."

He felt that that was a good time to establish his own power and importance with this official, to explain how his acts should be regarded as sympathetic, not criminal. After all, he had taken lives that would soon have become "extreme Marxists leading to the Islamization of Norway."

Wasn't he, Anders Breivik, a living symbol and hero fighting against the Muslim invasion of his beloved country? Although he was mentally prepared for the likelihood that these police officers would not immediately grasp his motives, he had to give it a try.

At this time during the interrogation, Breivik suggested a bargain. He would trade information on the two remaining cells he had referred to for the cessation of mass Muslim immigration into Norway. Whether he truly believed that any such agreement could be reached is doubtful. It could be that his focus on his mission was waning with the effects of the drugs he had taken that morning to keep him motivated. To bolster his strength against Tombre, he referred constantly to his manifesto. He'd had the entire manuscript saved on a USB thumb drive that he had stuck behind the Knights Templar flag on his combat vest, but now it was gone, lost in the day's constant action.

Well, he reasoned, there would be days and days ahead when he could prove how important his crusade was to the country. So far, he had done all he could. Learning that Prime Minister Jens Stoltenberg was still alive was disappointing, but now they would know of him and his cause—a cause he would defend until his death.

CHAPTER SEVEN

BREIVIK'S WAR ON ISLAM: BECOMING ONE WITH HIS IDEOLOGY

Multiculturalism is an anti-European hate ideology. As such, they are the Nazis of our time, not us.

—ANDERS BREIVIK MANIFESTO

Approximately 150,000 out of Norway's population of five million identify as Muslims, and Islam is the country's second-largest non-Christian
religion. In Book 3 of Breivik's manifesto, he goes on at length about his
frustration with immigration policies, and he ends by saying that Muslims
must be driven out of the country—and if that effort fails, then they must
be killed.

In an "interview" with himself, a simple question-and-answer session,
he writes that his best friend for many years, a Muslim who lived his life

in Oslo West, had only limited contact with the Norwegian-Pakistani community. Yet Breivik's friend refused to be integrated into Norwegian culture. He attended Urdu language classes from early childhood and went to the mosque occasionally after he had turned twelve.

According to Breivik, "He felt really torn between the Norwegian and Pakistani communities. I was wrong assuming that he would chose [*sic*] to follow my path and the Norwegian way. I understood early that he resented the Norwegian society. Not because he was jealous. After all, he could have conformed if he wanted to. He resented it because it represented the exact opposite of Islamic ways."

This is not an unusual story. Many Muslims in Norway—or anywhere else, for that matter—don't accept the culture in their host country. At best, they ignore it. Breivik writes that shortly after he and his friend broke contact, ". . . he started hanging out with his cousin and other Pakistanis. Since then he and his Muslim friends have beaten and harassed several ethnic Norwegians, one of them being my friend, Kristoffer."

Norway views itself as one of the world's most tolerant nations, yet it faces the same problems with its immigration policies as other parts of Europe. Siv Jensen, head of the Progress Party, has objected to moves to introduce special measures in order to accommodate Muslims' religious traditions. These include a Labor Party suggestion (in an attempt to attract more Muslim women to the police force) that officers could wear headscarves with their uniforms.

At a 2009 Progress Party conference, in a *BBC, Oslo* report by Thomas Buch-Andersen, Jensen said "The reality is that a kind of sneak-Islamization of this society is being allowed. We are going to have to stop this."

She told the *National Post* that freedom of religion is good for democracy. "But radical Islam is not religion. It is politics and it poses a danger to the free world and threatens the values that we appreciate so much. You find radical Islam in societies where people have failed to integrate. When you find terrorist cells in the United Kingdom or Germany or Norway, for that matter, it is always for some reason where people are not very well integrated." Yet Jensen remained frustrated as the Norwegian government did nothing to "crack down" on Norway's Muslim population.

FAILING TO MAKE A DIFFERENCE

Breivik dealt with the same frustration Jensen verbalizes. He tried to make a difference politically and failed. After attempting to change the status quo, he received no support from his countrymen, not even his own political party. In his self-interview in the manifesto, he asks himself about his views on moderate anti-immigration parties and replies that however noble their motives, they are counterproductive.

"They start out as idealistic but end up diluted and corrupt," he writes. "They should admit that the democratic struggle to save Europe has been lost, and the only way to proceed is to resist the establishment. Contributing to pacify the people gives them false hope."

Again, he is referring to his own false hope when he was involved in politics. He doesn't view himself as a racist; and since he feels that his views are not being listened to, he believes the only way he can express this is through violence. The violence will force people to hear him.

Kaczynski expressed similar frustration. After he had given up on having a social life, his goal was to live in a secluded place outside of society, and he began learning survival skills. He worked odd jobs and received financial support from his family, funds he used to purchase the piece of land in Montana that would be his home and the base for his bombing campaign.

Realizing that it was impossible for him to live completely outside of society, he complained in his journal about watching the wild land around him get destroyed by development and industry. Kaczynski began performing isolated acts of sabotage, initially targeting developments near his cabin.

One particular incident marked him.

"The best place, to me," he said in an interview with *Earth First! Journal*, from prison in Colorado in June 1999, "was the largest remnant of this plateau that dates from the tertiary age. It's kind of rolling country, not flat, and when you get to the edge of it you find these ravines that cut very steeply in to cliff-like drop-offs and there was even a waterfall there. It was about a two days' hike from my cabin. That was the best spot until the summer of 1983. That summer there were too many people around my cabin so I decided I needed some peace. I went back to the plateau and when I got there I found they had put a road right through the middle of it. . . . You just can't imagine how upset I was. It was from that point on I decided that, rather than trying to acquire further wilderness skills, I would work on getting back at the system. Revenge."

From then on, Kaczynski stepped up his campaign of sabotage. Violence, he concluded, was the only solution to what he saw as the problem of industrial civilization. In his interview with *Earth First! Journal*, he said he'd lost faith in the idea of reform and saw violent collapse as the only way to bring down the techno-industrial system.

"I don't think it can be done," he said about reform. "In part because of the human tendency, for most people, there are exceptions, to take the path of least resistance. They'll take the easy way out, and giving up your car, your television set, your electricity, is not the path of least resistance for most people. As I see it, I don't think there is any controlled or planned way in which we can dismantle the industrial system. I think that the only way we will get rid of it is if it breaks down and collapses. . . . The big problem is that people don't believe a revolution is possible, and it is not possible precisely because they do not believe it is possible. To a large extent, I think the eco-anarchist movement is accomplishing a great deal, but I think they could do it better. . . . The real revolutionaries should separate themselves from the reformers. . . . And I think that it would be good if a conscious effort was being made to get as many people as possible introduced to the wilderness. In a general way, I think what has to be done is not to try and convince or persuade the majority of people that we are right, as much as try to increase tensions in society to the point where things start to break down. To create a situation where people get uncomfortable enough that they're going to rebel. So the question is how do you increase those tensions?"

Conversely, McVeigh didn't think he had a choice.

"I didn't define the rules of engagement in this conflict," he later said, according to Michel and Herbeck. "The rules, if not written down, are defined by the aggressor. It was brutal, no holds barred. Women and kids were killed at Waco and Ruby Ridge. You put back in [the government's] faces exactly what they're giving out."

Breivik believes his politically correct country labels the political right as "evil fascists, racists, Nazis, and bigots." And he also believes that the only way to analyze the far right is to detach it from the politically correct narrative.

Again, Breivik emphasizes that he is not a racist and says that he still suffers from two decades of multiculturalist indoctrination.

"Also I am against the Marxist/multiculturalist alliance and the Islamic presence in Europe, so writing about skin color would be counter-productive. However we can't ignore NS (National Socialists) if we are to make a truthful evaluation. Western nations can never mount a defense against cultural Islamic demographic warfare unless we manage to convert the NS. This is why we must argue against their ideology instead of ignoring them."

Muslims feel this anger as well. In the same *BBC* interview, Khalid Mahmood, a Pakistani native and member of the Labor Party, calls Muslims "the Jews of our time." According to him, "It is not any longer immigrants who are targeted, but simply Muslims. We are portrayed as uncivilized people living double lives—orderly and behaved when in public, but at home fundamentalists suppressing and physically abusing women."

Most Muslims sense it. Most Norwegians deny it. And other than the Progress Party, few speak their frustrations at trying to blend two cultures that appear as incompatible, on the surface at least, as oil and water. Breivik's point about the lack of tolerance in this politically correct society of Norway is valid. If one doesn't agree with the Labor Party and the socially accepted opinion, one is labeled far right and a racist. One is immediately attacked by the group for having a different opinion on these issues. The more one reads the manifesto, the more one questions whether Breivik's frustration, anger, and ultimate plan for mass murder resulted from hatred toward Islam and multiculturalism, or hatred toward the country where he was raised and the Laws of Jante.

TIPPING THE SCALES

One question in his self-interview asks: "What tipped the scales for you? What single event made you decide you wanted to continue planning and moving on with the assault?"

Breivik replies: "For me, it was my government's involvement in the attacks on Serbia (NATO bombings in 1999). It was completely unacceptable how the U.S. and Western European regimes bombed our Serbian brothers. All they wanted was to drive Islam out by deporting the Albanian Muslims back to Albania. When the Albanians refused, they didn't have any choice but to use military force. By disallowing the Serbians the right for self-determination over their sovereign territory they indirectly dug a grave for Europe. A future where several Mini-Pakistans would eventually be created in every Western European capital. This is unacceptable, completely unacceptable."

It is important to remember that Breivik wanted to sound credible here. As he wrote, he believed people would read his manifesto after he was dead or in prison. He wanted to show them that he was sane and his actions justifiable. It's highly unlikely that the NATO bombings were the breaking point for Breivik. It is an excuse. The true breaking point was probably after he was rejected in politics, by every group he had tried to join, and he realized he was getting nowhere in Norway. After that, he gave up trying to fit in to society.

He had originally gone into politics, thinking he could still change the system; but after becoming disillusioned, he traveled to Liberia, where he probably heard the inside story from the Serb known as "The Dragon" about why the Serbians were killing the Muslims. He says that something changed in him when he met "The Dragon." The Serb was supposedly the one who sent Breivik to a founding meeting of the Knights Templar in London.

At that time, Breivik was a pot ready to boil over, and listening to "The Dragon" may have made him believe that the same fight was brewing in Norway. And he was the man to lead the charge. He was quite open to suggestion and might easily have taken on any cause, but this was the one that manifested itself at his most vulnerable moment. He needed to matter. Finally, he felt part of something.

"There have been several issues that have reaffirmed my beliefs since then. Among them: my government's cowardly handling of the Muhammad Cartoon issue and their decision to award the Nobel peace prize to an Islamic terrorist (Arafat) and appeasers of Islam. There have been tens of other issues. My government and our media capitulated to Islam several years ago, after the Rushdie event. Since then, it has gone downhill. Thousands of Muslims pouring in annually through our Asylum institution, or by family reunification. The situation is just chaotic. These suicidal traitors must be stopped."

Breivik is referring to editorial cartoons, depicting the prophet Muhammad, cartoons that were published in the Danish newspaper *Jyllands-Posten* in 2005. Muslim groups in Denmark complained, and the issue eventually led to protests in many countries around the world, which included violent demonstrations in some Islamic countries. Some of the protests escalated into riots that left more than two hundred people dead. As a show of support, *Magazinet*, a Norwegian publication that has since changed its name to *Dagen (The Day)*, published the cartoons.

Foreign Minister Jonas Gahr Støre, a leading member of Prime Minister Jens Stoltenberg's Labor Party, sent an e-mail to the Norwegian embassies, asking them to apologize for printing the cartoons, while keeping it a secret from the Norwegian press. He wrote:

"I am sorry that the publication of a few cartoons in the Norwegian paper *Magazinet* has caused unrest among Muslims. I fully understand that these drawings are seen to give offense by Muslims worldwide. Islam is a spiritual reference point for a large part of the world. Your faith has the right to be respected by us.

"The cartoons in the Christian paper *Magazinet* are not constructive in building the bridges which are necessary between people with different religious and ethnic backgrounds. Instead, they contribute to suspicion and unnecessary conflict.

"Let it be clear that the Norwegian government condemns every expression or act which expresses contempt for people on the basis of their religion or ethnic origin. Norway has always supported the fight of the UN against religious intolerance and racism and believes that this fight is important in order to avoid suspicion and conflict. Tolerance, mutual respect, and dialogue are the basic values of Norwegian society and of our foreign policy.

"Freedom of expression is one of the pillars of Norwegian society. This includes tolerance for opinions that not everyone shares. At the same time, our laws and our international obligations enforce restrictions for incitement to hatred or hateful expressions."

The e-mail was meant to be kept from the Norwegian public. According to the Foreign Ministry, "that would look rather stupid in the Norwegian press."

But it was fine to send it to everyone else. How must the citizens of Norway and Scandinavia have felt when they learned that their governments had apologized—secretly, at that—for caricatures typical of those that Scandinavian newspapers constantly publish about many other political and cultural figures?

Even today, the artists who created the cartoons, along with the editor-in-chief of the newspaper, live in secrecy under police protection. The fatwā, or ruling by Muslim leaders sentencing them to death, is still in effect. And with the shooting in Paris that killed almost the entire editorial board of *Charlie Hebdo*, these fatwās are to be taken seriously.

Also living in secret is author Salman Rushdie, in New York. Rushdie's fourth novel, *The Satanic Verses*, published in 1988, provoked protests and death threats from Muslims in several countries. A fatwā was issued by Ayatollah Ruhollah Khomeini, the Supreme Leader of Iran, in 1989, sentencing Rushdie to death (the ruling was lifted in 1998 but revived in September 2012). Direct threats against Rushdie's Norwegian publisher, William Nygaard, and translator, Kari Risvik, followed, and Nygaard was given police protection for a period of time.

Then, on October 11, 1993, Nygaard was shot three times outside his home in Dagaliveien in Oslo. Nygaard was hospitalized for several months, and he slowly recovered. His alleged Muslim assailant was never prosecuted.

All this was more fuel to people like Fjordman and, in turn, Breivik, who followed Fjordman closely. In one essay, Fjordman quotes linguist Tina Magaard, who believes that Islamic texts encourage violence more than those of other religions.

". . . there are hundreds of calls in the Koran for fighting against people of other faiths. [Quoting Magaard:] 'If it is correct that many Muslims view the Koran as the literal words of God, which cannot be interpreted or rephrased, then we have a problem. It is indisputable that the texts encourage terror and violence. Consequently, it must be reasonable to ask Muslims themselves how they relate to the text. . . .'"

This was the Norway in which Breivik lived and tried to make a difference. He describes his political stances of the past as "a complete nut job, due to the fact that I was ignorant about most issues then. But if you actually take the time to study the non-PC (politically correct) documentation available, you cannot avoid making many of the same conclusions I have made today."

He goes on to explain that "Fighting for your people's survival, when threatened, is the most logical thing to do. Defending your people and culture from genocide is the most basic and recognized human right and one of few causes actually worth dying for."

Breivik makes it clear that he doesn't regret his actions: "In fact, I would do it all again, without any hesitation, if I was given the chance." In this statement, Breivik is justifying what he had yet to do. He had become one with his ideology, his cause. Although he never participated in any of the violent activities with which he was associated, in his writings he has now crossed the line. He comes across as cornered, as if there is no other way out. It is as if, through his manifesto, he was able to write himself into a state where he could commit murder, mass murder. He needed to convince himself that these planned killings were warranted; and the more he wrote, the more he believed it. By the time he was gunning down teenagers execution-style, he was wholly convinced that he was in the right.

McVeigh had no regrets either. On the contrary, he was satisfied that he had accomplished his mission. He later admitted qualms about the children in the day-care center situated just above his Ryder truck. He had never intended to harm children.

"The day-care center," he later said, according to Michel and Herbeck. "If I had known it was there, I probably would have shifted the target." He claimed to take no pleasure in killing; however, he had no trouble justifying the bombing.

NOT A RACIST?

At one point, Breivik, the interviewer, asks Breivik, the soon-to-be killer, how he would describe himself as a person. Breivik refers to himself as a laid-back type and quite tolerant on most issues: "Due to the fact that I have been exposed to decades of multicultural indoctrination, I feel a need to emphasize that I am not in fact a racist and never have been." He points out that he was baptized at age fifteen, and that his godmother and her husband had come to Norway as political refugees from Chile. "In retrospect I understood that they were Marxist political activists, but I didn't comprehend these issues at the time. Our two families have been very close throughout my childhood and youth. I've had several non-Norwegian and Muslim friends. I spent a lot of time with Onor, a Turk, Jonathan, an Eritrean, Raol and Natalie from Chile, Arsalan Ahmad Sohail, Faizal and Wazim from Pakistan. I've had dozens of non-Norwegian friends during my younger years, Bashir from Somalia, Pablo from Chile, Odd Erling—adopted from Columbia, Lene—adopted from India have been good friends and a couple of them still are today."

Once yet again, Breivik is emphasizing that he is not a racist and that he was exposed to a multicultural environment when growing up. To him, it seems important to stress this point. In Norway, no one expressing racist views is taken seriously. He wants to gain the reader's recognition and sympathy.

When he asks himself why he has so many non-ethnic Norwegian friends, Breivik explains a moral code that had driven his actions since his teen years and into his adulthood. He reiterates how, when in trouble, he expected his friends to back him up. "The majority of people who shared these principles of pride was [sic] the Muslim youths and the occasional skinhead. However, even back then, the Muslims outnumbered the skinheads 20 to 1. Being a skinhead was never an option for me. Their dress codes and taste of music was unappealing and I thought they were too extreme. I hated rock then and I still do."

Most critics of immigration aren't Nazi skinheads. Yet many people who criticize the immigration politics in Europe are put in the neo-Nazi box, and Breivik was trying to work around this.

Breivik knew that if he was perceived as a racist, he wouldn't be taken seriously in Norway or in any other country. He knew that racism was a sign of uneducated people. He wanted to show that he had thought the matter through, and that he was reasonable and intelligent. The police confirmed that he did have Muslim friends, and that he had no problems with his multicultural relationships.

The next part of the "interview" goes on to establish his credibility and his sanity, an issue he knew would be a major question, regardless of whether or not he survived his attacks. He wanted it to shine through his manifesto that he was an educated, intelligent person, and that he had proven that by being a successful businessman and ultimately through the writing of his manifesto.

It's no surprise then that his next question to himself is this one: "Violent Muslim gangs in European cities are not exactly a new phenomenon. Tell us about your experiences growing up in the urban multicultural streets of Oslo."

In this answer, Breivik attempts to show the readers that the Muslims, not the Norwegians, are the racists. He adds more about his wanting to gain respect and credibility among the Western Oslo demographic. He also offers his take on tagging, hip-hop, and gang activity:

"Even at that time, the Muslim gangs were very dominating in Oslo East and in inner city Oslo. They even arranged 'raids' in Oslo West occasionally, subduing the native youths (kuffars) and collecting Jizya (loot) from them (in the form of cell phones, cash, sunglasses etc.). I remember they systematically harassed, robbed and beat ethnic Norwegian youngsters who were unfortunate enough to not have the right affiliations. Muslim youths called the ethnic Norwegians 'poteter' (potatoes, a derogatory term used by Muslims to describe ethnic Norwegians). These people occasionally raped the so called 'potato whores.' In Oslo, as an ethnic Norwegian youth aged 14-18, you were restricted if you didn't have affiliations to the Muslim gangs. Your travel was restricted to your own neighborhoods in Oslo West and certain central points in the city."

It is difficult to establish whether what Breivik describes here is reality, part of his imagination, or stories he had read and adopted as his own. Most likely it's somewhere in between. Oslo had a lot of problems relating to gang violence in the 1980s and 90s, but it is not clear whether or not Breivik was ever a part of that scene.

Anger begins to color his words as he recollects how the culture seemed to be changing: "I gradually became appalled by the mentality, actions, and hypocrisy of the 'Marxist-Jihadi youth' movement of Oslo disguised under more socially acceptable brands such as: SOS Rasisme and Youth against Racism. And the group, Blitz, who literally hijacked segments of the hiphop movement and used it as a front for recruitment."

He says he had heard of and witnessed hundreds of Jihadi-racist attacks, more than ninety percent of them aimed at helpless Norwegian youths "who themselves are brought up to be suicidally [*sic*] tolerant and therefore are completely unprepared mentally for attacks such as these." This happens while the Marxist networks in the hip-hop movement and the cultural establishment silently and indirectly condone it, he says, and he emphasizes that there is no political will to ensure that justice is served on behalf of these victims. "I remember at one point thinking, 'This system makes me sick.'"

Breivik was well aware, as most acquainted with the dark side of Muslim faith are, of the so-called honor killings where a family, usually a male family member, kills a daughter who dates, or even hangs out with, a non-Muslim man. A Muslim girl raised in Switzerland, Germany, the UK, France, or Norway has a good chance of encountering young men who aren't Muslims. Women's groups estimate twenty thousand women a year may be victims of "honor killings."

The interviewer (Breivik) then asks if Breivik ever contributed to violence against Muslims in Norway:

"During these years, I heard of hundreds of cases where ethnic Norwegians were harassed, robbed and beaten by Muslim gangs. This type of behavior was in fact acts of racism or even based on religious motives (Jihadi behavior), although I failed to see that connection then due to lack of knowledge about Islam; I saw the practical manifestations and I didn't like it at all. The only thing you could do was to take the necessary precautions, create alliances or be subdued by them. If you made any attempt to create a 'Norwegian gang' you would be instantly labeled as a Nazi and face the wrath of everyone, in addition to the Muslim gangs. They, however, were allowed to do anything while being indirectly cheered by society. So in other words, we were trapped between the 'wood and the bark.' This is still the case in all Western European major cities. They are allowed to consolidate, while we are not.

"I never took part in any of their activities and I never participated in any Blitz demonstrations either. To me, that would have been too hypocritical seeing that the Muslim gangs and their 'racist/Jihadi' behavior was toler-ated by the police, media and the violent left wing extremists (ANTIFA) like 'Blitz' and 'SOS Rasisme.' I left the hiphop community and the gangs when I was 16 and never looked back."

Finally, Breivik explains more about his involvement with gangs and how their music (metal bands) disgusted him. Again, he mentions people he'd grown up with, and their attitudes and ideology. He says: "The big irony was that they (skinheads) were a lot more 'normal' than us during this period. They were peaceful, while we were violent. They followed the law and rules while we broke the law and ignored the rules again and again." He explains that at the same time, "the hip-hop community was cheered by the media, praised as the pinnacle of tolerance among the new generation, while THEY (skinheads) were condemned for their political views, systematically harassed and beaten by non-white gangs, extremist Marxist gangs (Blitz etc) and the police. It's quite ironic and shameful."

He provides this last part as another example of how the so-called extreme right movement wasn't necessarily violent, but how, on the con-trary, they were the peaceful ones. The violent groups, according to Breivik, were the leftist, socialistic ones that responded to politics using their fists.

In the next part of Book 3 of his manifesto, Breivik writes from a diary he had been keeping. His personal reflections at this time were fueled by the excitement of keeping a log on the Knights Templar and to what he terms his "preparation phase."

Breivik had at that point written himself to murder. He was driven by his private war on Islam and his inability to effectively speak against it or take action through political channels. True, he hated the inequity of multiculturalism. And most of all, he hated being unable to express his anger and frustration. He would express it, though, and soon.

By not allowing those who disagree with the Norwegian policy of multiculturalism to express their beliefs, by putting them in a box labeled *extreme right* or *neo-Nazi*, society drives them elsewhere. To extremist groups, to the Internet, and perhaps to darker places within themselves. If people felt they could speak freely, the EDL (English Defense League), and other groups like it, would have fewer followers.

Because of Breivik's war on Islam, innocent people died. Yet it wasn't Islam or the Muslims that drove him to murder; it was his inability to openly protest and try to change, in a democratic way, what he saw as an inequitable system. He had a ready-made enemy, one his government dictated he must accept, even if that enemy didn't accept him and his culture. And that is the ultimate irony of multiculturalism. Although its intent is to bring people together, it all too often drives them apart.

When speaking to Steven M. Kleinman, Director of Strategic Research, The Soufan Group, I asked him why extremists such as Breivik pick this particular religion to hate. He replied that the question was both simple and deeply complex.

"The simple element has to do with proximity and opportunity," he said. "If we rolled back the clock a generation, I doubt Breivik (and people with his world view) would have invested the time in preparing extensive manifestos against Islam (much less taking such horrific action). By living in Norway, the probability that Breivik's life would ever be touched—directly or indirectly—by a single Muslim (much less a community) would have been remote." The absence of a Muslim community would not have stopped Breivik, because his ultimate enemy was the government that he felt repressed him. He would have found and embraced another ideology. His target might have been what he viewed as politically correct journalists. It might have been Labor Party politicians. Regardless of the ultimate adversary, he would have found a cause worth killing for.

Kleinman went on to point out that the discovery of deep resources of fossil fuels in the North Sea in the 1960s essentially shielded Norway—unlike Europe, the United States, and Japan—from the heated geopolitical issues surrounding the Middle East, because Norway wasn't dependent upon a constant flow of oil from that region.

He also pointed out that in the past thirty years there have been fifteen terrorist attacks on Norwegian soil, compared to more than two thousand incidents in the United States over the same period of time. The numbers are much smaller, but the social impact is greater.

"The complex element involves economics, geography, and, most important, psychology," Kleinman told me.

"The socioeconomic forces that produced the flow of émigrés, refugees, and displaced persons from the Middle East and North Africa into Europe changed everything. The geographic chasm that kept the type of extreme xenophobia operating in the mind of a person like Breivik in relative check was lost. As a result, Breivik and those within his 'in group' (that is, the many who were looking for scapegoats, enemies of the state, and threats to the prevailing way of life) finally found their 'out group' (comprising anyone not like them)."

Of course, Breivik didn't fit in his country's "in" fringe groups, but he continued to try. Islam was an easy choice as a target.

"I think a case could be made that Islam was simply the most appealing and accessible target of opportunity," Kleinman said. "If the immigrants who were establishing communities throughout Europe, competing for jobs, and taxing the region's social resources had been Jewish, Coptic Christians, Buddhists, or even followers of the Baha'i faith, the lethal combination of ethnic difference, competition for increasingly scarce economic resources, and the apparent deep-seated need to protect a way of life from what they viewed as foreign invasion would have spurred people like Breivik to act."

Kleinman said Breivik's manifesto can be described as extensive, but not extensively researched. "Rather than leading to rational conclusions, it seems he worked backward from his conclusions so that his sources and analysis would all lead the reader to a predetermined point," he said.

"One might go so far as to describe Islam as a gift to Breivik. He had an enormous capacity for hate, vitriol, and conspiratorial perspective; what he lacked, however, was an appropriate target for this heinous energy. He found one in Islam."

CHAPTER EIGHT

"...NO SAFER PLACE ON EARTH...." THE DAY EVERYTHING WENT WRONG

And we have a very clear message for you: We know who you are, where you live and we are coming for you. If not today, then tomorrow, if not in 10 years, then in 50 years.

—ANDERS BREIVIK MANIFESTO

One hundred eighty-nine minutes of terror. No one stopped Breivik from parking his van with the bomb in front of the entrance to the building hosting Norway's government and prime minister. Seven minutes after the bomb exploded, eight people were dead and more than two hundred injured. The lone wolf then had almost one and a half hours on the island of Utøya to slaughter his victims. Sixty-seven people were shot to death there, two others died trying to escape, and 102 were shot and injured. Breivik knew that no one would stop him, at least not before he had completed his mission. He was well aware that no one on the island, not even the security guard, would be armed.

In the end, even he thought the police took too long to come and stop the massacre. He called them himself to surrender. Numerous times. The two times he got through on the emergency line, the voice on the other end didn't appear to take him seriously. Breivik hung up and continued killing.

In the wake of July 22, 2011, the Norwegian government appointed a commission to study the details of that day and to find the answers to three key questions: *What happened on July 22? Why did it happen? How could our society have let this happen?*

The July 22nd Commission, as it was called, worked for a year to find out what went wrong that day. It concluded that the attack on the government buildings in the center of Oslo could have been prevented through effective implementation of already-adopted security measures. The authorities' ability to protect the people on Utøya also failed. Breivik could have, and should have, been stopped sooner. In addition, the Commission concluded that more security and emergency-preparedness measures should have been implemented. Surprisingly, it also concluded that the government's communication with the general public and media had been adequate in the aftermath of the attacks. Perhaps the Commission members felt they had to dilute their negative findings with *something* positive.

The Commission's oftentimes vague and repetitive findings, assembled in a report consisting of almost five hundred pages, focused on four areas. These were: ineffective preventive security intelligence; the false sense of security that prevails in Norway; lack of police preparedness; and, finally, law enforcement's failure to communicate with the victims and each other during the attacks.

INEFFECTIVE PREVENTIVE SECURITY INTELLIGENCE

"When initiating the 'chemical acquirement phase,' in end November/ early December, I must admit I was filled with some angst," Breivik wrote. "This was after all a critical phase, perhaps the most dangerous of all phases. If I messed this phase up, by being flagged, reported to the authorities etc. I would be neutralized before I could finalize my operation.

Even when taking all possible precautions; I estimate it is a 30% chance of being reported to the system protectors at the national intelligence agency during this phase."

Breivik was flagged by the Police Security Service (PST) for ordering chemicals, yet no one can explain why there were no follow-ups.

In the opinion of the Commission, several public agencies should get involved in, and take advantage of their expertise in, the efforts to detect terrorism. Interaction and information-sharing is essential in order to act effectively against threats, including solo terrorists.

"Our review indicates that legislative imbalances can present an obstacle to such collaboration." The confidentiality provisions in the general legislation, according to the Commission, in particular the Customs Act, prevent PST from doing its job effectively.

In 2005, parliament adopted new statutory provisions that gave PST broad authority to use radical methods in relatively early stages of suspicion where "there is reason to investigate whether someone is preparing a [terrorist] act." At the same time, the Commission criticized the fact that a higher level of suspicion is required for civil servants in other government agencies to submit a report to PST than there is within PST itself. As an example, the requirements for probable cause are lower for PST to use listening devices as preventive measures than for a customs agent to let the PST know if disturbing items are found in a person's luggage. Similarly, the requirements should not be stricter for the Police Security Service to procure information from customs records than to initiate an undercover search. "The Commission finds this to be inconsistent," the report stated.

There is no communication between the different agencies. Thus, if customs is suspicious of a package like the ones Breivik imported, they're not encouraged to report it unless they have solid evidence of probable cause.

Only to a modest degree has the Police Security Service utilized information and communications technology (ICT) to increase the capacity and quality of its work processes. Tips about unknown subjects are usually only checked against the service's own working register and police records before PST makes a decision on whether the case will be given priority. Because Breivik didn't have a criminal record, the fact that he was ordering suspicious chemicals didn't make him suspicious enough to investigate.

"Systems and work processes for knowledge management and advanced intelligence using open sources and public records appear to be rather crude," the Commission concluded. Despite the fact that it has been known for years that terrorists operate on electronic platforms, Norway has not yet established any regulations for when the Police Security Service is allowed to monitor potential terrorists' computers and closed forums on the Internet. The Commission also found that prior to July 22, PST did not take advantage of the information and capacity inherent in the postal and customs systems.

The Commission asserted that July 22 should not have happened; Breivik should have been checked out long before.

FALSE SENSE OF SECURITY

Norway should have been prepared for several aspects of July 22. A car bomb at the government complex and other coordinated attacks have been recurring scenarios in threat assessments and drills for many years. Why then was it possible to park an unregistered and unknown car outside the H-block or anywhere in the government complex? What were the underlying reasons that Grubbegata was not blocked off? Why weren't more security measures put into place? These were some of the questions the July 22nd Commission tried to answer in the year following that tragic day.

"Norway has established security and emergency preparedness legislation in recent years that is generally up-to-date, and it has a government administration with a reasonably clear distribution of responsibility for the prevention, aversion, and management of terrorist attacks," the Commission asserted. So what went wrong?

As Breivik was driving his van with the bomb toward Oslo's city center and the government buildings, he committed a traffic violation by driving up a street reserved for buses, taxis, and trams. He was not stopped. Arriving at Grubbegata near building H, he came to a halt and waited for two whole minutes with the emergency blinker lit on his car. Stopping there was also illegal, but no security guard paid any attention. Then he drove farther and parked the van directly in front of building H at 15:17. No physical blocks were set up to avoid cars entering the perimeter of the government complex, not even around the H building hosting the Justice

Department and prime minister. A chain with a no-entry sign partially blocked the road, but there was enough space for a truck to drive past it. Although Breivik would have preferred to park his van in a different spot — so that his bomb would destroy the structure of the building and cause it to collapse—he still managed to park directly in front of the entrance. After approximately twenty seconds, the time it took to light the fuse of his bomb, he got out of the car and started moving away. Dressed in a police uniform and helmet, he carried a handgun. During the seven minutes between the time Breivik left the van and the explosion, seventy people passed the illegally parked van. None of them was a police officer or security guard.

That afternoon, two security guards were present in the government complex. At 15:20, a receptionist noticed the van and called one of the security guards, who located the car on his surveillance screen but didn't react fast enough.

The security cameras recorded Breivik walking and sometimes running to get away from what was about to happen next. Once he stopped, turned around, and took a last look at the white Volkswagen Crafter. Then he continued. As the security guard picked up his phone to deal with the illegally parked van, it exploded. The clock showed 15:25. Eight minutes had passed, from when Breivik parked his truck until the explosion. In addition to the people who were killed or injured, buildings within a radius of 350 feet were damaged beyond repair.

Breivik got to his flight car, a silver-gray Fiat Doblò, and drove away. However, one witness found it suspicious that this man, dressed as a police officer, with a helmet, and carrying a handgun, was getting in a civilian car and driving away from the scene. Furthermore, the suspect took a one-way street in the wrong direction. The witness called the police emergency line and reported a description of Breivik and the license plate number of Breivik's getaway car. This message was delivered directly to the chief of emergency operations. The security guard who observed Breivik's Volkswagen Crafter briefly before the explosion also called the police and told them it was a car bomb. He described the man getting out of the van and moving away from the area before the explosion. The police then had two corroborating tips on what the perpetrator looked like and the license plate number of his flight car.

Because of a traffic accident, Breivik's trip to Utøya took sixty-five minutes. No roadblocks were set up, and Breivik had no problem getting away. It would take twenty minutes from the time the tip with the license plate number was called in until someone at the police decided to check it out. Breivik had by then left Oslo and was well on his way to Utøya. When the tip was followed up, smaller police stations near Oslo were contacted, but none of these acted on the information or did anything to set up roadblocks. The police there declared the tip too vague to take action. The focus was on the bombing of the government complex.

Forty minutes after the police received the call with Breivik's license plate number, the police sent out a national alarm. *None* of the local police stations in the country took notice of the alarm. By this time, Breivik was nearly at his next target.

"There are no indications that the police in the first hours after the terrorist attack in Oslo in any way attempted to make use of the press or media to notify the population or its own staff about the presumed perpetrator's description and license plate number," the Commission reported. "Only at 18:26 [that is, three hours after the explosion] did Oslo police station send out an alarm to its staff that any police officer in uniform, unable to identify himself, should be stopped, by force if necessary."

Though all of these systematic failures took place in 2011, the government had actually adopted procedures, in case terrorist attacks should occur, several years earlier. According to the Commission's report, the security council had decided in 2004 to implement measures to secure the H-block and the entire government complex against attacks. "The work was to have high priority," the Commission wrote. "Nonetheless, seven years later, it was possible to detonate a car bomb close to the entrance of the H-block. No professional routines had been established to ensure that the project was implemented with the intended speed and quality. Adequate and relevant provisional measures were not implemented."

In the summer of 2010, the Office of the Prime Minister and the Ministry of Justice and Public Security were informed by the National Police Directorate that the work to secure the government complex gave cause for concern because several measures of great importance for security had not yet been put into practice. This concern, however, never reached the leadership of the ministry in charge of national security.

Utøya, which is owned by the Labor Party's Youth Unit (AUF), has been the venue for the organization's summer camp for more than sixty years. It should have been conceivable that if someone wished to harm the political power in Norway, he might also attack this island during the summer camp. All Labor Party leaders have taken part in the summer camp, and the current prime minister, Jens Stoltenberg, has been at Utøya every single summer since 1974. Yet only one security guard—unarmed at that—was present. Former prime minister Gro Harlem Brundtland—whom Breivik wished to kill and behead—had visited the island in the morning and left around 3 P.M. No security reinforcements in connection with her visit were put in place. After the bombing of the government buildings in Oslo, no one thought of sending forces to the island of Utøya to protect the political future of the country.

According to the Commission report, "Hardly anyone could have imagined that a secondary attack would have been made on the youth camp on Utøya Island. Sadly, however, after repeated school massacres in other countries, an armed desperado who shoots adolescents is indeed conceivable—even in Norway. This is the type of mission that every Police District drills today, and is expected to be able to deal with."

At the same time, the Commission asserts that through public reports and legislative work, Norway's parliament and government have had security and emergency preparedness high on their agendas for the past fifteen years. New directorates and oversight bodies were in fact in place, and higher expectations could reasonably have been asked of the authorities. In 2002, PST accorded the fight against international terrorism highest priority. PST stated that ". . . the terrorist acts in the United States on September 11, 2001, marked the beginning of an era in international politics with increased uncertainty and a higher threat level. It appears that the United States is the primary target, but it cannot be excluded that other countries, also Norway, may be hit in the future."

LACK OF POLICE PREPAREDNESS

The Security Act, adopted in 1998, sets standards based on "vital national security interests." According to the Commission, "Many had views on questions related to the Act, and one took the liberty of using 13 years to develop regulations that were to provide clarifications. During this period, there was no oversight that could have identified significant shortcomings with a view to security."

After the NOKAS cash-depot robbery in 2004, where an officer was killed, the National Police Directorate decided to set up a system for swift, secure, and efficient notification between police districts in connection with major events. Although the police in the NOKAS case had been notified of an imminent robbery at the cash depot, the perpetrators got away with $10 million, making it the biggest theft in Norway. The local police station in Stavanger was understaffed and unprepared due to Easter holidays. Only six years later, in 2010, did the system become operational.

"The National Police Directorate was warned about weaknesses in the chosen solution," the Commission reported. "The system was never tested systematically, and although experience indicated a number of problems, no improvements were made." On July 22, the system failed miserably.

Likewise, the police developed a special set of plans for use in the event of terrorism and sabotage. The measures in these plans included roadblocks to prevent terrorists from getting away and initiatives for the immediate mobilization of police personnel to reduce the response time for any further attacks, and would be of the utmost relevance in the case of a large bomb detonating in the government complex. These plans, developed to facilitate procedures in a chaotic situation, were ignored on July 22.

"Different understandings—or more accurately, different *acknowledgement* of risk and vulnerability*—stand out as one important explanation," the Commission states in its report, and also illustrated its point with some examples including the fact that it was underestimated that solo terrorism could cause such devastation. The police's emergency preparedness has not improved since the NOKAS robbery, the Commission further concluded. "Despite the fact that experience and repeated exercises have pointed out that this translates into vulnerability, the situation has not changed. The notification and mobilization of personnel are based more on coincidence than on emergency preparedness schemes."

Even though there were indications of further attacks after the explosion, law enforcement took too long to put security measures in place.

"Helicopters and the Armed Forces' other resources were requested so late that they did not provide much help for the police operation. Many hours passed before military troops were called out to secure civilian objects. . . . Instead, people gradually accepted that the probability of new attacks was small."

The Delta police forces that arrived from Oslo had no boat at their disposal when they got to the dock near Utøya, and they were unsuccessful at finding a tourist boat. The local police finally arrived with a tiny red Zodiac, but it was too small for the men and their equipment. First Lieutenant Terje Klevengen explained that because of the gravity of the situation, Delta wished to bring as many arms and as much equipment as possible. As a result, the small boat was too heavily loaded and stopped in the water. Delta had no choice but to wait until a tourist boat picked them up.

Another boat that could have been useful to the police that day, according to the July 22nd Commission report, was AUF's own ferry boat, MS *Thorbjørn*. The ferry had taken off from the island right after Breivik started shooting and the captain contacted the police, who told him to get away from the island and to safety. The ferry therefore continued north and was inaccessible to take part in the rescue operation until after Breivik was apprehended.

Because it was July and vacation time, the Oslo police's only helicopter was unavailable to assess the situation in Oslo and to go to Utøya. As was the case in the NOKAS robbery, authorities acted as if there existed a tacit agreement that terrorists don't strike during holidays.

The 720th Army platoon in the south of Norway had, however, started preparing three helicopters ready to be deployed in the operation, but the Oslo police did not reach out to ask for any assistance. Only forty-five minutes after the first report about the shooting on the island did the police contact the Army for help. A helicopter belonging to the national news channel *NRK* was already circling the island, but the police did not attempt to obtain it.

The Commission puts it this way: "When the Armed Forces' emergency helicopter services were reassigned to Afghanistan in 2009, the police's access to helicopter support was reduced. The police's own helicopter service experienced reduced availability during the same period of time. While the consequences of this aggregate shortfall of capacity, not least to transport the Delta forces, were acknowledged, they did not trigger any measures to compensate for the shortfall."

LAW ENFORCEMENT'S FAILURE TO COMMUNICATE WITH THE VICTIMS AND EACH OTHER

When the news of the Oslo bombing spread to Utøya, a meeting was held at 16:00 to inform the participants about the bombing and to reassure everyone that "we're safe. We're on an island. There is no place safer on earth from terrorism than Utøya."

The parents of Håvard Vederhus, leader of AUF Oslo, Kirsten and Alf Vederhus, were in contact with their son while he was hiding near the pumping station on the island. He kept asking his parents to call the police and have them send helicopters to save them. The last time Alf Vederhus spoke with the police, he was told a helicopter was on the way.

"According to our son," Håvard's father said, "that doesn't sound as if it's true." The operator then finally admitted that there was only one police helicopter in the whole of Norway, that they should assemble the family and keep calm. That was their last conversation with the police that day.

"We were in touch with him for forty minutes," Alf said, "and it was as if we watched our son slide through our fingers and away from us. We were helpless. We couldn't do anything." Håvard's parents kept waiting for their son to send them a message saying he was okay, but that message never came. Breivik murdered fourteen teenagers, including Håvard, at the pumping station.

The Commission keeps repeating in its report that the police operation on Utøya was poorly coordinated, and as a result it took much longer than necessary to get there. The understaffed emergency operations center, which was designated in the plan to lead and coordinate, was overwhelmed by telephone calls. Communication problems caused different police units to miss each other. "Informal language usage and non-compliance with basic requirements for accurate communication in a crisis helped make a poor communication situation even more challenging," the Commission reported.

Seventeen minutes after Breivik started killing, the first police car left Hønefoss police station for Utøya. By this time—at 17:43—Breivik had already killed thirty-eight people. The main police station in Oslo dispatched more cars toward Utøya. Twenty-six policemen in total were at this point on their way.

"The police had to rely on telephone calls to notify and mobilize personnel," the Commission stated. Valuable time that could have been spent analyzing, planning, and managing the operation was lost. The police driving from Oslo didn't know exactly where Utøya was, and with the police radio not working, there was no communication between the cars and the police station closest to the island. Police cars drove toward the island from different directions without knowing each other's plans.

"Weak local communications and a lack of coverage by the Norwegian Public Safety Radio played a part in how there was a misunderstanding about where the mustering place was to be," according to the report. "The police did not have access to even the simplest technology for transmitting written mustering information to personnel and official vehicles. Most of Delta force's cars did not have electronic map systems."

The local police, consisting of eight armed men, arrived first at the port closest to Utøya, and although they were trained for battle, when they heard the gunshots from the island, they hid behind a container and decided they should "observe and report" from the mainland instead of getting themselves over to the island. They also heard over the radio that the Delta forces were coming from Oslo and decided it was best to wait.

After Breivik's first recorded call to the police emergency number, one of the police cars driving from Oslo was able to contact the local police station. Thirty-eight minutes had passed since Breivik's arrival on the island. The officers agreed to meet at a place called Storøybrua, almost two and a half miles from Utøya, and not at Utøya port, which would have been closest to the island, and where the local police were waiting. According to Terje Klevengen, head of the Delta forces on their way to the island, they believed they were dealing with three to five perpetrators, all armed with guns and possibly with explosives.

Sixty-six minutes after Breivik started shooting, Klevengen and his Delta forces set foot on the island. They ran toward the northern part while, unaware of their presence, Breivik walked toward the south. He called the police again, saying he was ready to surrender. Then he hung up and continued to kill.

The second boat arrived with more Delta forces; hearing shots coming from the south tip of the island, they moved toward the sound, where they met Breivik walking calmly with his hands out to the side, ready to surrender. Breivik was apprehended at 18:34, one hour and thirty-four minutes after he killed his first victims on the island.

For more than an hour, tourists had risked their lives picking up and rescuing the desperate teenagers struggling to swim and stay afloat in the cold water. Tourists and the local population had also stood on the shore on the mainland to receive the ones who managed to swim or were picked up by the boats, many of them wounded and freezing.

The ambulances with doctors and paramedics were still not allowed to go down to the dock, as the police didn't think it would be safe. Only twenty minutes after Breivik was caught were the ambulances permitted to enter the dock and treat the wounded. No doctors or paramedics were allowed to go over to the island to treat the injured there. The police were still looking for other perpetrators.

In the evening, as the police and paramedics searched the island trying to find survivors and count the dead, there were cell phones ringing and lighting up everywhere. Parents tried to contact their children without getting responses. Adding to their anguish, officials were uncertain how to interpret the confidentiality provisions in the Health Personnel Act. As a result, hospitals were unable to provide police information regarding the victims' identities. As police counted the dead on the island, they counted some victims more than once. By the following morning, the incorrect death count reported was as high as ninety bodies.

HUBRIS AND DENIAL

The "contrast between the inconceivable and the conceivable presents a challenge for a commission appointed to gain knowledge from 22 July," the report concluded with typical vagueness. Hindsight was not an option, it said, and "no one wants a terrorist to be able to change what is unique, transparent and worthwhile about this 'little country of ours.'" This ironic statement points out that in spite of its criticism of an obviously flawed system and law enforcement's reaction to the attack, the Commission members are Norwegians, after all. They do point out that leadership must start at the top, and that the main challenges relate to Norway's culture and the attitude of its people.

They state: "We are therefore of the opinion that the country's leadership, represented by the Government Security Council and the Government's Emergency Council, must spend more time on awareness of threat and risk levels and on ensuring good interaction and responses in the light of the challenges. . . ."

The Commission writes that individuals' actions are influenced by, and depend on, the extent to which the leadership has paved the way for their duties to actually be performed in a satisfactory manner. In society's quest for scapegoats, the report says, it is easy to forget that imperfect systems can help put individuals in a position to make fatal mistakes. Meanwhile, it is essential to understand the details.

"A system is by and large the sum of the individuals who take decisions and perform actions."

The Commission attempted to put a positive spin on coincidences that had nothing to do with the law-enforcement efficiency. For instance, the summer vacation season worked to the public's advantage, the Commission pointed out. Had Breivik managed to detonate his bomb earlier that day, or at a different time of the year, several hundreds more would have been present at the scene and possibly dead.

As unbelievable as it sounds, the Commission also concluded that the call-out response for Utøya was quicker and with a larger operational force than what was normally available on a Friday afternoon. Because of Breivik's bombing of Oslo, the Delta forces were on high alert and already mobilized. They concluded that had the massacre on Utøya taken place as an isolated incident, fewer and less well-trained officers would have been at work at the police station in Hønefoss.

For many, the mobile-phone network was the only well-functioning mode of communication that day, but a few weeks earlier there had been a serious outage in large parts of the mobile-phone network in eastern Norway. Again, the Commission concluded that the consequences could have been even more dramatic.

The attack on July 22 was, according to the report, "exceptional, and a day unlike any other day." It seems to be saying that the tragedy is in the past, and nothing like it will ever happen again in Norway. But with regard to that day in 2011, "With better ways of working and a broader focus, the Police Security Service could have become aware of the perpetrator prior to 22 July," the Commission wrote. "Notwithstanding, the Commission has no grounds for contending that the Police Security Service could and should have averted the attacks." This contradictory statement attempts to appease the outraged population, but at the same time fails to place the blame where it belongs.

Although the Commission's proposed changes look good on paper, they are not specific enough. Even in the original Norwegian language, the suggestions for change are vague. What must change—and the Commission touches on it half-heartedly—are the hubris and the culture of denial.

The Commission found that any failures were primarily due to:

- The inability to acknowledge risk and to learn from training.
- The inability to implement decisions and to use plans.
- The inability to coordinate and interact.
- The inability to utilize information and communication technology.
- The inability and unwillingness of leaders to clarify responsibility, set goals, and adopt necessary measures. In other words, the Norwegians think they are untouchable.

"The Commission believes that the measures recommended will put society and individuals in a better position to face future challenges," they wrote. "They are inevitable. Accordingly, it is crucial to address the basic challenges. This is urgent."

"We are a small country," Prime Minister Stoltenberg said in a speech right after the attacks, "but a big people. We have a lot of questions. We all demand honest answers. Not to put blame on someone else but the perpetrator. But to learn and to move forward." It is now up to every Norwegian to ask him or herself: What am *I* willing to do about it?

This horrific day has not changed much in Norwegian society. Many of these structural deficiencies have not been remedied, whether it is safety measures around public buildings or police standby in case of terrorist attacks. When the next killer strikes—and he will—Norway's preparation or lack of it will once again be painfully obvious.

Norway was not prepared for what happened on July 22, 2011 and, in the immediate aftermath, remained numb and in denial. The price the victims and their families paid for the country's negligence was tragic.

CHAPTER NINE

MADMEN OR CRAZED GENIUSES?

Our shock attacks are theatre, and theatre is always performed in front of an audience.

—ANDERS BREIVIK MANIFESTO

As darkness began to veil the island of Utøya, Anders Behring Breivik was held and interrogated in the island's main building, while, outside the guarded quarters, groups of police, medical staff, and volunteers kept working, using any electric or battery-powered lights available to collect the dead and offer aid to the wounded before they were eventually evacuated by boats and helicopters back to the mainland. Oslo had known of the rampage for hours. Breivik's name was already on thousands of lips throughout the city and spreading quickly across the country.

News travels fast in Norway, a small country with just five million citizens. One out of every four Norwegians getting word of the massacre would soon learn that they knew, or were in some way connected to, at least one of the victims in the bombing of the government building or in the shooting carnage on Utøya. And a surprising number of citizens had, at some point, come in contact with Breivik in one way or another.

All the various foreign groups represented on the "island paradise" that day had lost at least one of their representatives during Breivik's moment of terror.

THE MOST HATED MAN IN NORWAY

As the death toll rose, even Breivik later agreed that he, at that moment, must have been the most hated man in Norway, and it wouldn't be long before his notoriety would spread worldwide. But in the first few hours of the night following the terror, nobody knew with certainty that an Islamic terrorist cell wasn't involved. The horrors in New York on September 11, 2001, were still fresh in the minds of the Norwegian citizens. The Norwegian government, through the media, instructed the people of Norway to remain calm. There would be no outright criticism of Islam or the Muslims currently living in Norway.

Then there was Breivik, the man who was being held as a suspect. The only means anyone had of truly rejecting and punishing him was to reserve their outrage. In this way, the country would show that they bore the accused no sign of harbored hatred and animosity. Such prejudices would be avoided, in order that Breivik be left alone with his murderous soul, deprived of the attention and acknowledgement he craved. A short address by Prime Minister Jens Stoltenberg declared that his country would not respond with premature calls for vengeance, as the United States had done immediately after the attacks in 2001.

"We must show that our open society can pass this test too," he declared. "The answer to violence is even more democracy. Even more humanity." Then, in a moment of what could have been his reflection on the enormity of Breivik's crime, he added: "But never naïveté."

As the night wore on, and Breivik was held on the island, the Norwegian citizenry searched the Internet and watched for reports that would add brushstrokes to the mass murderer's portrait. Had the prime minister's words acted as a balm to the outraged? Would anyone be able to eventually get over the horror that had occurred that day? The dead would never come back to their families.

On Facebook, the curious found postings made two days prior to the attacks. They contained photos of a nice-looking blond man wearing a casual polo shirt in one pose, a full military-type uniform in another, and a formal dinner jacket in still another. The man's Facebook page revealed his name, Anders Behring Breivik. He listed his religion as Christian, his political views as conservative, and his favorite book as George Orwell's *1984*.

Not much there. Certainly nothing that pointed to a madman.

If anyone searched further, they might have discovered that he had posted a warning of sorts on a right-wing website which could have ignited their interest. It seems that this 32-year-old businessperson was warning his audience of a gradual takeover under way in Europe by the forces of Islam. And on his lone Twitter message, he quoted British philosopher John Stuart Mill: "One person with a belief is equal to the force of 100,000 who have only interests."

The next morning, Breivik awakened from a short sleep. Superintendent Ørjan Tombre and other investigators must have been fatigued from Breivik's self-aggrandizing and his self-righteous requests to barter special information about future attacks for certain privileges, such as access to a computer in his prison cell. Tombre, by this time, was probably wondering how they would get this man, accused of killing close to a hundred innocents the previous day, back to Oslo before one of his men decided to break Norway's ban on the death penalty and carry out a personal execution.

On Saturday morning, the international media began to swarm into Oslo. Word of a possible third attack had made its way from the island, and most city dwellers were glued to their TVs and discussing the news among themselves. The city had been partially closed down, to discourage the over-curious, but mostly because it wasn't safe to wander near buildings that might or might not collapse due to the impact of the bomb, not to mention the possibility of another bomb attack. At this point anything was possible. It wasn't the time to be outside, meandering about, unless one was involved in the official business of restoring order and safety to the city. Near the government center, the area remained stark evidence of the destruction: the building's front entrance had been sheared off. International media personnel, who knew of this city's open peacefulness, walked in silence as police and military troops lined the streets, acting as sentinels.

As citizens and tourists alike took in the devastation, one could feel the questions hovering in the air, which still smelled of sulfur. Who? Why? What would happen next?

Police had notified Breivik's mother late Friday night, hoping she might shed some light on why her son would have committed such an act of violence.

"It could not be my son," she repeated over and over. She told the police that she had seen him that morning and that he had slept in his room on Thursday night. He had been so calm, she reported. "He's not the type [to kill anyone]," she insisted. Finally, after being informed of the massive evidence that pointed to her son's guilt, she did admit that it might have been possible. She blamed mental illness. Far easier than blaming any part of his life that she might have touched.

When the FBI had visited McVeigh's father in Pendleton, New York, after his son's apprehension, Bill McVeigh admitted that it was possible that his son was the perpetrator of the Oklahoma City bombing.

"Because he's been so upset about Waco, it probably wouldn't surprise me if he was involved in this," Bill McVeigh had said.

"THAT AIN'T ME"

Unlike Breivik, who deliberately called the authorities and knew they would not use deadly force on him if he surrendered, McVeigh knew that he had to get away from the crime scene in order to have a chance of surviving, so he kept on driving his escape car away from Oklahoma City.

About seventy-five miles from the disaster area, nineteen-year-old Oklahoma Patrol trooper Charles J. Hanger noticed a battered Mercury Grand Marquis without license plates passing by. He directed the driver to pull over, and McVeigh complied. Hanger wanted to know why McVeigh had no license plate. McVeigh explained he'd just bought the car. When Hanger asked if he had insurance, registration, or a bill of sale, McVeigh explained that everything was being mailed to his address.

As he handed over his driver's license, Hanger noticed a bulge under McVeigh's jacket. "What's that?" the trooper asked. When McVeigh said it was a gun, Hanger held his own weapon to McVeigh's head and confiscated the 9-mm Glock, as well as a clip of ammunition and a knife attached to his belt, and told McVeigh he was under arrest.

McVeigh had a concealed-weapon permit in New York, but it wasn't valid in Oklahoma. Hanger put the handcuffed McVeigh in the police car and called his dispatcher to run a computer check on the driver's license and the Glock. McVeigh did not have a criminal record, nor was the pistol stolen.

Hanger locked up the Mercury and took McVeigh to the Noble County Jail in Perry, Oklahoma, where he was booked on four misdemeanor charges—unlawfully carrying a weapon, transporting a loaded firearm in a motor vehicle, failing to display a current license plate, and failing to maintain proof of insurance. No one had any idea that he was the bomber.

Although the charges were relatively minor, McVeigh had to wait for his day in court. Because Judge Danny G. Allen was tied up in a lengthy divorce case, McVeigh's bail hearing was delayed until Friday, April 21, two days after the bombing. Had he been tried in a timely manner, McVeigh might well have escaped. As the sheriff's office was listening to the news of the bombing and the first description of a possible suspect was given (a white male, somewhere between five feet nine and six feet one), one deputy looked over at McVeigh. "That ain't me," McVeigh laughed. "I'm six-two. Listen to that description." But the delay of the bail hearing allowed more time to be devoted to the identification of the bomber.

In Virginia, at the FBI's behavioral-science unit, specialists were working hard to establish a profile of the bomber. Most of the investigators were convinced that the bombing was the work of foreign terrorists, but not Special Agent Clinton R. Van Zandt, a psychological profiler who had worked as chief FBI negotiator at Waco, Texas. Van Zandt noticed that the date of the attack, April 19, 1995, was exactly two years to the day after the deaths at Waco had occurred.

He believed the perpetrator would be white, male, and in his twenties. Furthermore, he was convinced that the suspect would be a military man and possibly a member of a fringe militia group. Terrorism expert Louis R. Mizell, Jr. noticed that the date coincided with that of Patriots' Day—anniversary of the Revolutionary War Battle of Concord, which was celebrated by those who believed in the militia movement.

Van Zandt had also been involved in identifying Kaczynski. That investigation was still ongoing when McVeigh bombed Oklahoma City. Linda Kaczynski, who was married to Ted Kaczynski's younger brother, David, urged her husband to read the published manifesto. Given the numerous FBI press conferences where the Unabomber was described as someone from the Chicago area (where he began his bombings), with connections in Salt Lake City and the San Francisco Bay Area, Linda had connected the dots.

Although he at first dismissed her theory, David read the manifesto and began to accept the likelihood that his estranged brother was indeed the Unabomber. He then went through old family papers and found letters written by his brother. Dating back to the 1970s, they contained phrases similar to what was found in the Unabomber Manifesto. David, still not certain about Kaczynski's guilt, voluntarily gave the letters to the FBI to protect his brother from the danger of an FBI raid.

Van Zandt believed the letters and the manifesto were the products of the same author. The FBI arrested Kaczynski on April 3, 1996, after a manhunt of nearly two decades, at his remote cabin outside Lincoln, Montana.

Searching his cabin, the investigators found a wealth of bomb components and forty thousand handwritten journal pages that included bomb-making experiments and descriptions of the Unabomber crimes. The FBI also found, hidden underneath his bed, yet another explosive device ready for mailing.

In the last months before the Oklahoma bombing, McVeigh had used different aliases, just as Breivik had, to avoid apprehension. But he did use his own name at the motel where he had parked his Ryder truck the night before the blast, and the fact that his escape car didn't have license plates was an invitation to the authorities to arrest him. So was the envelope with anti-government documents that he left in the Mercury and the hateful messages he had written on his sister's computer. Yet when apprehended, McVeigh didn't confess to the crime. He wanted to take every opportunity to inconvenience and embarrass the authorities along the way.

On Friday, July 22, 2011, Attorney Geir Lippestad had been out on the Oslofjord waterway, on his way back from vacation with his wife and children in his private boat, when he heard the rumbling sound coming from the city. Looking up at the rain clouds, he dismissed the low roar as thunder. But at the same time, he thought it was weird that he didn't see any lightning. He noted that it was almost 3:30 P.M., and minutes later he answered a call on his cell phone. It was one of his employees, sounding excited. A bomb-like explosion had ripped off the front of the government building not more than a hundred yards away from his offices.

Assured that his building hadn't been damaged, he ordered his staff to evacuate and continued sailing toward shore. That night and into the morning, he watched and listened as the news came in about the bombing, then the shootings on Utøya.

The 48-year-old tried to coax his stocky, fit body into sleep. Four hours later, his phone woke him. He listened as the voice of a policeman, who'd been interrogating Anders Behring Breivik, informed him that the accused had personally requested him, Geir Lippestad, to be his attorney. His first inclination was to say *no*, but he ran a hand through his short clipped gray hair and said, "I need some time to think."

Lippestad had been relatively unknown until Breivik asked him to be his attorney. After he graduated from the University of Oslo Faculty of Law in 1990, he had been hired by a small law firm in the outskirts of Oslo. Later, he started his own firm with some colleagues in downtown Oslo. Breivik had at some point rented office space in the same building as Lippestad, and they shared the same canteen. In 2002, Lippestad's name appeared in the national press when he defended Ole Nicolai Kvisler, who was sentenced to seventeen years of prison for his participation in the racially motivated murder of Benjamin Hermansen. Breivik was impressed by the way Lippestad had defended Kvisler, and knowing he would be an even more hated public figure than Kvisler, he felt that Lippestad was a suitable choice. Breivik also thought that Lippestad would let him use his trial as a marketing tool.

Lippestad's first thought was that he couldn't deal with this case, nor the man, if he indeed was responsible for such mayhem. But Lippestad didn't have much time to think about it. Breivik wouldn't, he was told by the policeman on the phone, reveal any information of other terrorist cells and hidden bombs until his attorney got there. He decided he must discuss the matter with his wife, who always seemed to know what to say and do in tough situations. His wife, a nurse, reminded him of his job as an attorney, and that she, as a nurse, would have treated Breivik had he been brought into the hospital wounded.

"It is your job as an attorney to defend him and to protect his interests," she said. Lippestad went for a long walk, to think, and when he came back home he had made up his mind. He had convinced himself that this was a case just like any other, and that the rules of criminal law and procedure were just the same. And maybe, in the back of his mind, he realized what this case might do for his career. He immediately called the policeman and told him he was on his way. He would meet with Breivik, speak with him, and then decide.

SHOCK, GRIEF, AND DENIAL

On Monday evening, still in a state of shock and grief, Norwegian citizens responded in rallies calling for unity to mourn the dead. More than two hundred thousand people assembled in Oslo alone, while other large groups gathered across the country. In front of Oslo's City Hall, amid the people carrying flowers, cards, and candles, Crown Prince Haakon announced "Tonight our streets are filled with love." Crown Princess Mette-Marit, who had lost her stepbrother on the island, cried as many onlookers in the crowd held up roses.

Prime Minister Jens Stoltenberg, who had almost overnight become something of a father figure to the country, said he was confident that Norway would pass this test. "This is a march for democracy, tolerance, and unity," he told the thousands. "Evil can kill people but never conquer a nation."

One woman in attendance raised her voice, saying "We are more than the evil within us."

Her husband added "We must and will stand together now."

But amid the country's collective unity, questions were being raised. Why hadn't Breivik's plans been detected? His name had appeared on a Norwegian Police Security (PST) watch list for buying chemicals needed to build a bomb, and nothing had come of it. Why had security failed in so many ways? How could one man commit all this evil without being stopped?

Not only was Breivik's state of mental health discussed among the prosecution and defense teams, but many pro-government political views were being expressed. Just days after the massacre, novelist Jostein Gaarder and Professor Thomas Hylland Eriksen wrote an op-ed for the *New York Times*, "A Blogosphere of Bigots," in which they claimed Breivik wasn't a lone wolf–type madman, but a product of the extreme right wing. Much of the essay indicated that Breivik's disgust with multiculturalism and his hatred for Muslims had driven him over the edge.

Other political activists claimed that the Labor Party, while taking advantage of a stunned community, was exploiting July 22 in order to maintain its power. Breivik, they reminded the public, had killed fellow Norwegians, and his derangement shouldn't be recognized as a product of the right-wing Progress Party. Author Mora Levin, a respected member of Norway's Jewish community, wrote that the *New York Times* piece was "the ugliest thing I have ever read since *Mein Kampf*."

Bruce Bawer wrote that this political debate was "plainly a new Norwegian order that the political and media establishment, led by the Labor Party, was trying to ram down the country's throat in the wake of the atrocities."

Geir Lippestad would soon agree to defend Breivik. No one was sure of his motives or strategy at that time, but he must have been thinking that Breivik was already being discussed as a phenomenon. In his first press conference, Lippestad faced the cameras and gave short, concise answers to the waiting crowd.

- Yes, Breivik had admitted to his acts.
- Yes, Breivik thought his acts gruesome—but, to his mind, necessary.
- No, he (Lippestad) hadn't officially met with his client.
- Yes, he planned to meet him that afternoon.
- Yes, if he agreed to defend Breivik in court, he would defend him to the best of his ability.

And the world had finally met the man who might be willing to defend such a monster.

Later that afternoon, in Oslo's central police station, he faced the man who had stolen Norway's spirit and sent its citizens into their homes, broken and fearful for their country. Had all their progress directed at peace and equality for all been in vain? Had one of their own proved that madness and evil existed in every human mind?

After spending about three hours with his client, Lippestad texted the message that the court had been waiting for. He assured them that he would officially represent Anders Behring Breivik in the upcoming trial. Then he immediately granted a second interview to the hungry media.

His client was in a war. That was his message to the crowd. His client believed that the Western world wouldn't understand him, that it would take sixty years for his actions to be fully understood and appreciated. Then Lippestad raised his voice as he briefly explained his client's mindset. "Everything," he said, raising his eyes to level them on his audience, "indicates to me that he is insane."

Meanwhile, Inga Bejer Engh, a 41-year-old attorney in the Oslo Prosecutor's Office, had been driving to her summer cabin when she learned of the killings. She followed the case with interest. Within a month, she and her colleague Svein Holden were officially assigned as prosecutors for Breivik's case. What followed would be far from a typical Norwegian trial, but it would follow the Norwegian mindset to a frightening degree.

A copy of Breivik's manifesto began to surface through an anonymous post on various Internet forums. Immediately it went viral, and a surge of anxiety rushed through the nation and beyond. With the live drama about his upcoming trial, his written diatribe was discussed in many tones, most of which were aimed at how he would be tried. The majority wanted him quickly convicted and imprisoned. Since there is no death penalty in Norway, the call was for life in prison, to lock him up and throw away the key.

As the peaceful parades continued, the full impact of what her son had carried out on that deadly Friday struck Wenche Behring. She collapsed in her apartment, where Breivik had so often slept, and was admitted as a patient in the psychiatric ward at Diakonhjemmet Hospital.

For more than a month, too shocked to face the outside world, she talked to the police and gave what would later be considered crucial evidence at the hearing. Too ill to attend, she allowed her remarks to be read to the court a few months later by her far-from-unbiased doctor. "I thought [my son, Anders] had turned completely crazy," the doctor would read to a visibly shaken Anders Breivik. "I thought there was something wrong with his head."

Like Breivik, McVeigh was unashamed of his crimes. He admitted to his attorneys that he was responsible for the bombing; however, he claimed that his actions were a justifiable response to the tyranny of the government. Much like Breivik, he wanted his lawyers to craft a "necessary defense" pleading and create a platform for him to get his message through to the public. And as in Breivik's case, McVeigh's attorney, Stephen Jones, attempted to use insanity as a defense in spite of his client's opposition. The psychiatrist Jones hired to evaluate McVeigh, however, quickly came to the conclusion that McVeigh had known exactly what he was doing when he detonated the bomb. He was legally sane, and it would be difficult to argue otherwise.

The question of sanity was also crucial to Kaczynski. Forensic psychiatrist Sally Johnson, appointed to examine Kaczynski's mental state for competency, diagnosed him with paranoid schizophrenia. Furious at this finding, Kaczynski attempted to fire his attorneys and refused to accept a diagnosis of mental illness. In the end, he pleaded "guilty" to avoid being characterized as insane during the trial.

A QUESTION OF SANITY

In order to understand the farce that followed July 22, 2011, it is imperative to study the meaning of the insanity ruling in Norway. In most countries, including the United States, it is a defense, meaning that being judged insane might *reduce* one's sentence. In Norway, however, insanity excludes the assailant from punishment altogether. Under Norwegian law, a person who is guilty of a crime, but considered psychotic, cannot be imprisoned or even punished for his actions. Had Breivik been sent to a mental institution, he could pretend to regret the murders and secure a release as soon as five years later. That was the fear that filled the Norwegian population. No one wanted this monster to go unpunished.

However, statistically, only one of five insanity pleas in Norway was successful; and of those, many involved subjects who were deemed mentally deficient without contest.

Had Breivik killed his countrymen because, as his manifesto suggested, he was a rebel against the multiculturalist left? Certainly, when he committed the murders, he was mad. That was what I thought at first. It was as clear as black and white to me. A moral middle ground did not exist for him, especially not in Norway, where black and white fade into noncommittal shades of gray. Perhaps Breivik's destiny was predicted early on, when Kristian Andenæs, a renowned criminal-law professor at the University of Oslo, wrote: "In a way, he [Breivik] is obviously insane, but not in the sense of [Norwegian] criminal law."

Later, though, as I conducted my research, my opinion changed, as I learned that Breivik is a textbook example of a lone wolf killer, and that he was perfectly sane before, during, and after his gruesome acts. Just like Kaczynski and McVeigh.

CONFLICT OF INTEREST

Breivik's first psychiatric examination was arranged by court-appointed Torgeir Husby, the 61-year-old head of psychiatry at Oslo's Diakonhjemmet Hospital. Known for his tough medical approach rather than his attention to his patient's veracity, or lack thereof, he was joined by Dr. Synne Sørheim, a former assistant of his at Oslo's facility. Ironically enough, the hospital Dr. Husby headed was the same facility that had treated Breivik's mother in the past and was treating her now, after her breakdown. Clearly, Husby was no impartial expert. Breivik's mother had long insisted that her son was insane, as a way of avoiding taking any blame for his actions.

The panel's conclusion was made public on Tuesday, November 29, 2011. They diagnosed Breivik as suffering from paranoid schizophrenia. This disorder had developed over a period of time, they concluded, and he had been criminally insane during the attacks and still was during their examinations days later.

According to the report, Breivik offered unfitting dialogue that lacked empathy. He spoke and acted compulsively, alluding to himself as Europe's warrior in "a low-intensity civil war." He described himself as a grand master in the Knights Templar and claimed that the organization would commit further executions.

One might think this would take care of the question as to Breivik's state of mind when he slaughtered seventy-seven people and left well over a hundred more collectively suffering on the street, at the camp, in the fields, and in the water. Yet the Norwegian people were shocked by the realization that he could, in essence, go free. That was what their legal system offered them. A person, in this case Breivik, could either be sane and imprisoned or insane and unpunished. It was too much to fathom.

This shock created a huge outrage in the media. On December 8, 2011, on behalf of the surviving victims of the attacks, their attorneys challenged the panel's bias and demanded a second opinion.

Meanwhile, Dr. Randi Rosenquist, a renowned psychiatrist who had observed Breivik during his initial days in prison, spoke for the first time about the case on national television. It was her opinion that someone who, like Breivik, was in the midst of an active psychosis like the panel had concluded, most likely couldn't have pulled off such a complicated and well-organized plan of attack.

When she learned how Breivik had manufactured the bomb, coordinated its blast, and directed his attack on the island, she paused to ponder the totality of horror he had accomplished. The time it must have involved just to plan the attack. The energy he must have expended. The precise manner in which he had executed his mission. All these factors suggested that he was probably sane. The full scope of Breivik's act seemed too complex to be compatible with an active psychosis.

In January 2012, the court appointed a second panel of psychiatric experts, Dr. Tørrissen and Dr. Aspaas, in an attempt to appease the media and population. Right after Easter break in April, the panel's conclusion was made public. They deemed Breivik sane, in the criminal sense of the term. Their conclusion didn't come as a surprise, and critics of the insanity circus have pointed out that both panels had political agendas.

One such critic, author/psychologist Ellen Kolsrud Finnøy, pointed out that both panels had ulterior motives for their conclusions. In her book *The Envious Murderer*, she portrays four possible motivating factors that address both panels. First, a diagnosis of insanity was the ultimate revenge against Breivik because he feared lack of credibility above all else. Second, the insanity conclusion would prevent uncomfortable discussions about the Norwegian legal system and justice for the victims. No one would have to think about how sentences in Norway can be reduced after a few years if the prisoner behaves well, or that the goal is to rehabilitate, not to punish, the prisoners. Third, the diagnosis of schizophrenia may have been an attempt to discount Breivik's political views and motivation for the attack as expressed in his manifesto.

On the other side, as a fourth point, she points out that the second panel's motivation was appeasement of the victims, their families, and the population in general. The second panel was bullied by the media into coming to their conclusion. And so the debates continued to rage, leading up to Breivik's formal trial.

A CIRCUS

On February 6, 2012, after Breivik had attended a number of subsequent custody hearings, he was brought into the court to face presiding judge Wenche Elizabeth Arntzen, for his final preliminary hearing. Both his team of defense attorneys and the state's group of prosecutors sat at their appropriate tables. In attendance were many expert witnesses for both factions of the insanity debate. Also, many surviving victims of the massacre watched with differing degrees of passion. Upon entering the courtroom, Breivik swung his cuffed hands out in a ceremonial gesture.

He pleaded not guilty and claimed that the attacks were perpetrated upon a nation planning on destroying its own culture and ethnicity. After rambling on for what seemed to be an eternity, he said that he deserved a medal of honor for his deeds.

During the hearing, Dr. Rosenquist pointed out that although Breivik's manifesto was highly influenced by America's infamous Unabomber, Theodore Kaczynski, Breivik couldn't be compared to him in any full measure. Kaczynski had been a child prodigy who had entered Harvard University at sixteen and had acquired a professorship at the age of twenty-five. Breivik, Dr. Rosenquist insisted, was no genius, though he possessed an above-average intelligence and—like the Oklahoma City bomber, Timothy McVeigh, whose bomb recipe he copied—had had all of his faculties while planning and committing his heinous crimes. Not even Rosenquist fully understood the similarities between the three killers.

One fact became evident to most involved with the case and with the decision on how to try Breivik. He, above all those following the case, hoped the verdict was sanity. There was to be no mental hospital for him. No bed where doctors could experiment with his superior mind. No drugs to fog his thoughts. He wanted a place where he could stay properly fit and eat from a menu designed just for him, and where he could have a computer upon which he could begin his first book as a Knight, a savior of his country.

His next court date would be on April 16, 2012, when the full trial would be called into session. The court hadn't yet decided which panel of experts it would follow, and no one would know which until the final verdict was given. In the Norwegian legal system, insanity or sanity is usually determined before the trial begins; but, unusually in this case, it was not resolved until after the trial was finished.

This sequence of events was a first in Norway's history.
- An unprecedented second panel to decide Breivik's mental state.
- A conflicting decision that this mass killer was indeed sane.
- No immediate acceptance of either panel's findings by the court.

The court system, encouraged by the media, had created a circus, one that would continue throughout the trial.

CHAPTER TEN

THE TRIALS: "UNLIVABLE INJUSTICE"

Saturday, June 11—Day 41: I prayed for the first time in a very long time today.

—ANDERS BREIVIK MANIFESTO

The trial began with handshakes.

On April 16, 2012, in Oslo's contemporary-style, monumental District Court Building, both the prosecutors and the defense counsel for the accused, Anders Behring Breivik, shook the defendant's hand to begin the day in a show of courtesy, as they would for the next two months. Breivik, before taking his seat at the defense table, touched his heart with a clenched fist and then extended it in a straight-armed salute aimed at his accusers.

His face was as calm and unyielding as the courthouse's white granite exterior. Now minus handcuffs and wearing a black suit and pearl-gray tie, he listened as Judge Wenche Elizabeth Arntzen asked if he understood the charges against him. He stated that he did not recognize the legitimacy of the court because its authority came from parties supporting multiculturalism, and that the judge herself was a close friend of the former prime minister's sister.

In a quick, formal address, Judge Arntzen, in her lightweight black robe, made stylish only by its lace collar, said that his protest would be so noted. Then she offered him the opportunity to speak. It was as if the air had been sucked from the room. A man who had admitted to killing more people in one day—singlehandedly—than any other mass murderer in the recorded history of the world, was being asked if he would like to say something on his own behalf, as though he were being questioned about why he had rolled his vehicle through a stop sign.

At this point, many wondered why this trial had proceeded. After all, as already noted, forensic psychiatrists had found Breivik to be suffering from schizophrenia and said that he should have pleaded insanity and been sent to a mental hospital. The court had been bullied into appointing a second panel of experts, and that panel had accommodated public opinion and come to the opposite decision. In that second analysis, the two psychiatrists concluded that Breivik was sane and could be held responsible for his actions. Before the trial had even started, the debate about whether or not a trial should even be happening was already raging.

The court would decide the insanity question when they came back after deliberation on August 24. In the meantime, the trial was going to proceed.

A KIND OF NUMBNESS

During the ten-week-long trial, no one knew what the outcome would be. Those worldwide, who watched this process taking place a five-minute walk from where the government building had been bombed by this madman, wondered where the anger was, the desire for revenge on the part of the Norwegian people. One of the lay judges, before the trial began, had been excused because he expressed his feeling that the only punishment that fit the crime was the death penalty.

Unlike in the United States, there is no jury in the Norwegian court system. The two professional judges were assisted by three (usually four, but the one who was excused was not replaced) lay judges representing the people. Selected randomly, similar to a jury, lay judges are normal citizens of any profession; however, lawyers, police officers, and members of parliament are excluded. In addition to being at least twenty-one years of age, lay judges must speak Norwegian, have a basic knowledge of the Norwegian legal system, and have lived in the country at least three years. Norwegian citizenship is not a requirement. When ruling upon a case, a lay judge's vote equals the vote of a professional judge.

"I can still tell you Breivik's exact route on Utøya, and in which order his shots were fired," one of the lay judges, Diana Fynbo, said, according to an *NRK* article from December 20, 2012. "It was strange sitting so close to him in the courtroom and feeling all the energy he took in the room."

Fynbo also said it was daunting to have the press around them at all times, covering the case. Another one of the lay judges, Ernst Henning Eielsen, was caught on camera playing cards on his computer during Lippestad's questioning of an expert witness on Islam.

Yes, the people of Norway were outraged, but at the same time most seemed to exhibit a kind of numbness. Dismayed with constant television images of the horror, Norwegians just wanted to get on with their lives.

And here was Breivik, now in the courtroom, answering lead prosecutor Svein Holden's countdown of his failed business ventures with a smile that suggested his boredom about such misunderstood matters. Defense attorney Geir Lippestad, who was relatively unknown before this case, stared back at the accused impassively. Holden, undaunted, mentioned how Breivik had been living with his mother for four and a half years, playing the video game *World of Warcraft*.

The day ended on a series of notes not befitting the sheer severity of what one would believe a trial of this magnitude deserved. At one point, the only videographer filming the proceedings had caught Breivik showing his first sign of remorse. About five minutes into watching a video he had prepared on his manifesto, he was caught shedding a tear. A tear of what? Pride at his own image? The sorrow that he couldn't have brought about more deaths before being apprehended? Certainly, it wasn't related to the victims of his slaughter.

BREIVIK'S TESTIMONY

Day 2 commenced with Breivik's outthrust hand salute. At that time, he began his testimony, which was expected to go on for about six or seven days. The courtroom remained silent, but one could feel the vibrations of protest against such a lengthy diatribe. The defendant added to the unrest when he asked to be allowed to read a document he deemed essential to his defense.

His lead counsel, Geir Lippestad, said it would take about thirty minutes to read the text. This was a considerable understatement, as the entire reading lasted seventy-seven minutes. This scene in a way previewed the days ahead, where the court seemed to be lured into Breivik's monologues on his ideology.

Much of what he read echoed his manifesto. Breivik said he would have preferred to target a group of journalists instead of the island camp. He went on to say "There should be only two outcomes from this case: the death penalty, or an acquittal." Then he added to the public's resentment by telling his weary audience that Norway's maximum sentence of twenty-one years' imprisonment, no matter the crime, was "pathetic."

He quoted Norwegian social anthropologist Thomas Hylland Eriksen: "Our most important task ahead is to deconstruct the majority, and we must deconstruct them so thoroughly that they will never be able to call themselves the majority again."

Breivik believed Eriksen and the rest of the multiculturalists wanted to deconstruct the Norwegian ethnic group so that they would never again constitute a majority.

Prosecutor Inga Bejer Engh asked Breivik why he had broken into tears on the opening day of the trial, and he responded that he had been weeping for Norway and his perception of its deconstruction. "I thought," he said, *"my country and my ethnic group are dying."* Breivik had connected with his ideology and would remain its most loyal defender.

THE ROLE OF COMPUTER GAMES

On Day 4, Breivik didn't make his appearance with his aggressive clenched-fist salute. Lippestad had become upset with him on the previous day because of his fascist salute, and in his frustration yelled at Breivik: "Don't you realize what it does to the victims' families?" According to Lippestad, Breivik turned to him with a surprised look on his face and responded that if that were the case, he would of course discontinue the gesture.

During the prosecution's questioning, he retained his superior persona as he denied Holden's team's assumptions. *No*, he said to the idea that computer games, stressing violence, could be linked to his actions on that fateful day. This activity was, for him, simply to learn "strategy," not "violence." He did concede in interviews prior to the trial that the games did help him go through with his mission in that he put his mind into game-mode.

He testified that the guns he used at Utøya were inscribed with names using Runic script, as he had often done in his computer games. His rifle had the name "Gungnir," the same as Odin's spear that returned to its owner upon use. His Glock pistol was "Mjölnir," the same as the hammer of Thor, the warrior god.

Breivik maintained that he had tried more peaceful methods to convey his ideology; but when he felt that the press and political parties had rejected him, he resorted to violent means. Possible targets he had considered included the actual Labor Party's convention or a Norwegian journalists' annual conference. Because he lacked the time to detonate more bombs in Oslo, and because his bombing of the government quarters had failed, he claimed that he had decided to carry out his backup plan, which was the shooting spree on the island.

The courtroom was visibly shaken, and many of those present wept openly, when Breivik said that his goal at Utøya had been to kill everybody. He wanted to frighten the young people there, enough so that everybody would get into the water to escape. The water would then function as a weapon of mass destruction, because everyone would be too panicked and cold to swim the 600 yards to the mainland.

Breivik's original plans involved three car bombs and shooting sprees across Oslo—"a very large operation," as he called it. He considered placing a bomb near the Labor Party's headquarters, the Parliament of Norway Building, the *Aftenposten* (Norway's main newspaper) offices, and Oslo City Hall. He also considered bombing the Norwegian Royal Palace. Of course, he explained, he would have forewarned the royals. His battle wasn't with the symbol of Norwegian royalty but with the Norwegian government.

His goal, he said, was the murder of all members of the Norwegian government cabinet. He also wanted to behead Gro Harlem Brundt-land, the former Prime Minister of Norway and former Director-General of the World Health Organization. She is often referred to as the "Mother of Norway," but to Breivik, according to his manifesto, she was the "Murderer of Norway." He added that he imagined handcuffing her and then beheading her using the bayonet on his rifle, recording the killing on an iPhone, and posting it online. Breivik might have modeled his plan on al Qaeda's execution of journalist Daniel Pearl in 2002. The court noted that when describing how to kill the former prime minister, Breivik seemed excited. To Breivik, Brundtland was the ultimate symbol of the Labor Party and the "multicultural pack," which had bullied him and the rest of the population into silence. Maybe his wish to kill her was a subconscious wish to kill his own mother, who had been the cause of so many of his attachment issues.

He then made an abrupt shift to talk about his video games. *Call of Duty*, a game he admittedly played for sixteen straight months, was one he actually didn't like. "It was necessary," he said, to gain what he called "targeting skills." One can only imagine how this statement must have sounded in open court, let alone to the survivors of his sharpshooting, who were following his testimony.

A "SMALL BARBARIAN ACT"

Breivik, on the fifth day of the trial, asked the court to distinguish "clinical insanity" from what he alleged as his own "political extremism," and conceded that what he did had caused huge suffering. He could potentially comprehend the human suffering resulting from his actions, he said, but had managed to block this from his "immediate consciousness in order to cope."

On that day, something in the courtroom's atmosphere seemed to darken. It was as if the first gray clouds had passed, but now the true storm was on its way. People began to flinch as Breivik talked and went into great detail about what he had done on the island. The victims' families and survivors heard it all as he described his hesitations and feelings of unease as he set out. Then he described how his victims had reacted. He said he had never seen on television how people in such circumstances might become effectively immobilized. He then described how he found some of the young people lying on the ground pretending to be dead, and how he shot them too.

Breivik said that there were gaps in his memory of some of the approximately ninety minutes he spent killing on the island. He also said that he had considered wearing a swastika for the operation, to provoke further fear, but chose not to because he didn't want to appear to be a Nazi sympathizer.

The mass murderer insisted that he was ordinarily a nice person. He said that he very nearly backed out of doing the operation on the island, and that while he was carrying it out, he was in a state of what he described as shock, so he focused simply on functioning. He had managed to distance himself from the reality of the horror and put his mind in a computer-game mode. He spoke as if he were the one who deserved sympathy, as if the audience would understand his struggle and that he, in the end, was a saint for having had the guts to go through with it. He also maintained that he spared a few people on the island because they were so young.

One could almost hear the approaching thunder, crawling through Oslo's business center. As much as the court's dignitaries wanted to control the tempest, to shield their citizens in this place of justice, they weren't prepared, and it was as if an ill wind had shaken the beautiful structure's artful exterior.

"No one," someone in the courtroom said, as if predicting the following days, "should be expected to bring justice to this madness."

Breivik's story of horror continued into the next day. Unbelievably, the prosecution wanted more. "What I've done," Breivik went on in his twisted logic, "was create a small barbarian act to prevent a larger barbarian act."

He had lost everything that day, his family, his friends, his life as it had been, he told the court. Yet he had felt a compulsion to kill, but only because it would prevent something worse in the future.

Everyone listening must have been thinking how insane this monster was, or how they wished the police had killed him on sight once they'd found him brazenly walking toward them in his war suit, his guns and ammo still clinging to his person, asking for a bandage.

Breivik must have smelled the instinctual aggression riding this otherworldly wind. He was the "victim" of a racist plot, he said. Wasn't it obvious? The prosecution still wanted him declared legally insane so they could drug him into silence. The prosecution, he insisted, was out to delegitimize his ideology.

At this, the judge looked aghast at her lead prosecutor, her fine features earnest but perplexed, her short blondish hair not brushed that morning. Something faded in her normally lively eyes when she removed her glasses for a moment to touch her temple.

And Geir Lippestad scratched the top of his clean-shaven scalp, and probably reminded himself for the sixth time in six days that he'd taken this job because every criminal, regardless of his or her crime, deserved a proper defense. Or so he had said.

Breivik's trial stands in deep contrast to the trials of Kaczynski and McVeigh, where the considerations for the victims were the focus. The need for justice and punishment of this kind has no place in Norway's penal system. In the United States, trying and sentencing a perpetrator is about making him or her take responsibility for his or her crime, and it's about trying to achieve justice for the victims. "Punishment" is not a taboo word.

On Tuesday, May 5, 1998, Kaczynski was sentenced to four life terms in prison after agreeing to a plea bargain to avoid the death penalty.

"Lock him so far down that when he dies, he will be closer to hell," Susan Mosser said, according to a May 5, 1998 article in the *Washington Post* by William Booth. Mosser's husband's body had been ripped open by an exploding package mailed by Kaczynski.

Lois Epstein expressed a similar sentiment: "May your own eventual death occur as you have lived, in a solitary manner, without compassion or love." Epstein's husband, a professor of pediatrics, had lost his hand to another bomb.

McVeigh was sentenced to death and executed by lethal injection on June 11, 2001, at age thirty-three.

Both Kaczynski and McVeigh were frustrated that their trials didn't allow them to tell the public their story. Their acts of terror, the bombings, were their twisted way of communicating with a world that wouldn't otherwise listen. The lone wolf has a need to be heard and for the world to see how important he is, but McVeigh and Kaczynski did not receive this. Norway, however, gave Breivik exactly what he wished for.

THE SURVIVORS SPEAK

In the following days after Breivik was finally done, the lead prosecutor called on witnesses to the bombing, and the courtroom settled into an almost hypnotic trance as the awful stories of horror droned on.

On Day 8, Breivik took the stand again. He said that it had been a difficult task, listening to testimonies of those who were at the blast site. But he also let the court know that it was the Labor government, with its lax immigration policies, that was to blame. Then he contested the contents of the second psychiatric report, concluding that he was sane, insisting that although the conclusion was correct, the report was meant to portray him in a bad light. He alleged that almost all of it was false and spoke to several points in the report that sounded petty against the weight of the eyewitness accounts earlier rendered. No one seemed to care if it was untrue that he feared radiation or that his psychiatric evaluation wasn't recorded.

More survivors gave testimony on the following few days. Harald Fosker, who worked at the Ministry of Justice, had been caught in the blast. He described how he would need surgery to reconstruct his face, hearing, and vision. So great were his injuries that he hadn't felt any pain until the following day.

Meanwhile, forty thousand protesters gathered in Oslo. Singing a song called *Children of the Rainbow*, which Breivik had claimed brainwashed Norwegian children, they marched, in a respectful demonstration of unity, to the courthouse. Not because they were critical of the legal system and Breivik's trial. They gathered in front of the courthouse to demonstrate their sympathy for the victims and their disapproval of Breivik's political views. Many more such protests took place in other cities around the country.

On Day 10, Tore Raasok, employed in the Ministry of Transport, spoke of his injuries that had required ten surgeries, including the amputation of a leg. Shards of glass had flown into his eyes, and he had lost the use of one arm.

On the 11th of May, the autopsy reports were concluded, and again the court seemed to sway in an agitated state of remorse for the victims. Suddenly, someone shouted "Go to hell! Go to hell! You killed my brother!" Then the cursing man stood and threw a shoe toward Breivik. Instead, he hit Vibeke Hein Bæra, a member of his defense team.

The disrupter, Hayder Mustafa Qasim, was escorted out of the courtroom to a round of spontaneous applause and handed over to the medical staff. Many present knew that shoe-throwing marked extreme contempt among the Arab people, reserved for villains not worth the dirt one steps on. The footage captured by the videographer wasn't released to the public.

After a break, Breivik announced to the court that if someone wished to throw something, they could throw it on him as he entered and left the courtroom. "Do not throw anything at my lawyers. Thank you."

The mood in the room darkened again the next day as fifteen-year-old Ylva Helene Schwenke displayed her scars from wounds she had received on the island, saying that the four bullets marked "the price for democracy" she had paid. She concluded her statement by saying that democracy had prevailed. And in the nightmarish atmosphere, Anders Breivik was caught smiling at her commentary.

He merely shook his head slowly as another young female spoke of being saved by a young man who had thrown himself into Breivik's line of fire to save her life. "Breivik laughed with joy as he continued his bloodbath," she said.

Mathias Eckhoff testified to demanding that Breivik show his identification when he and others encountered Breivik, dressed in full combat gear, outside the island's café, where they had been discussing news of the downtown bombing earlier that afternoon. Eckhoff, along with the others who had assembled, had been shot. Bullets had ripped through both of his legs and his scrotum, yet the 21-year-old had managed to escape once he jumped into the water, by using only his arms as he swam away from the carnage.

Also twenty-one, Mohamad Hadi Hamel asked that Breivik be removed from the room as he testified from his wheelchair. He had been shot in the abdomen, shoulder, and thigh. He had endured amputations of an arm and a leg. The price he had paid had been enormous, and he didn't want to face the man responsible for all the wreckage to his young body.

The next witness, Adrian Pracon, however, looked straight into the defendant's eyes as he answered questions about how, after shooting him in the shoulder, the shooter for some reason hadn't finished him off.

"Breivik made an error when he decided to spare me," he said, gazing steadfastly at his attacker. "Now, I really understand how fragile our society is. I see how much it is worth and the importance of politics. I will continue with politics," he said, as if making a promise to Breivik, "and the Labor Party remains close to my heart."

It didn't go unnoticed that his comment made Breivik visibly uncomfortable, and that Pracon had been the only victim to look at the defendant in such a challenging way.

STRIVING FOR SANITY

Breivik, McVeigh, and Kaczynski each wanted to be taken seriously. Thus, they all rejected insanity as a defense, even when their lawyers argued otherwise. On Day 35, the fifth of June, Breivik's defense attorneys invited right-wing extremists to testify at the trial as a way of portraying him as sane. Ironically, these were the last people Breivik would have wanted speaking in his defense.

Tore Tvedt, founder of Vigrid, and Arne Tumyr, of Stop Islamization of Norway (SIAN), insisted that many people shared Breivik's political views, without being violent and certainly without being insane. The extremists distanced themselves from Breivik's actions, yet they openly supported his political views. Arne Tumyr said "Islam is an evil political ideology disguised as a religion."

Ronny Alte, another witness, said that although he didn't personally know anyone who supported Breivik's actions, "there could easily be around a hundred that I know about" on the Internet who did.

The extremists were there to show that the madman was truly sane. What they showed were the first signs that Breivik, regardless of the trial's outcome, was on his way to political rock-star status. None of the extremists appeared remorseful regarding Breivik's killings.

On June 17, the first panel's testimony consisted of a long and dreary description of how Breivik was psychotic and suffering from paranoid schizophrenia. Breivik rolled his eyes and smiled throughout, as if amused by how ridiculous it all sounded.

On June 18 and 19, the court-appointed psychiatrists from the second panel, Aspaas and Tørrissen, said that they acknowledged the political context of Breivik's thoughts and actions. Thus, they saw no sign of psychosis. Standing by their previous report, Breivik was a political terrorist with a psychological profile that made it possible to comprehend his terrible acts.

The trial of *United States v. Timothy J. McVeigh* began on April 24, 1997. McVeigh didn't deny the bombing, but he never acknowledged any guilt either. Perhaps because of the magnitude of his crime, this trial was also a media circus, created by McVeigh's defense team and the press. The media published some stories, partly leaked by his own defense team, that McVeigh thought damaging to his chance of a fair trial. Several times he attempted to have new attorneys assigned to his case. The defense team maintained conspiracy theories as a strategy, much to the frustration of the prosecutor, who claimed that these various theories sent the prosecution on a far-fetched fishing expedition. McVeigh was also frustrated. He wanted Jones, his lead attorney, to argue necessary defense and to stop trying to blame someone else for the attack.

Kaczynski was equally unhappy with his attorneys, who—instead of letting him use the trial to promote his philosophy—wouldn't let go of arguing insanity as a defense. In the end, Kaczynski interrupted the trial and asked to speak with the judge. The private session lasted hours before the judge finally allowed Kaczynski to defend himself.

Like Breivik, McVeigh refused to show any emotion during the prosecution's testimonies. While the prosecution recalled the stories of the different victims of the Oklahoma City bombing, including the small children who died, he remained unfazed, smiling and joking with his lawyers, making eye contact with attractive female journalists, or breaking into a grin when something he heard struck him as funny.

Conversely, Breivik, during his trial, would take turns looking directly at each of the fifteen press photographers following his trial and posing for their cameras.

McVeigh said something about his lack of emotions during the trial that might shed a light on Breivik's state of mind: "The victims are looking for some show of remorse. I understand and empathize with the victims' losses, but at the same time, I'm a realist. Death and loss are an integral part of life everywhere. We have to accept it and move on. To these people in Oklahoma who lost a loved one, I'm sorry, but it happens every day. You're not the first mother to lose a kid, or the first grandparent to lose a grandson or granddaughter. It happens every day, somewhere in the world. I'm not going to go into that courtroom, curl into a fetal ball, and cry just because the victims want me to do that."

On June 2, 1997, after twenty-three and a half hours of deliberations over four days, the jury had reached its verdict. McVeigh was found guilty of conspiracy to use a weapon of mass destruction, use of such weapon, destruction of government property with explosives, and eight counts of first-degree murder of the federal law-enforcement agents killed in the blast.

McVeigh remained expressionless as the verdict was being read. Both McVeigh and Breivik used the term "collateral damage" to describe their victims. Neither of them had any remorse.

On Friday, June 13, 1997, Timothy McVeigh was sentenced to death by lethal injection. According to Michel and Herbeck, McVeigh felt that he hadn't gotten a fair trial and was frustrated that America had not been told his side of the story. At the sentencing, he made a statement quoting U.S. Supreme Court Justice Louis D. Brandeis, a hero to advocates for individual rights: "He wrote," McVeigh said, "'Our government is the potent, the omnipresent teacher. For good or ill, it teaches the whole people by its example.' That's all I have."

Then he was taken by helicopter to the U.S. Penitentiary Administrative Maximum facility in Florence, Colorado, known as "Supermax," where Kaczynski would soon join him.

Breivik never denied the killings, the defense made clear in its closing speech. Thus, he was sane. Svein Holden, the prosecutor, argued that because the first psychiatric report was written in a non-falsifiable manner, it was impossible to disprove that Breivik was insane. Thus, he should be committed to psychiatric care because there would be more harm in sentencing a psychotic person to an ordinary prison than a non-psychotic person to a psychiatric facility.

On the forty-third and last day of the trial, Breivik delivered a forty-five-minute defense speech, as if his days of promoting his political ideas during the earlier days of the trial had not been enough. Although the court had refused video or audio transmission of this speech, it appeared on YouTube on July 26, 2012 by a German man who claimed he had received the video from an elected member of the Norwegian Progress Party. A Norwegian man had originally posted the recording on YouTube on June 27, according to the Norwegian news media. The man told media he didn't know he was breaking the law and removed the video, but not before many people saw Breivik speaking in his own defense.

The trial had gone on for more than a month. At one time or another, everyone, even the officers of the court, including Judge Arntzen herself, had shed their share of tears. Everyone, that is, except the defendant. He seemed to be quite pleased with the process, as it continued to advance toward the closing arguments. "Unlivable injustice," he had claimed as a motive and rationale. But as the trial progressed and came to an end, one question remained: unlivable justice for whom?

CHAPTER ELEVEN

SENTENCE:
21 YEARS FOR 77 DEATHS

Was Sitting Bull a terrorist because he fought for the indigenous rights of his people[,] or was he a hero? That is the question that you will decide during this trial.

—ANDERS BREIVIK MANIFESTO

Four months after Anders Breivik's trial had begun, a panel consisting of five judges ruled him sane. This meant that he would serve his sentence in a regular prison, not in a mental institution where, in his mind, he would be considered a monster, a beast never again to see a day of freedom. He even got a break he hadn't counted on. Instead of having to serve his sentence in Ringerike, a prison located about twenty-five miles northwest of Oslo, reserved for Norway's most hard-core criminals, Breivik would be sent to Ila Prison, only about ten miles outside the capital. Many of Ila's inmate population required maximum security, but its reputation as being "cushy" and more dedicated to rehabilitation than punishment dismayed those wanting Breivik to suffer for his crimes.

Most of the public, their very souls still torn by the tragedy, took the verdict as paradoxical. Many concerned citizens thought it would be better to send Breivik to prison than to place him in a mental institution where he could be deemed cured at any time. Most of all, they wanted him to be held responsible for his slaughter. But would Norway's lenient approach to its penal system allow a convict of Breivik's notoriety too many advantages? Would the country's maximum sentence be enough penance for a man whose constant threats indicated that he had wished to kill more? After all, he could be released in 2033, at the age of fifty-three. The reaction to Breivik's age, if released, stirred immediate protest from the liberal idealists who believed he should, after serving his prison term, be set free as a changed and rehabilitated man. After all, they argued, this is how the system is supposed to work. The goal with prison is not punishment but rehabilitation. A law professor at the University of Oslo, Mads Andenæs, agreed with Bård Solvik in that the goal was to return a rehabilitated Breivik back onto the streets one day if he were no longer considered dangerous. Solvik claimed that those who believed Breivik would never be liberated were wrong. Insisting, as others had done in an attempt to calm the public's worries, Solvik said the purpose of such claims was "either to conceal to the people what kind of system we have, or to undermine the system."

Many people, on the other hand, thought the killer should be silenced forever. In various articles and social media posts, others warned that Breivik should not be able to participate in intra- or inter-prison networks, where he could spread his anti-cultural, right-wing views through an underground criminal system that both the left and the right believed existed worldwide.

The survivors, the bereaved family members, and those just generally outraged by the bombing and shootings, would now know that the perpetrator of these crimes would be put away. But in that packed courtroom, when the verdict was announced, those injured and interested parties had plainly witnessed the smile on Breivik's face as he watched them hug one another in their rather pathetic celebration.

When does Norway not want to see a murderer back on the street? Breivik's case isn't one of car theft or breaking into a bank. It is mass murder. The last time Norway had such a disaster was World War II, and the traitors and war criminals were executed by a firing squad. Norway demonstrated with Breivik that it knows no limit in any cases. In that country, rehabilitation is the only goal of incarceration. One wonders how the Norwegian government would handle another Hitler today. How many people must one kill to warrant life in prison? What type of message does Breivik's treatment send others who may be contemplating similar crimes?

NORWAY'S SOFT-TOUCH APPROACH

"Too weak a judgment upon the worst killer in Scandinavian history," many who had followed the trial reported. The United States, considered by many abroad to be a land with a cruelly punitive criminal-justice system, voiced its outrage at the sentencing. Media from across the world questioned Norway's soft-touch approach. Had the rights of the accused outweighed those of the victims? One could almost hear the echo of Breivik's rants about the "deconstruction of Norway at the hands of cultural Marxists," his anti-Muslim lectures, and his anti-multiculturalist views, all of which he had given after entering the courtroom with his arm straight out in a fascist salute.

In the modern age of Facebook, Twitter, and YouTube, one blogger summed up the outrage of many citizens around the globe. His calculations made the argument that Breivik would serve less than four months for each death. Where was the justice in such a sentence? Not only would Breivik's taunts and rants live on, but the vision of his arrogance would remain indelible in the minds of millions of people. Breivik's guilt, neither doubted nor disputed, hadn't seemed the issue at any point, and clearly he would be considered sane. And now the world would have to live with that fact.

As days passed, order replaced chaos, and even the most disenchanted appeared to wilt a bit and see the verdict as fair punishment.

"Now we can have peace and quiet," Per Balch Sørensen, whose daughter was killed in the Utøya shootings, told the Associated Press. Sørensen no longer felt any personal rancor toward the accused. "He (Breivik) doesn't mean anything to me," he said. "He is just air." This was his attempt to invalidate Breivik and his political views.

In general, most reports agreed that the court's decision was in keeping with the country's penal system, one of the most progressive in Europe. One of the establishment's talking points championed their focus. "Our emphasis," they said, "is on rehabilitation rather than punishment."

Still, the massacre haunted some. "The thoughts of murder were evidently stimulating for the defendant," Judge Arne Lyng said, reading from the ninety-page verdict summation. "This was clear when he talked about decapitating ex-Prime Minister Gro Harlem Brundtland," he continued. "It was hard to imagine that such a term-limited sentence is sufficient to protect this country from this man."

THE LEVEL OF DETAIL

Conversely, many people interviewed claimed that they were satisfied with the court's declaration that Breivik, now that he was on his way to prison, would finally be forced into some kind of accountability. The majority of Norwegians felt that their society would eventually heal, that their beliefs in their country's liberal justice system would prevail, and that it would remain fundamentally unchanged. If there was to be justice for such a man convicted of committing crimes this heinous, their nation's court system had found it in their verdict. At the end of the long and exhausting trial, Norway would put away the man who had slaughtered so many of its most hopeful youths before they could reach their dreams. That would have to suffice for now.

"I am relieved to see this verdict," said Tore Sinding Bekkedal, who had managed to survive the Utøya massacre by hiding in a storeroom. "The temptation for people to fob (Breivik) off as a madman has gone," Bekkedal said. "It would have been difficult to unite the concept of insanity with the level of detail of (Breivik's) planning."

The above quote interested those close to the case. It brought to mind much about the entirety of Breivik's character, the exactness of his arc from young boy into young manhood. *The level of detail in his planning.* How many times had those words been used to describe Breivik's approach to gain an advantage? During Breivik's quest to succeed in life, he himself must have thought of those words as his credo, his reason for living—no matter the horror it might eventually bring to his family and friends.

He still must feel this today, for there isn't an ounce of remorse in his character, only more desire to complete his goal as a Knight Templar, a soldier against Islam.

CUSHY JAIL QUARTERS

Many discussions have ensued about how this self-described "noble soldier" will spend his incarceration in prison, out of sight and out of reach from Oslo. Breivik began living out his sentence in Ila Prison, a high-security penitentiary, where his quarters consisted of three 86-square-foot cells. All in all, it resembled a typical student dorm space.

Below is his routine from the early days of his incarceration, according to a recent Facebook post on *Daily Mail*:

> Anders Breivik starts each day in Ila Prison with a wholesome early breakfast of porridge or homemade brown bread served with cheese or ham, and a jug of black coffee.
>
> The isolated prisoner then spends time exercising at his adjoining gym, where he has a treadmill. He enjoys a "suite" of three adjoining 86 sq ft cells—bedroom, gym and a study containing a computer without internet access.
>
> He then reads the newspapers and plays a non-violent computer game, or watches a DVD or TV show on one of 15 channels.
>
> The killer is able to ring a room-service bell to have ciga-rettes delivered and often enjoys some fresh air in an enclosed yard after lunch.
>
> He is also allowed to write letters, or practice meditation, before a dinner of typical Norwegian fare such as meatballs and potatoes, or cod.

Those who observed him said he slept soundly at night. A court psy-chiatrist who assessed Breivik said the killer had compared prison to being in "kindergarten." Breivik even went so far as to say in a letter that "I'm still in isolation, and I will probably remain here for many years ahead. This is of course unproblematic as ending up here was my own choice. I'm used to living ascetically so continuing to do so will not be that hard." He continued: "The officers who work here are actually nice people, and as long as one follows orders and acts in a nice and polite manner, living here is easier than I would have thought."

When Kaczynski was incarcerated after his trial, the federal Supermax prison in Florence, Colorado, was a step up compared to the crude cabin in the Montana woods that had been his home for three decades. In prison, according to the Associated Press, Kaczynski now had a shower, toilet, electricity, and television. His cell is larger than his cabin, and he can order books from an extensive library, is served three meals per day, and receives freshly laundered clothes and sheets three times per week.

Kaczynski is a model prisoner who is not permitted to work "due to his medical condition," according to *The Smoking Gun* on October 27, 2003. That classification puzzled Kaczynski, according to a notation, dated May 3 that same year, that he made on one report.

"I have no idea what this 'medical condition' could be. I run 5 miles a day, 4 or 5 days a week, so I ought to be fit to work," Kaczynski wrote. "But if they don't want me to work that's fine with me since I have too much to keep me busy as it is."

A MINI ABU GHRAIB

Then, in a *thestar.com WORLD* article dated November 23, 2012, Breivik compared his incarceration to a "mini Abu Ghraib." His prison guards, he declared, were driving him to insanity by giving him cold coffee and banning his candy supply.

In a twenty-seven-page letter obtained by the Norwegian newspaper *Verdens Gang*, Breivik told penal officials that he had endured eight hundred strip searches, and not one of them had shown any sign of his holding an object "between the buttocks." According to the letter, he needed more social interaction after spending "23 hours and 55 minutes" alone on a typical day.

"Such treatment isn't humane," said his new lawyer, Tord Jordet, to the Agence France-Presse news agency.

An additional issue involved Internet access. Prison officials had commented that their refusal to offer such service to the prisoner would prevent him from spreading his ideology of racial hatred. Breivik expressed many other concerns in his letter. The "mental strain" of being supervised while shaving and brushing his teeth had forced him to limit those activities to once a week. And they no longer permitted him to keep his hydrating skin cream in his quarters. The quarters were drab, he wrote, the windows without a view. The electrical switches for his lights and television were outside his suite of cells, obliging him to summon guards to turn them on and off. Breivik wrote that he disliked having to be handcuffed. He stated that the steel edges cut into his wrists, and he dreaded having to wear the cuffs for each trip outside his cell. He wrote that his coffee frequently went cold without a thermos, and his phone calls and mail were unfairly censored.

"His freedom of speech is being violated," Jordet said.

"Only correspondence from the *New Testament Christians* and other people who do not like me has reached me in recent months," Breivik wrote. "I highly doubt that there are worse detention facilities in Norway."

About the time Breivik's letter was leaked, a prison spokeswoman said he had been given an electric typewriter. According to the Associated Press, the spokeswoman denied that the machine was, in any way, a response to Mr. Breivik's letter.

BORN FOR THE PRISON SYSTEM

Many questions remained about Ila Prison's new isolated inmate. Normal prison protocol didn't fit this man who seemed to challenge the rules at every junction. During the trial, he'd been given ample time and opportunity to argue every aspect of the proceedings. In his mind, he had cooperated in an illegal trial, where his rights as a patriot against an invading force were violated. As a Norwegian citizen, he called for the police to investigate his imprisonment—and, as a citizen, he got his wish. The police responded and immediately informed him that his rights hadn't been infringed upon, and he would have to comply with the verdict handed down by the court.

At this point, the people who hadn't yet put Breivik out of their thoughts wondered how he would be treated as time went by. In the past, his resolve had proven that he would continue to battle the penal system for as long as he was able; and under Norway's progressive philosophy of prison-inmate correction, he must have felt confident that the sky would be his only limit.

In June 2013, Breivik attempted to form a fascist organization from his prison cell. Basically, he tried to register a political association aimed at "a democratic fascist seizure of power in Norway." This endeavor also included the forming of an independent state from where he could operate.

Evidently, his request went too far, the *Aftenposten* newspaper reported, even for Norwegian policy. His request was denied because he included only one signatory—himself. Regulations stipulated that he needed two. His attorney, Tord Jordet, acknowledged that his client was pursuing other political activities and would appeal the rejection.

Insufficient paperwork had stopped Breivik this time, but what about future attempts? A representative from the Anti-Racist Center in Norway was quick to point out that any further pursuits of this kind would be banned on the grounds that they would be considered terrorist groups.

Following Breivik through the years, one must marvel at his perseverance. He had proven how dedicated he could be while laboring over his lengthy manifesto and planning his attacks. In a way, he is perfect for a prison system, an environment in which he can relax among his own private thoughts. A few years would be easy for him to endure. With his goals so cemented in place, several years would be a cakewalk, as long as he didn't disappear in the minds of those who both despised and admired him. All he needed was a platform from which to expound his ideals.

In March 2013, Breivik's mother died after a lengthy battle with poor health and her lifelong mental demons. Breivik requested leave to attend her funeral; but after much debate among those still outraged, this was denied by the prison board.

His attorney, Jordet, explained that Breivik had said good-bye to his mother in prison earlier in the month. She was the only visitor who had been allowed to see him since his incarceration at Ila. Jordet also said that Breivik appeared to be deeply saddened. His mother, who had been the cause of so many of his attachment issues, was the only person who could still emotionally unravel him.

After numerous complaints about Ila Prison, Breivik was finally moved to a different facility in September 2013. But this high-security correctional facility in Skien, about 80 miles southwest of Oslo, didn't suit him for long. On November 5, 2013, Breivik wrote yet another complaint demanding immediate changes in his living conditions.

"For twenty-seven months," he wrote, "I have been denied permission to present my case before the prison managers, as you have been unwilling to arrange an interdisciplinary meeting in which I may participate. The main objective of such a meeting is to create a 'rehabilitation plan' in order to solve the problems that keep me isolated. Such a plan should also facilitate an increased offer of activities in the cell, increased social contact with custodial staff and individual prisoners, and visits from friends and supporters."

He then cites the European Prison Rules, points 25.1 and 25.2, as well as Norwegian law specifying that isolation and other extreme measures are to be compensated. No such compensation has been made, Breivik claimed.

"As of today there are at least 100 right-wing radicals in Norwegian prisons, out of a total of approximately 2,600 prisoners. About 60 of these are defined as National Socialists and about 40 as classic fascists (like me). I can with great probability socialize with all of these. Unfortunately, they are spread all over the Norwegian prisons (one to five per prison, depending on the size). It's inhumane to deny me interaction with like-minded people. (Even Hitler showed a greater degree of humanism in that his regime allowed like-minded people—whether ethnic or ideological—to be imprisoned together.) Many of them are interested in getting to know me, and I them."

In the letter, Breivik also threatened to go on a hunger strike if his demands were not met.

Reports suggesting that Breivik may someday be headed for the Halden Prison have surfaced from time to time. This newly constructed "luxury prison," spread over seventy-five acres of woodlands outside Oslo, boasts a system that focuses on human rights. The facility's sound studio, jogging trails, and a two-bedroom house on the grounds for conjugal visits continually ire the general population, many of whom continue to question Norway's stance on rehabilitation.

Breivik's sentence of twenty-one years can be extended in five-year increments if he is still considered a danger to society. But what most people don't know is that any such extension is subject to appeal and will lead to a new trial if opposed by Breivik. The extension isn't supposed to work as a replacement for life in prison: its only purpose is to protect society if it can be proven that Breivik is, in fact, not rehabilitated. The government might also have a different opinion on Breivik and his heinous crimes after twenty-one years, if not before. After all, the importance of the role of the perpetrator in the victims' lives tends to diminish over time. Breivik will also be eligible for supervised or non-supervised leaves toward the end of his sentence, designed to prepare his re-entry into society. This will also be the case during any five-year extensions of his imprisonment. It is therefore very possible that Breivik will one day, sooner than one might think, be released and free in Norway.

All of these possibilities mean little to those who have put the massacre behind them. People who want to forget tend to do just that. They forget.

Recently, an American acquaintance of mine, speaking about the 1969 Charles Manson murders in Los Angeles, had this to say:

"Charles Tex Watson, under Manson's influence, led the random slaughter upon seven innocent individuals. Given a life sentence in Texas, he later was extradited to a prison in California and eventually married a prison groupie, fathered four children, wrote a couple of books, and formed a nonprofit ministry, all while incarcerated."

My source continued, as if adding a warning: "Watson was granted many leaves from lock-up to accomplish his preaching and conjugal rights. Has he repented? Was justice served? His victims might not think so if they were still alive. He will be due for another parole hearing in 2016. To most people, the proceedings will amount to little. Watson will be more than seventy years old, a man far from the 'crime of the century' he once belonged to. If he were set free, it's doubtful anyone would recognize him, let alone give his sighting much thought if they did."

Out of sight. Out of mind. Time erodes the awfulness of crimes. How much are we going to be asked to forget? And is forgetting the same as forgiving?

DEAR RUSSIAN BROTHER

A letter from Breivik to a Russian follower, dated July 5, 2012, recently surfaced. It contains startling information as to just how extensive a network Breivik has already managed to develop. Below, I've listed just a few of the plans he has been able to kindle after the massacre and during his retention. I will edit sparingly, so that one might consider and study his very words.

I'm in the process of contacting the German National Socialists who killed twelve from 2002 to 2011, and Peter Mangs in Sweden who shot ten, killed maybe three.

I'm already in contact with a couple of Norwegians and a patriotic brother in Denmark.

One positive thing . . . the massacre media has enabled me to be in contact with key individuals around the world.

I estimate there are at least a thousand prisoners in Western Europe who will join us.

Muslims are dominating many prisons, making Christians convert to stay alive. The Muslim brotherhood and al Qaeda are now the most successful revolutionary movement in the world.

As for naming our movement, I suggest we build the network for ten years before we choose a name. I must clear my own political conviction. I am not a militant national conservative. I am a national crusader nationalist.

I support ethnic and cultural protectionism. Women should have a secondary role, similar to Japan and South Korea.

All Asians, African [sic] and Southern Europeans against Nordics should be deported, which will include eighty percent of the Jews. I believe Christendom can be reformed into an ethnocentric military, like it was before the enlightenment reforms.

Vladimir Putin is either our best friend or our worst enemy. It seems he is trying to destroy European Russia, and is trying to create an Asian empire . . . so, no, I don't support him.

Russia [sic] militants are the most organized ideological group in Europe. To illustrate . . . there are ninety thousand skinheads in Russia, whereas there are less than nine thousand in Northern Europe.

My network, the Knights Templar network, has embraced al-Qaeda methods . . . the glorification of martyrdom and what follows with it . . . the "spectacular effects."

In order to contribute to a struggle, there must be a "we." I believe we should create a network that includes all indigenous rights activist, anti-Marxists. And anti-Islamist individuals.

Our long term goal should create a brotherhood against all Muslim[s] in prison, and encourage our brothers to learn English and essay writing. The pen is just as powerful as the sword.

Lastly we should create an economical fundament to support the wives and children of our Martyrs.

You must be aware I could be in prison for several decades . . . as my network is only beginning to take shape.

I risk being sent to a mental hospital. My lawyers are doing all they can to prevent this. In the worst case scenario I will be forcibly and chemically lobotomized, so that I'm unable to function, but as of now, I believe . . . I'll be able to build my network.

STILL AN EXTREMIST

Breivik's father, Jens Breivik, confirms that his son has not lost his political ambition or his extreme political views. After Jens attempted to visit his son in prison, he finally received a letter from Breivik. In *My Fault? A Father's Story*, published in October 2014, Breivik's Norwegian letter is printed. The letter, dated February 11, 2014, is addressed to Jens David Breivik, not "Father" or "Dad." Businesslike and cold, it is a formal good-bye to his father. It also shows the state of mind of a lone wolf who not only doesn't regret his acts, but who has grown even more extreme with the passage of time.

"This is the first letter I've sent you in many years, and it will probably be the last," Breivik wrote. "I have many ideological brothers and sisters with whom I correspond in France [where his father lives]." In Breivik's opinion, Jens was a good father but a victim of the social democracy's "extreme state feminism." By this, he no doubt means Norway's focus on empowering women. Breivik believed this bias was the reason his father lost custody of him to his ill-equipped mother.

"Your comments in the aftermath of my mission were predictable. Very cowardly but understandable. A nationalist with few years left to live, and in addition residing relatively protected in France, you should have taken advantage of the rare opportunities for propaganda you were given to do something for *nordisisme*, and for the fascist and anti-communist ideology. We both know, however, that you are and will remain as far from being a nationalist as is possible. . . . Your irrational behavior may best be compared to the Stockholm Syndrome, where you defend and submit yourself to your abusers. Fjordman suffers from the same syndrome, as did Mom."

Breivik invited his father "to take part in the Norwegian fascist movement." "If you yet again choose to take 'the broader path,' this will be the last contact we'll have. . . . Visiting me has no purpose as long as you share the majority's attitudes and opinions."

In his letter, Breivik once again complained that he was being kept prisoner "under inhumane conditions."

Breivik rambled on about historic events and al Qaeda. "Brainless shells, and you give the impression of being one, you bow your heads in agreement when steps are taken to protect the ideological bubble, utopia. . . . Are you completely retarded, or are you acting in this irrational role as practical idiot to your abusers?"

He continued that he felt ashamed that no one in his family had chosen to fight with Vidkun Quisling—the Norwegian who cooperated with Hitler—during World War II.

"I am proud of the fact that I'm participating in saving my people," he wrote, "and I continue to work 70 hours per week for this cause. . . . I am and remain extremely proud of my participation in the battle against communism and liberalism. . . . I will continue to work to ensure that the fascists acquiring power will be *nordistic* fascists."

Nordistic and *nordisisme* are words Breivik created to describe his utopia. He ended his letter by wishing his father the best. "Live well, no matter which side you choose. I will always be thankful that you gave me the opportunity to fight. My door will always be open to all *nordisists*, you included. But we both know you will never choose the narrow path.

"With kind regards,

"Anders Behring Breivik"

∞

Also at the beginning of 2014, Breivik sent a thirty-page letter to selected international press and to the Chinese and Russian embassies. According to *ABC Nyheter* on January 10, 2014, Breivik claims that although he has no regrets about his acts of violence on July 22, 2011, he now renounces the use of violence to achieve his goal. On the contrary, his intention is to start his own political party and campaign for his politics the democratic way. Perhaps this strategy will prove effective when the time comes to prove that he is no longer a threat to Norwegian society.

In the letter, he also complains about inhumane conditions at Skien prison and writes that he won't survive unless major improvements are made to his environment. Among the torturous conditions, he mentions the fact that he's not allowed to establish a political fascist party, that he doesn't have access to the books necessary to study political science, and that he has an old computer.

His attorney, Tord Jordet, is uncertain when his client changed his attitude concerning the use of violence. "But he is clear on the fact that he will be using democratic means," Jordet said to *ABC Nyheter*. "That's the reason freedom of speech is so important to him. I won't say the change in him happened on that day, but Breivik surrendered voluntarily on July 22; and since his terrorist acts on that day, he has not attempted to use violence or encourage others to violent acts."

Although he's in prison, Breivik has not lost his voting rights. Norway's laws contrast with those of the United States, where most states prohibit prisoners from voting. Jordet confirmed that his client voted in the last regional election in 2011; however, he wouldn't confirm whether Breivik used his voting right in the 2013 Parliamentary election. "He has attempted to found his own political party, and it's therefore likely that he will present himself for election and take advantage of his voting rights."

The reason Breivik was unsuccessful in creating "Norway's Fascist Party and its Nordic League" was that his former prison at Ila refused to let him try to collect the necessary second signature in accordance with Brønnøy-sundsregistret's rules. To present himself for election, he would also need five thousand signatures from eligible voters.

"Until now, the prison has prevented him from sending out letters with a political content," Jordet says. "It's a problem for democracy that the Norwegian Correctional Service imposes such limitations. Founding a political party is a human right." As long as Breivik doesn't provoke hatred, violence, or any illegal activity, his attorney sees absolutely no problems with Breivik running a political party from prison.

"He has not shown any aggressive behavior against corrections officers or others, and he's been very clear on the fact that he'll continue his battle using his pen." When *ABC Nyheter* asked if Breivik is discouraging the two remaining terrorist cells—he still claims they exist—from violence, Jordet's response was unclear.

About Breivik's claims about the conditions in prison, Jordet confirmed that visits are restricted and that Breivik is not free to invite visitors. In addition, there are unannounced body and room searches on a regular basis.

"One might ask if it's necessary, with such comprehensive surveillance of someone who is locked up in isolation without contact with anyone except the corrections officers," Jordet says. "In my opinion, it's not. And he experiences these clearly inhumane conditions as torture."

Breivik's attorney added that Breivik is emotionally strong and said that his client is not broken. "He has never expressed any remorse, and still vouches for what he said during his trial—that his acts were gruesome, but necessary."

When asked why Breivik sent his thirty-page letter to the Russian and Chinese embassies, Jordet answered that since Norway criticizes those countries for human-rights breaches, Breivik thought it important that they receive information about how Norway treats its own prisoners.

Some still think Breivik's sentence wasn't harsh enough. Norway actually has a law that allows a thirty-year sentence in extreme circumstances. The law is supposed to be used against terrorism and crimes against humanity. Although the law was passed in 2008, it hasn't yet been enforced, due to bureaucracy and political unwillingness, and Breivik was sentenced under the regular law where the maximum is twenty-one years. Perhaps, in this world today, where a single terrorist like Anders Breivik can cause such mass chaos and destruction both in and out of prison, Norway will change its attitude toward criminals and start enforcing the thirty-year law. However, that is yet to happen.

Prime Minister Jens Stoltenberg expressed after the trial that he was proud of how the court and the Norwegian people handled Breivik's trial. "It was handled with a lot of dignity," he said.

Perhaps in our time, dignity will not be enough to keep us safe.

CHAPTER TWELVE

AFTERMATH

*But this trial is also about finding the truth. The statements I have
made, the comparisons I have drawn—are they true? Because, if
something is true, how can it be illegal?*

—ANDERS BREIVIK MANIFESTO

Warning signs that might have prevented a tragedy like the July 22, 2011
attacks were everywhere. Breivik's early life, if one were to examine it
closely, offered hints as to how he might have veered from what is frequently
viewed as "normal" behavior. Psychiatrists point out how disorderly his
home life was, especially his relationship with his mother. Social Services
even recommended that he be sent to a foster home. Recent evidence
would lead one to believe that his half-sister, Elisabeth, warned her mother
about his odd behavior. She believed that Breivik, in moving back home
and playing computer games all day, was signaling his strange existence.

His friends also worried about him and tried time and again to get him to come out of his room at his mother's apartment. Those who knew Breivik best spoke of how adept he always proved to be when going into one of his planning phases. Before the attacks, he had slipped into a state of near-hibernation socially, but his mind and body continued to explore and activate his diabolical plot.

"The reason these killers don't show up in police blotters is because they are not technically in the criminal life," said Dr. Kathleen Puckett. "Usually in law enforcement, including the FBI, most cases are studied on a case-study basis. You never really have a portrait of the internal mechanisms of their psychological states."

Apart from making a few mini-bombs in high school, there was nothing in Kaczynski's life to draw law enforcement's attention to him.

"One day in the laboratory," he wrote in a high school article, "having finished my assigned experiment early, I thought I might as well spend the extra time pursuing my favorite line of research . . . a mixture of red phosphorus and potassium chlorate seemed promising."

The first six of Kaczynski's bombs were made in accordance with that article from high school.

"He may have been brilliant," according to Robert D. McFadden's *Prisoner of Rage*, published in the *New York Times* on May 26, 1996, "but what they remembered about him at Harvard were his annoying trombone blasts in the dead of night, the primordial stench of rotting food that drifted from his room, his odd metronomic habit of rocking back and forth on a chair as he studied, and his icy aloofness as he strode through the suite, saying nothing, slamming his door to shut them out."

Not much there to indicate a mass murderer in the making.

"He was so young and so lacking in social skills," Kaczynski's mother, Wanda, said to the FBI. "It was always hard for him to make friends. I think he grew even more isolated while he was at Harvard."

Kaczynski cut himself off from social life after he left his teaching job at the University of California, Berkeley and secluded himself in the Montana woods, where he began plotting murder.

After the explosion of his first primitive homemade bomb in 1978, Kaczynski would terrorize the United States for the next two decades, mailing or hand-delivering a series of increasingly sophisticated explosive devices that killed three people and injured twenty-three others.

He sent the first mail bomb in late May 1978 to materials engineering professor Buckley Crist at Northwestern University. The package was found in a parking lot at the University of Illinois at Chicago, with Crist's return address. The package was "returned" to Crist, but when Crist received the package, he noticed that it was not addressed in his own handwriting. Suspicious, he contacted campus policeman Terry Marker, who opened the package, which exploded immediately. Marker survived but required medical assistance for injuries to his left hand.

The bomb was made of metal that could have come from a home workshop. It contained smokeless explosive powders, and the box and the plugs that sealed the pipe ends were handcrafted from wood. Later, as Kaczynski's methods became more sophisticated, he used batteries and heat filament wire to ignite the explosives faster and more effectively.

He followed the initial 1978 bomb by targeting airline officials, and in 1979 he placed a bomb in the cargo hold of American Airlines Flight 444, a Boeing 727 carrying seventy-two passengers and a crew of six from Chicago to Washington, D.C. According to authorities, it had enough power to "obliterate the plane," but it failed to explode due to a faulty timing mechanism, and the pilot was able to make an emergency landing. Apart from twelve passengers treated for smoke inhalation, no one was harmed.

Bombing an airliner is a federal crime in the United States, and an FBI-led task force was formed to investigate the case. Assigned the code name UNABOM (UNiversity and Airline BOMber), the task force grew to more than 150 full-time investigators and analysts. This team made every possible forensic examination of recovered components of the explosives. These were of little use, as the bombs were essentially made from scrap material available almost everywhere. The victims, investigators later learned, were chosen irregularly from library research. Because Kaczynski had no criminal record, there was nothing to lead authorities to him.

In 1980, chief agent John Douglas, working with agents in the FBI's Behavioral Sciences Unit, issued a psychological profile of the Unabomber which described the offender as a man of above-average intelligence with connections to academia. This profile was later refined to characterize the offender as a neo-Luddite holding an academic degree in the hard sciences, but this profile was discarded in 1983 in favor of an alternative theory developed by FBI analysts concentrating on the physical evidence in recovered bomb fragments. In this rival profile, the bomber suspect was characterized as a blue-collar airplane mechanic. In truth, the FBI didn't have a clue.

A 1-800 hotline was set up by the UNABOM Task Force to take any calls related to the Unabomber investigation, with a $1 million reward for anyone who could provide information leading to the Unabomber's capture. But it was the publication of Kaczynski's manifesto—almost two decades later—that led to his arrest.

"The terrorist group FC is planning to blow up an airliner out of Los Angeles . . . ," Kaczynski threatened, "during the next six days" if his manifesto was not published by a major national newspaper.

After a heated debate on whether to agree to the terrorist's demands, the United States Department of Justice, along with Attorney General Janet Reno and FBI Director Louis Freeh, recommended publication in hopes that a reader would identify the author.

McVeigh had also been a law-abiding citizen until April 19, 1995.

He was obsessed with *The Turner Diaries*, a novel by former American Nazi Party official William L. Pierce. Writing under the name Andrew Macdonald, Pierce writes about Earl Turner, who demonstrates his contempt for gun-control laws by truck-bombing the Washington FBI headquarters. He was clearly an inspiration for McVeigh.

After McVeigh left the Army, his anger against the government increased. He railed against gun control and the abuse of power. He spouted conspiracy theories and appeared to believe in UFOs. He even told a friend from the Army that he'd seen documented evidence that the government was importing drugs from Canada in mini-subs. When his friend asked to see a copy of the document, McVeigh claimed it was on secret paper that couldn't be copied. But what concerned his friend so much that he wrote it down was McVeigh's statement that he knew how to steal guns from the military. McVeigh had said it would be "very easy to rob a base of guns . . . two people could easily get away with it."

ABOVE: Government building H, housing the prime minister. Breivik's van exploded in front of this building. It didn't collapse but was torn down later because it was deemed unsafe. Here, the building was covered up to hide the damage. *Credit: Samuel Turrettini.* BELOW: Utøya in the background with the ferry boat MS *Thorbjørn. Credit: Samuel Turrettini.*

ABOVE: Utøya in the background with the ferry boat MS *Thorbjørn*. *Credit: Samuel Turrettini.* BELOW: MS *Thorbjørn* being used the day following the massacre to transport police to the island and dead bodies off it. *Credit: Rune Folkedal.*

ABOVE: Despair as rescuers discover all the dead bodies on the island. *Credit: Rune Folkedal.*
BELOW: Dead bodies covered up at the south tip of the island. *Credit: Rune Folkedal.*

ABOVE: Prime Minister Jens Stoltenberg holding his first press conference the day after the massacre. *Credit: Rune Folkedal.* BELOW: Procession of roses. Prime Minister Jens Stoltenberg in focus. *Credit: Rune Folkedal.*

Roses in honor of the victims in the center of Oslo. *Credit: Rune Folkedal.*

ABOVE: Oslo District Court House where the trial took place. *Credit: Samuel Turrettini.*
BELOW LEFT: Anders Behring Breivik during the trial. *Credit: Rune Folkedal.*
BELOW RIGHT: Breivik doing his fist salute at the trial. *Credit: Rune Folkedal.*

ABOVE: Psychiatric expert panel during the trial. *Credit: Rune Folkedal.* BELOW: Judge Wenche Elizabeth Arntzen shakes hands with Breivik at the beginning of each trial day. *Credit: Rune Folkedal.*

Utøya memorial. *Credit: Samuel Turrettini.*

McVeigh was less careful than Breivik, who did not share his anti-government rhetoric. He discussed his thoughts in depth with his former Army comrades Michael Fortier and Terry Nichols. Both knew McVeigh had planned something big, and Nichols even helped him build the bomb. He had even discussed his ideas with his younger sister. No one seemed to take him seriously enough to warn the police.

Perhaps Breivik could have been stopped early had Norway been more awake and aware. As is the case with many children, he displayed malevolence at times. His offbeat scheming methods to get his way had raised questions, but nothing pointed to his becoming a monster.

When Breivik isolated himself outside Oslo to perfect his bomb, buying up suspicious chemicals, his country snoozed. He was able to purchase enough fertilizer to blow up a big portion of downtown Oslo. This collecting of material that contained certain combustible ingredients automatically placed him on Norway's Police Intelligence List and flagged him as a suspected terrorist. However, authorities didn't follow through on his case simply because he didn't have a criminal record. His "farm" was never checked out, and his manufacturing continued. Nor were the authorities alarmed that his company, in the official register, had a different purpose than farming. His farming neighbors said, in hindsight, that Breivik had acted suspiciously, that he had covered the windows of his house, and that he didn't seem to know much about farming. Yet it would have only taken one phone call to the PST and his quest might have ended right then and there.

NO HEALING; ONLY DENIAL

Adrian Pracon was as unlike Breivik as anyone on the island that day; gay, Catholic, son of Polish immigrants, county secretary for the Workers' Youth League of Telemark. Supposedly unprovoked, Pracon beat a man and woman after leaving an arraignment hearing for Breivik in November 2011. In August 2012, he was sentenced to 180 hours of community service and the equivalent of $1,700 in damages for his aggravated assault. He was given leniency in his sentence by the court because of the trauma he had suffered on July 22 the previous year.

Pracon later explained in his book, *The Heart Against the Rock*, written with Erik Moller Solheim, that he suffered from a kind of survivor's guilt, especially after realizing why he had been spared. In the water, he was convinced that he would die. He wrote:

I stopped breathing. My heart was beating so hard that it must have been visible through my wet T-shirt. Where was he going to hit me? In the head? In the heart? I hoped for the heart. And that it would be quick. I had never had a gun aimed at me before. It was a feeling of complete inferiority. He could do to me whatever he wanted.

Dead or alive. It was up to him.

I searched for a response from the man behind the weapon, but all I could see was the open black chasm in his telescopic sight. My body prepared itself for the bullet that was going to penetrate it. My skin stung around my heart and on my forehead.

He closed his eye.

Now it was over.

Then he lowered his weapon, turned on his heel, and vanished. I gasped for air. At the same moment, my knees gave way beneath me. With shaking steps, I only barely managed to get up onto the island before I collapsed on the rock.

For some reason, I was still alive.

Pracon was later shot at the end of Breivik's massacre, and he was probably the last victim. Breivik had decided to come back, and as Pracon was still lying on a rock, playing dead, he shot him in the shoulder. Pracon remembered feeling Breivik's shoe and hearing him breathe directly above him. Right after he fired his last shot at Pracon, Breivik went to surrender to the police. In his final day of testimony, Breivik revealed the reason he had allowed his victim to live.

"Certain people look more leftist than others," he said. "This person appeared right-wing; that was his appearance. That's the reason I didn't fire any [more] shots at him. When I looked at him, I saw myself."

In his own twisted, narcissistic way, perhaps Breivik felt some sort of tenuous connection with this victim.

Pracon fought with his own emotions long after the massacre, and is still doing so today. Unable to express his anger and confusion, he turned to a response that had nothing to do with candles and roses.

Several of the survivors have expressed difficulty dealing with their feelings of anger and hatred. Crown Prince Haakon said in his speech on July 23, "Tonight, the streets are filled with love." In the messages given by the authorities in the days and weeks after July 22, it was as if there was no room for any other feelings. The message was clear. If you had dark emotions, such as anger or hatred, you were put in the same evil category as Breivik himself. Pracon and other victims of the massacre have admitted that they struggle with feelings of guilt and shame, because they had been expected to respond to their injuries with flowers and love, not with hatred and a desire for revenge.

Lara Rashid survived Utøya, but her sister, Bano, was killed. "It has become taboo to hate," she said, "because there is so much talk of love and dignity. I'm so angry with him, I want to. . . . There is a lot of aggression. But it is very difficult because I can't do anything about it, and then I take it out on others. But I hate him. After all, he has ruined my life."

Lars Weisæth, professor of disaster psychiatry at the University of Oslo, told *TV2*: "For those directly stricken, a red-glowing hatred is more natural. If they felt that they had to suppress it, that they could not show it, that could have been a burden for some. It could have been made clearer that one is allowed to have such strong feelings of hatred, that one has a wish to kill."

Another survivor with anger issues is Eskil Pedersen, head of AUF. Pedersen had left the island soon after Breivik started shooting, on the same ferry Breivik had arrived on. He, too, has mentioned feeling guilt for surviving when so many of his friends didn't. "Toward someone who has taken that many lives, one should be allowed to plunge down to the darker parts of the human mind," he told *TV2*.

"When I feel inside that it boils, and it has been boiling often," Pracon said. "One feels very alone and excluded when one goes around feeling angry over time."

Pracon regrets his outburst on those innocent bystanders in Oslo and says that he takes full responsibility for his actions. At the same time, he believes it is important that other victims who might be feeling this rage seek help to deal with it before it's too late.

"I'm not saying that there are other ticking bombs out there," he said, "but there are many that spend a lot of unnecessary energy to control those feelings."

Maybe Pracon, without knowing it, is on to something. This suppression, always controlling one's feelings and opinions, always living within the designated limits of society, always being politically correct, is the very cancer of our society that helped create the monster Breivik.

A NEW "WE"

It has been said that on that day in July 2011, Norway lost its innocence. But has it changed anything? And if something has changed, what?

Knut Arild Hareide, head of the Parliament's July 22 Commission, hesitated when he was asked this question by NTB (the Norwegian News Agency). Although he immediately thought the massacre would change Norwegian society drastically, he is no longer so certain. He did experience an increased solidarity and camaraderie, a new "we," in the Norwegian people in the weeks after the attacks, but he also says the long-term effects shouldn't be overestimated.

Wakas Mir, a Norwegian-Pakistani radio host for the program *Voice of Oslo* on the Norwegian-Pakistani radio channel, said to NTB that many immigrants are disillusioned by the reactions of ethnic Norwegians after the attacks. "We have received a lot of response from our listeners about this," he said, "and they claim that July 22 has not led to less discrimination or racism in Norway."

Many immigrants are saddened by the fact that if not even "such a huge tragedy as July 22, that happened because of hatred of immigrants, can reduce racism, nothing will," he said.

Jon Reichelt, lieutenant colonel and chief of psychiatry (KPS) in the Norwegian Army, isn't surprised. "Big crises are not usually enough to create a permanent change in a people's mentality," he said to NTB. "Incidents such as July 22 make impressions, but one soon gets back to normal. It's not the case that we become nicer, more tolerant, or more suspicious because of such one-time incidents."

Former Prime Minister Jens Stoltenberg's statement to *Samtiden* sums it up in this way: "With time I have learned to live with the fact that I'm fumbling to find an answer that will do. . . . I think the correct response will come much later. And it will come in pieces that will be carefully put together into an expanded and nuanced mosaic."

That is, if anyone really wants to get to the truth.

WHERE ARE THE ANSWERS?

Questions persist. Can Breivik be compared to others? Why is he Norway's first such madman when other countries' histories are marked with many? According to the *New York Times*, the FBI's survey over the past thirteen years concludes that mass shootings like those in 2012 at the Sandy Hook Elementary School in Newtown, Connecticut, and the movie theater in Aurora, Colorado, are occurring with greater frequency. The average annual number of shooting sprees with multiple casualties was 6.4 from 2000 to 2006. That jumped to 16.4 a year from 2007 to 2013, according to the study of 160 incidents of gun mayhem since 2000.

Could it be that this small society that has given the world the Nobel Peace Prize has itself been in the process of changing? Are Norwegians as nice and kind to each other as has been portrayed for so many years, or has something evil been able to work its way below the surface? In a country that prides itself on being picture-perfect, have social rules become outdated compared to real time?

It is imperative to answer these questions honestly before another Breivik with another cause begins killing.

ROLE MODELS

Experts in the field of terrorism believe Breivik could be an inspiration for countless repressed young souls who, in this threatened atmosphere we live in, wish to seek a level of martyrdom. Breivik was the first in Norway. He will not be the last. Presently, he has become a mega-superstar, attaining a status to which those following in his footsteps aspire. The new mass murderers are anything but silent, and Breivik is no exception.

Norwegians seem to be in a state of denial. They believe—or say they believe—that the massacre was a one-time event, never to occur in their country again. Most citizens will not say nor do anything that might bring them criticism. They don't want to discuss—or even think about—the killings and the reasons behind them. Most individuals join *en masse* to light candles and walk in the streets with roses, their voices insisting "Let's meet the hatred with love."

What about the anger? The wish and the need for justice? No one can truly mourn the dead and the injured. The perpetrator upon their lives remains free of any real punishment for his crimes, and instead has managed to obtain exactly what he wanted. Martyrdom. A voice. The power to influence.

Now, in the aftermath of Breivik's trial, Norway's response to this act of terrorism will be closely examined. The people of this small nation chose to act without any revised measures. Rather than reacting with hysteria, the people acted within the rules of established law. This proved to be a different approach than how the United States, after the September 11 attacks, bypassed its own criminal justice system in numerous ways. Both the United States and some European countries, including the United Kingdom and France, relied on administrating detention and deportation to other countries where torture was used upon suspected terrorists. Which would Breivik choose?

Ironically, despite his desire to be treated like a warrior, he was prosecuted under Norwegian law as an ordinary criminal.

POLITICAL FURY

The multiculturalism debate in Norway is almost evenly divided between the political parties. After Anders Breivik's atrocities, the anger continued to rise along both the liberal and conservative fronts. The liberals (left-wing) maintained that authorities ignored the dozens of anti-Muslim messages from Breivik. *"We have not really been prepared for right-wing extremism in Norway,"* a Peace Research Institute representative said.

Conservative observers directed their ire at the government's open-door policy on immigration in numerous blogs and Twitter feeds. Some analysts believe the shootings may reflect growing national disillusionment with the country's immigration policies. *"The political establishment of Norway consists of relatively well-off people who live in areas where there are simply no immigrants, so it's just poor people that are being pushed out of places they used to live and whose jobs are in jeopardy,*" Norwegian terrorism expert Helge Lurås said.

Norwegians are said to be fed up with their country's brand of what has been dubbed "radical liberalism." In the growing debate over multiculturalism, many on the right believe the liberal policies have set the government against its own people. Nabila Ramdani, a political journalist, said: "In Norway, far-right sentiment is wider than Norwegians are ready to admit. And there is a polite and respectful attitude toward those kinds of views in the mainstream media. But the reality is that 50 percent of Norwegians are against multiculturalism."

As Norway attempts to heal after the massacre, the two sides continue to battle over a type of immigration the world has never before experienced—multiculturalism. Talking heads on international media point out how easy it will become for Islamic terrorists to impose their knowledge of destruction and their will to carry it out upon innocent countries. The Islamic State (ISIS)—the self-proclaimed caliphate and state in Iraq, Syria, and the Middle East—is using social media as one of the methods to intimidate and attract new members to its cause. This terrorist organization is known for its use of death threats, torture, and mutilation to compel conversion to Islam. It executes clerics refusing to pledge allegiance to ISIS, as well as prisoners of war, and it sexually enslaves Iraqi women and girls. Despite its brutality, ISIS manages to attract new members, especially teens, from Western countries who are converted by ISIS members sent out to recruit.

On the other hand, much of the media expect a police crackdown on the growing number of far-right groups worldwide, fearing that their actions will escalate and add undue tension among the Muslim communities. Both sides of the political debate agree that Breivik's attack might not be the last one in Norway. With multiculturalism comes rage on all sides, especially when that rage cannot be openly expressed.

Bruce Bawer, in his book *The New Quislings*, insists that Norway has never really had an open debate about multiculturalism because the left, by using Breivik's massacre as a premise, has silenced any true discussion.

Quoting a "wise observer," Bawer says: "If you want to know who is responsible for Breivik, it's not the people whose books he read. It's the people who refused to debate and discuss the contents of those books." Bawer goes on to point out how the liberal establishment continues to exploit the massacre in hopes of restoring its control over the parameters of public debate. This, he claims, is what caused the problem in the first place.

A summary of Norway's dialogue policy regarding multiculturalism was presented at the CRONEM Conference, University of Surrey, in June 2012 by Christian Stokke, of Buskerud University College. This study found that Norway's integration debates paralleled those in many European countries where multiculturalism was under attack. Although Norway promotes tolerance toward gender equality and emphasizes the need for individual rights, there is really no true policy on how to manage the influx of Muslims moving into Norway in great numbers who are not integrating into Norwegian society in the way other immigrant groups have in the past.

MANY FACES OF MULTICULTURALISM

In a September 2011 article, Irene Bloemraad, of the University of California, Berkeley's sociology department, addresses far-right groups in Northern Europe, such as Geert Wilders's Freedom Party in the Netherlands, the Sweden Democratic Party, the True Finns Party in Finland, the Danish Peoples' Party, and the Progress Party in Norway. These political factions insist that multiculturalism undermines social cohesion, and this has fueled their political success.

In October 2010, German Chancellor Angela Merkel proclaimed that Germany's multicultural approach had "utterly failed." In February 2011, French President Nicolas Sarkozy called multiculturalism a failure, and British Prime Minister David Cameron described his country's policies in much the same way.

Bloemraad writes: "Revealingly, in seven of nine studies tracking anti-immigrant attitudes over time, researchers found stable or increasingly negative attitudes toward immigrants, especially in Western Europe, while only two studies reported positive trends."

Another article, this one by Prithi Yelaja, examines Canada's recent experiences with multiculturalism. Titled "Multicultural Canada: A Haven from Norway-style Violence?" it contains a warning.

"There's no reason for Canadians to be smugly confident," says Barbara Perry, associate dean of the Faculty of Social Science and Humanities at the University of Ontario, Institute of Technology. "Pockets of resistance to changing demographics exist in Canada —most notably in Quebec and Western Canada—just as they do in Europe, particularly in Scandinavia."

Canada has been perhaps the most welcoming of all nations to immigration. Multiculturalism has remained a touchstone of Canada's identity and a point of pride for its people. Perry suggests that a resistance is building against this identity: "Everyone doesn't welcome multiculturalism. It's not universally loved, this notion of being open to all comers."

"So it's both an anti-immigrant and an anti-Muslim sentiment they are dealing with, which are both new features for [the Canadians]," Perry continues. "It's a trend that makes me fearful—the connection between political imagery and negative political rhetoric and public opinion."

In many ways, Canada, which is part of the Commonwealth and is under the Queen's reign, is more like Europe, a class-designated society. In the United States, where one's title (such as count or duchess) means next to nothing, multiculturalism occurs through exposure, marriage, and frequently choice. No doubt, the United States has incredible ethnic diversity, and that may be the reason there is no formal label or policy of "multiculturalism" to ostensibly counteract a class-designated society.

Society and global interaction have changed since the United Nations started encouraging multiculturalism following World War II, when the ideology seemed so noble. That practice, which can be simply defined as assimilation into another culture, is one more way that Breivik—and the Tsarnaev brothers—were isolated into their own worlds. Multiculturalism made them feel even more remote from the culture they were expected to embrace. Breivik felt he was being discriminated against in his own country. And from the viewpoint of those worlds, the only way to change society was murder.

CHAPTER THIRTEEN

THE LONE WOLF KILLER

To be honest, if I felt that other people could do my job I would not do what I do, that I can guarantee you. I don't want to do what I do, I would rather focus on starting a family and focus on my career again. But I can't do that as long as I feel like a person caught in a burning spaceship with nowhere to go.

—ANDERS BREIVIK MANIFESTO

A person caught in a burning spaceship. That is how Anders Breivik described his life, and it is a common feeling among such killers. In truth, Breivik could not focus on starting a family or reviving his career. If he could have, he would not have chosen the path he took. But trapped in that burning spaceship that was his own head, he could not escape and establish meaningful relationships with anyone. All that remained was a cause that could show everyone who had betrayed him how wrong they had been.

Mass murder is not unique to any one country. The worst massacres have been recorded over centuries in the various wars that were propagated, not by the conquest of land, but by the desire to spread ideology. One might suggest that a holocaust perpetrated by armed legions is a far cry from those caused by one individual's planning. But are they?

A DIFFERENT KIND OF KILLER

The lone wolf shares qualities of mass murderers, but he also differs in important ways.

- Attachment—Someone failed him at an early age. At the same time, and perhaps because of this early failure, he had difficulty establishing meaningful attachments to others.
- Intelligence—He possesses medium to high intelligence. What he can't learn in a group, he'll learn on his own.
- Victim of bullying or some other form of social injustice—He was injured early and won't forget it.
- Rage—He wants to strike back.
- Inability to connect or have meaningful relationships—Not even in extremist groups.
- Misplaced attachment—Because of his intelligence, he has the capacity to connect to a cause/ideology as a surrogate for connecting with other people. He becomes its true believer and most faithful keeper.
- Narcissistic—He is the most important person in the world.
- Desire to live—He is not suicidal. In his narcissistic view, he is too important and too essential to that cause to be sacrificed.
- Not in a hurry—He is smart enough to avoid detection and takes his time to plan his attack and execute it to perfection.
- Needs release—Killing is the ultimate rerouting to intimate gratification.
- Kills on a societal level—It is not enough for him to just kill a neighbor or former teacher. He needs to be seen, to matter. Thus, the killings must be on a mass scale and in a high-profile place.

Study this description and Kaczynski, McVeigh, and Breivik will emerge.

Breivik toyed with cosmetic surgery until he had the face he felt he deserved, and he believed that only he could save Norway from the Islamization of society, both compelling signs of his narcissism. Like other lone wolves, Breivik has a strong need to matter; and the nature of his attacks reflects that, given their scale and high visibility. Because he believes he is such an important person, however, he didn't want to die when he committed his acts of violence. He was not a candidate for suicide-by-cop, nor would he commit suicide at the end of his killing spree. Self-preservation ranked high on his list of values. However, first place on that list belonged to the ideology he had embraced. It was what he connected with more than anything—or anyone—else.

Breivik said that he dreaded getting up that morning on July 22, 2011, and that he knew that dying was a possibility, that the police might shoot him. He was ready for it. Yet, willing as he was to perish for his ideology, he was not suicidal.

The same was true for McVeigh. He realized that there was a chance he would be killed if someone discovered the bomb in his truck before he could light the fuse, or that he would run into law-enforcement officers while escaping the explosion. He had even been ready to drive his car into the building to cause an explosion if there were no available parking spaces in front of the entrance. Like Breivik, he was willing to sacrifice his life for his cause. But he had no wish to die.

"Rampage killers" may also want to be known, and they may sometimes leave a manifesto or some other explanation of their motives. Like the lone wolves, they too may have been isolated or bullied as children and have similar feelings of rage, as well as a desire for revenge, that can play a big part in their motivations. But unlike a lone wolf killer, they are often suicidal. An example of a rampage killer is Adam Lanza of the Sandy Hook Elementary School massacre in Connecticut.

Serial killers tend to have low to average intelligence, and most have a history of criminal misdemeanors or worse. They also may have been isolated and/or bullied as children, and often were abused. Killing provides them with psychological satisfaction. They feel no empathy and no guilt, and they prefer to do their killings in private and have no wish to be caught or recognized. Whereas a lone wolf wants to make a statement, a serial killer often kills for his own personal fulfillment.

According to Dr. Puckett, the lone wolf is not a psychopath. Unlike a true psychopath, he has a conscience, albeit a misguided one. Nor is he necessarily mentally ill. Even the Norwegian expert panel of psychiatrists got this wrong in Breivik's case. Breivik's lack of empathy at times does not, according to Dr. Puckett, come from psychopathic tendencies, but narcissism. Breivik's displays of empathy over his lifetime also show that he is not a psychopath. A true psychopath would have displayed a complete lack of empathy since childhood, often torturing animals or even other children or siblings as an early-warning sign.

Because the lone wolf is not a psychopath, he does not necessarily take pleasure in killing or view it as a game. In fact, Breivik dreaded having to murder for his cause. But since he was so disconnected from anything else, and because of his rage and desire to make the biggest statement possible, he murdered those young people on Utøya in a gruesome and callous manner. In the police interrogations of him, Breivik admitted that he had shot his victims' sexual organs and executed them with up to five shots in the head. He had also shot some teens in the back and then turned their lifeless bodies over to fire his gun down their throats, then finally shot and destroyed his victims' eyes. It was "uncomfortable" for him to do this, he claimed to the police and his attorney.

In his manifesto, he castigated his mother and sister, and then later told his attorney he had done that to protect them, so they would not be associated with him. The attorney fell for it. If Breivik had actually cared for them, he would have found a less painful way than character assassination to distance himself. Instead, he pretended to be connected because he didn't know what true connection feels like.

He acts in a similar manner throughout his entire manifesto. He is such a good leader, he claims, that his friends are going to miss him. He is the glue. In reality, he only pretends to know what it feels like to care about and connect with others. He speaks about relationships but has never experienced them.

His need to matter on a societal level, along with the fact that he had become completely subsumed by his ideology, blinded him to anything else. Although he pretended to understand the pain he inflicted and to regret the suffering he caused, he was merely mouthing platitudes—because he didn't know how to do anything else. He stopped doing his right-arm salute at the beginning of each court day during the trial after his attorney made him aware of the sorrow the gesture caused the parents of the young people he had killed. Was it because he truly had regrets, or because he wanted to be perceived as a sane human, capable of compassion? His trial was a strategy to promote his own cause; in order to do that, he needed to appear rational, even caring. Breivik did not regret the massacre, however. In his mind, he was fighting a war and his acts were necessary.

Because the lone wolf is sane and generally law-abiding until he acts, and because he is intelligent and has a high sense of self-preservation, he is extremely difficult to identify and, in some cases, like with Kaczynski, to catch.

DEVASTATING CONSEQUENCES

Our political leaders now double as military leaders. Or is it the other way around? Countries act out of a mass hysteria brought upon them by a singular leader and his/her tight circle of devotees. All people live in a collective limbo between political policies that, at their most modest levels, subliminally strengthen division. Division, at high levels, turns citizens into soldiers. Soldiers are easily cultivated into killers. History has proven that to be true. What history has not told us is what happens when the technology of killing has changed so drastically that one person can, without an army, kill so many.

According to Ramón Spaaij, in his book *Understanding Lone Wolf Terrorism: Global Patterns, Motivations and Prevention*, this phenomenon is increasing. Spaaij found that beginning in the 1970s, there has been a gradual yet observable increase in lone wolf terrorist attacks in the United States and a much more rapid increase outside the United States. Between the 1970s and 2000, according to Spaaij, "the total number of lone wolf terrorist attacks per decade rose by 45% (from 22 to 32) in the United States and by a massive 412% (from 8 to 41) in the other 14 countries [that were included in his study] combined."

One individually motivated massacre could devastate an entire citizenry. No country's war against terror is completely effective. Many believe that the growing governmental agencies employed against such unspeakable devastation can't possibly protect a nation.

Collecting data on terrorists is more advanced now than ever before. A demented person wanting to cause great havoc cannot hide easily if he has already committed a crime. Authorities alerted to a suspect will sift through his past, examine his life, spot his evil tendencies, and try to stop him before he strikes—or, at least, before he can strike again. For every terrorist, or terrorist group, there are experts whose job it is to stop him, or them.

But what about the ones who manage to escape the radar? Remember, the lone wolf does not generally display criminal behavior before his great act, as was the case with Anders Breivik. He was not previously in the criminal world, nor did he have any mental issues to speak of. He was not a rampage killer, and neither were Kaczynski and McVeigh. Rather, all three were highly meticulous.

THEODORE KACZYNSKI, THE UNABOMBER

Although Kaczynski's first attempts at mailing bombs failed, he was ultimately responsible for killing three people and injuring twenty-three others. As is the case with many lone wolf killers, Kaczynski came from a troubled home. His mother probably didn't give him enough attention after his younger brother David was born, and she was not sensitive to the fact that although Kaczynski had the intellectual capacity to skip grades, he didn't have the mental maturity to fit in with the older students. When his father, upon learning that he had terminal cancer, committed suicide, Kaczynski never acknowledged any sorrow, nor did he attend his father's funeral. He was convinced that both of his parents had made him a "social cripple" because they had made him enter Harvard when he was an unready sixteen-year-old.

His seven-year-younger brother David told the *New York Times* that he thought his brother's issues had started in his childhood. "I think that truth from my point of view is that Ted has been a disturbed person for a long time and he's gotten more disturbed," David said. It was he, the person closest to the suspect, who turned Kaczynski in.

"I think he's a person who wanted to love something and unfortunately, again, it gets so complex," David said. "He failed to love it in the right way because in some deep way, he felt a lack of love and respect himself."

Although Kaczynski wasn't close to his parents, he had a good relationship with his brother, at least to a certain degree. But when David got married, Kaczynski saw it as a betrayal.

"I always had a sense that something was missing," David said about the relationship between his brother and his parents. "The bond was never completely there, the way it had been with me"—although the fact that Kaczynski felt betrayed by David getting married hints that this relationship was unbalanced and not a healthy brother-to-brother relationship.

Highly intelligent, Kaczynski graduated from Harvard, earned a Ph.D. in mathematics from the University of Michigan, and became an assistant professor at the University of California, Berkeley, at age twenty-five.

Although he desperately wanted to connect with others, he continued to flounder and left Berkeley after two years, despite his innate intelligence. He could write in fluent, elegant Spanish, which he had learned from textbooks, and he had learned German the same way.

According to Dr. Puckett, such killers frequently reject authority: "They're going to go out and learn on their own." Kaczynski was more than capable of doing that, as were McVeigh and Breivik.

To Puckett, it wasn't the relentless anger Kaczynski expressed that was most striking; it was the searing loneliness, and his tormented longing for a woman to join in his voluntary exile from society. Again and again, he wrote agonizing passages about his inability to understand or engage in normal social relationships with people, especially women. He confessed in his journal that he had never experienced a sexual relationship with a woman, except for one kiss with a woman from his workplace in Chicago in 1978.

In 1971, Kaczynski moved to a cabin in Lincoln, Montana. Lacking electricity or running water, he lived as a recluse. By 1978, he began sending bombs, a total of sixteen, to universities and airlines. He chose his targets from newspaper articles, people who represented everything he hated. In his Unabomber Manifesto, he said that he wanted to attract attention to modern technologies that eroded human freedom.

Kaczynski spent eighteen years killing, maiming, and terrorizing his country in a fanatical battle to stop technology and punish those who did not fit his distorted model of the world. Extremely intelligent and careful, he took extraordinary steps to avoid leaving any trail back to himself and his cabin in Montana. In April 1995, he sent a letter to the *New York Times* and said that if the *Times* or the *Washington Post* published his manifesto, he would "desist from terrorism."

Turned in by the brother who had once idolized him, Kaczynski ultimately changed his plea to guilty to thirteen counts for attacks in three states that killed three and injured two. Like Breivik, he could not tolerate being diagnosed as mentally ill and having that as his defense. As of this writing, he is serving his life sentence at the ADX Florence "Supermax" penitentiary in Colorado with no chance of parole.

It is no wonder that Breivik was deeply influenced by Kaczynski. They have much in common, whether it is their loneliness or their devotion to their ideologies and the importance they place on their respective manifestos. And both continue to inspire copycats.

TIMOTHY MCVEIGH, THE OKLAHOMA CITY BOMBER

McVeigh's parents separated when he was ten years old, and he was raised by his father in Pendleton, New York. McVeigh—who, like Breivik, was bullied in school—took refuge in a fantasy world where he imagined retaliating against those bullies.

Most who knew him described him as withdrawn, but some said he was outgoing and playful. Again, like Kaczynski and Breivik, he was not successful in his relationships with girls. McVeigh had an awkward relationship with women, Dr. Puckett said. "He was bitter about his mother and blamed her for his parents' divorce. But he expressed interest in girls, one in particular, he seemed to put on a pedestal and toward whom he never really made any overt moves."

In high school, McVeigh was named Starpoint Central High School's "most promising computer programmer." Highly intelligent but bored with the school curriculum, he was interested mainly in guns, gun control, and the Second Amendment.

"He was a super soldier in the Gulf War—from a distance," Dr. Puckett said. He shot Iraqi soldiers, but there was no hand-to-hand combat. Indeed, the reason he quit the military was self-preservation, she said. "He dropped out of training because he got blisters on his feet. This is the total opposite of the school shooters who go in expecting to be fully engaged and to be killed. This killer is the most important person in the world. He cannot be hurt or even discomforted." This fixation on minutiae parallels Breivik's current behavior in prison, where he is massively vocal about the smallest of discomforts or slights, oblivious to the irony of these claims while in prison for murdering seventy-seven people.

When, on April 19, 1995, McVeigh exploded a truck bomb outside the Alfred P. Murrah Federal Building in Oklahoma City, it was the worst terrorist attack on United States soil until the attacks on September 11, 2001. It killed 168 people and injured over six hundred.

Puckett was struck by the visits McVeigh made to the Michigan Militia a year or two before he and Terry Nichols assembled the bomb in the Ryder truck that McVeigh would drive to the Murrah Federal Building on April 19. McVeigh attempted to inspire the group to violence, saying "massacres at Ruby Ridge and Waco" demanded payment in kind to the U.S. government. "They were told to leave more than one meeting," Militia leader Norman Olsen said, according to *All-American Monster: The Unauthorized Biography of Timothy McVeigh*, "because of that type of talk of destruction and harm and terrorism." This parallels Breivik's failed attempts to engage with, and join, Norway's Progressive Party and, later, right-wing online groups. Later, McVeigh tried unsuccessfully to recruit members for his own "patriot group." In the final days before the bombing, he tried several times to reach the National Alliance, a radical militia organization. He also hung up a note at a gun show that read "I'm looking for fighters."

Like Breivik, he never gave up trying to make a human connection.

Terry Nichols and Michael Fortier, whom McVeigh had met in the Army and who shared his views, helped him obtain the bomb materials and check out the site. But neither of them wanted to take part in actually executing the attack. In the end, McVeigh was alone in his operation.

ERIC RUDOLPH, THE OLYMPIC PARK BOMBER

Eric Robert Rudolph, another homegrown lone wolf, was responsible for a series of bombings across the United States between 1996 and 1998. He killed two people and injured at least 150 others. His bombings were motivated by his religious beliefs against abortion clinics and gays.

He was given his nickname after he bombed the Centennial Olympic Park on July 27 during the 1996 Atlanta Summer Olympics. A massive explosion ripped through the crowd of people celebrating on that summer night. A bomb concealed in a military backpack and placed under a bench had detonated. Although security was supposedly tight, no backpacks had been searched and there were no metal detectors.

Rudolph had made his bomb from three metal pipes filled with smokeless powder, similar to Kaczynski's, capped with end plugs and 8d masonry nails for shrapnel, according to FBI Agent Terry Turchie. "A Big Ben alarm clock and 12-volt battery provided the timing and ignition system."

Atlanta Police had received an anonymous call before the explosion, saying "There is a bomb in Centennial Park. You have ten minutes." Rudolph also sent letters to the news media claiming the "Army of God" was responsible.

Over the next eighteen months, three more bombings followed: In January 1997, an abortion clinic in Atlanta was attacked. In February the same year, a gay nightclub in Atlanta exploded, and as emergency personnel and police arrived at the scene, a second bomb detonated, aiming to kill the first responders. The "Army of God" also claimed credit for these.

Then on January 30, 1998, an off-duty police officer, Robert Sanderson, was killed at a Birmingham abortion clinic by a bomb triggered by remote control. This time Rudolph was standing just a few yards away.

As Rudolph walked away from the scene, a young man thought he looked suspicious and decided to follow him to his pickup truck. He wrote down his license plate number, and Eric Rudolph was identified as the suspect, although he wasn't apprehended for five more years.

He later explained that the purpose of the bombing was to "confound, anger and embarrass the Washington government in the eyes of the world for its abominable sanctioning of abortion on demand."

As with the other lone wolf killers, Rudolph needed to matter and to attack on a societal level, after merging with his cause. Extremely careful and diligent in his planning, he managed to remain hidden in the Appalachian forest for more than five years and was on the FBI's Ten Most Wanted Fugitives list until he was apprehended in 2003.

Dr. Puckett characterized Breivik as a combination of Kaczynski and Rudolph when it came to his approach to his attacks. Breivik was absent when his bomb exploded but present during the killings on the island. Kaczynski mailed his bombs, effectively detaching himself from the bombs' destructive results, while Rudolph always remained close enough to witness the damage his explosions caused.

Rudolph was born in Merritt Island, Florida; but when his father died in 1981, he moved with his mother and siblings to Nantahala, North Carolina. When he was eighteen, his mother took him to a Christian compound in Missouri known as the Church of Israel, in search of an alternative to suburbia and traditional religion. Later, Rudolph enlisted in the U.S. Army, but was discharged two years later because he was caught smoking marijuana. A typical lone wolf, he was unable and unwilling to adapt to any group. He was a loner who relied exclusively on his own abilities to deal with the world. On one of his solitary breaks, he disappeared for more than two weeks in the Nantahala forest. He told no one where he had been, not even his own family. His mother encouraged her children to think and live outside mainstream society, and Rudolph was secure in a large family that tolerated his solitary nature. Unlike Kaczynski, he expressed no frustration over not finding a suitable mate. According to Puckett, Rudolph was by all accounts successful with women sexually, but he didn't seem to need them to complete his world. Where Kaczynski was puzzled by society, Rudolph was indifferent to it.

Like Kaczynski and Breivik, Rudolph used the word *we* when conveying his ideology, referring to the "Army of God" when taking credit for his bombings. After he was caught, Rudolph entered a plea bargain and revealed the location of 250 pounds of dynamite hidden in the forests of North Carolina. He later said that he only agreed to the plea to avoid the death penalty.

Rudolph is serving his life sentence at the ADX Florence "Supermax" penitentiary on the same row as Kaczynski. In a letter to his mother from prison, he wrote: "Many good people continue to send me money and books. Most of them have, of course, an agenda; mostly born-again Christians looking to save my soul. I suppose the assumption is made that because I'm in here I must be a 'sinner' in need of salvation, and they would be glad to sell me a ticket to heaven, hawking this salvation like peanuts at a ballgame. I do appreciate their charity, but I could really do without the condescension. They have been so nice I would hate to break it to them that I really prefer Nietzsche to the Bible."

Like other lone wolves, he feels no regret for his acts and continues to hold firmly to his ideology.

THE ULTIMATE BULLY

At the end of his life, McVeigh said that the United States government was the ultimate bully. This is an important part of Dr. Puckett's theory, one that separates these types of killers from others. McVeigh's stated reason was that he sought revenge against the government for its handling of the 1993 Waco siege, which ended in the death of seventy-six people exactly two years prior to his bombing of the Murrah Federal Building. He also sought revenge for the Ruby Ridge, Idaho incident in 1992.

Ruby Ridge was the site of the deadly confrontation and siege in Idaho against Randy Weaver that led to the death of Vicki and Sammy Weaver, Randy's wife and son, along with Deputy U.S. Marshal William Francis Degan. The Waco siege involved many of the same agencies as Ruby Ridge, among them the Bureau of Alcohol, Tobacco, and Firearms (ATF).

McVeigh, much like Breivik, hoped to inspire a revolt against what he considered a tyrannical federal government. The Oklahoma federal building housed many federal agencies, among them the ATF.

Many parallels exist between Kaczynski, McVeigh, Breivik, and—to a smaller extent—Rudolph, enough to suggest that they all fit the profile of the lone wolf. These individuals were victims of bullying. Isolation was imposed upon them at some point in their lives, and that isolation was also self-imposed due to their own characteristic problems of fitting in with other people. When they killed, "they were righting a wrong," Dr. Puckett explained, "but they were so grandiose that the government itself had to pay for what they had suffered."

Contrary to the lone wolf, the rampage killer is not on any particular mission except to commit suicide and take as many people with him as possible. And contrary to the sociopathic murderer, the lone wolf does not take pleasure in taking lives, nor does he do it in secret. He wants impact above all else. Kaczynski even described in a letter from prison that he thought McVeigh's bombing was "unnecessarily inhumane."

"A more effective protest could have been made with far less harm to innocent people," according to Kaczynski. "Most of the people who died at Oklahoma City were, I imagine, lower-level government employees—office help and the like—who were not even remotely responsible for objectionable government policies or for the events at Waco. If violence were to be used to express protest, it could have been used far more humanely, and at the same time more effectively, by being directed at the relatively small number of people who were personally responsible for the policies or actions to which the protesters objected. . . . Moreover, the protest would have earned far more sympathy than the Oklahoma City bombing did, because it is safe to assume that many anti-government people who might have accepted violence that was more limited and carefully directed were repelled by the large loss of innocent life at Oklahoma City."

Kaczynski seems to forget that had his bomb onboard American Airlines Flight 444 exploded, he could have killed more innocent people than McVeigh did.

"Kaczynski picked his victims out of *Who's Who in America* and the newspaper. Breivik picked children," Puckett says. The lone wolf thinks *No one's safe from me because I can reach out and touch your society.*

Actually, the lone wolf—who has never been able to connect with anyone or anything but an ideology—cannot even connect with the person or people who caused him such early pain on a deep enough level to just focus on killing these individuals. He can't take out the school bully of his youth, so he takes out a school. He can't kill his mother, so he decides to kill "the Mother of Norway." Narcissism may be part of the equation, but the other part is the inability to connect with other people, even when one is deciding upon whom to take revenge.

NEW MEANS OF DETECTION

Kaczynski, McVeigh, Rudolph, Breivik: they all managed to evade early detection. How many times were these odd characters on the radar? And how many times did the authorities drop the proverbial ball? Certainly, it can be argued that this type of neglect had aided Breivik in carrying out his atrocities. Richard Cottrell, ex-Euro Parliamentarian and author of *Gladio: NATO's Dagger at the Heart of Europe*, and others hint of a possible conspiracy between the criminal, the governments, and their intelligence gatherers.

"We are seeing a massive extension of synthetic terror organized for political purposes," Cottrell says. He believes (after his study of the Aurora shootings on July 20, 2012) that the endless "no one is safe anywhere" mantra preached by the Department of Homeland Security will eventually invade public events and delve into the privacy of America's communication.

These new mass murderers have a ready audience in the digital age, and most take advantage of that. Almost always, they employ a manifesto or a journal to share their frustration and anger with an imagined audience. These documents often begin in a rational way, as Breivik's did, and then the authors almost always write themselves into murder.

They want fame, and the digital/blogging/YouTube age gives them a fair amount of that. Perhaps that need to be heard can make them easier to spot as well. Finding them before they strike is the challenge of the future if we are to prevent more from turning into lone wolves or international terrorists, as was the case in the Boston Marathon bombings of April 15, 2013.

"Boston is where the two dovetail," said Dr. Puckett. "We knew it was a matter of time before the domestic lone wolf merged with the international terrorist. The fact that these guys are acting on their own suggests they still have unmet social needs, so they continually try to re-engage people in extremist groups."

Dr. Puckett believes that spotting potential killers can start at the community level, when they attempt to become a part of local groups and cannot handle even those connections.

Local law enforcement doesn't have time to spot them, she says. "An organization like the FBI could bring people in, school them in this stuff.

Soon the conversation will get around to, 'Next time you talk to [the] head of local militia, make your usual connection, and eventually, he'll tell you which whackos show up on their radar.'"

Such an approach could also lead to witch hunts, yet Dr. Puckett and others in her profession have a point. Killers like Anders Breivik must be detected prior to their crime, because the first crime they commit will almost certainly be the one that destroys a large part of a community or a nation.

Breivik is an excellent example of that. In the relative freedom of his Norwegian prison, how many others who believe as he does has he already located? Is he planning for later when he's supposed to have been rehabilitated? Most certainly prison is the safest place for him to live, write, and motivate others. The danger here is that Breivik's fans can continue his work while he is incarcerated. And when he gets out—if he gets out—how rehabilitated will he really be?

CHAPTER FOURTEEN

COPYCATS AND KINDRED SPIRITS

Choose targets wisely and ensure that the secondary effects will have devastating effects.

—ANDERS BREIVIK MANIFESTO

On August 1, 1966, an angry engineering student and former Marine by the name of Charles Joseph Whitman murdered his wife and mother in Austin, Texas, and then shot and killed sixteen people and wounded thirty-two others in a massacre in and around the Tower of the University of Texas in Austin. He spent ninety-six minutes picking off his targets from the tower the way Breivik would, decades later, pick off his from the shores of Utøya.

Reporters of the time had difficulty explaining how much his incomprehensible actions shocked citizens of the United States. No one knew what to make of such madness. In those pre–September 11 days, they didn't understand how such a violent act could take place in their country.

After the killings, a psychiatrist Whitman had visited released all his records. They included information about Whitman's fantasy of killing people from the tower. Nothing else indicated that he was a danger, the psychiatrist argued in those more innocent times, when something like that might have been a red flag. But would experts have truly been able to spot a Whitman today?

His father had abused his wife and children, and Whitman confessed, in his journal, to striking his own wife. He also complained of unbearable headaches, and an autopsy confirmed that he may have suffered from physical, as well as mental, disabilities that led to his crime.

Regardless of the cause, Whitman's actions stunned the country in a way that few have since. The first in a long line of killers, he wasn't a lone wolf. His massacre was a form of super-suicide. He had no cause, no motive other than his own misery. Despite his brilliance, he wanted only to end his tortured life and to take as many people as possible out with him. He set the tone for the new mass murderer and mass killings to come.

Statistics show that in the weeks and months following an event such as the attacks of July 22, 2011, mass murders increase.

According to Richard Cottrell, "the Aurora, Colorado shootings were in the same line as the Norwegian mass murderer, Anders Breivik."

Cottrell points out that the parallels between the mass shooting by college student James Eagan Holmes (during a midnight screening of the new Batman movie, *The Dark Knight Rises,* in Aurora's Century Movie Theater on July 20, 2012), which killed twelve and injured seventy others, are aligned with Breivik's bombing in Oslo and, especially, his shooting mania on the island of Utøya.

"We seem to be looking at an American copycat version of Norway's Anders Behring Breivik," Cottrell wrote. "The same picture of a deranged lone gunman with a vengeance against society." Cottrell also makes an important point: "Like Breivik, he survives to tell his tale in court."

Cottrell lists a series of shootings and bombings across Europe that erupted soon after Breivik's massacre.

- The killing of two Senegalese street vendors in Florence, Italy in December 2011 by a suspected right-wing extremist.

- The rampage by an alleged solo assassin, who killed two shoppers at a Christmas fair in Liège, Belgium, in 2011.
- The murders of three Jewish schoolchildren, a rabbi, and three off-duty servicemen in Toulouse, France, during a presidential election campaign.
- Bombings at a school in Brindisi, Italy, in May 2012, in which a teen girl died and five others were horribly injured.
- The 2012 bus bombing in Bourgas, Bulgaria, which claimed the lives of the driver and five Israeli tourists and injured another twelve.

Cottrell notes that, in every instance, subliminal motives are aimed to ignite racial and religious tensions. More curious, he suggests, is how close this type of lone terrorist may be to the scrutiny of the police and intelligence services.

On August 10, 2012, Vojtěch Mlýnek, a 29-year-old Breivik sympathizer, was arrested in the Czech Republic while planning to carry out a series of copycat terrorist attacks. The man, who had been convicted five times in the past of explosives-related charges, had built up a stash of weapons, explosives, a detonator, and an automatic rifle at his home. Because he had used Breivik's name as a pseudonym in e-mail communication, the police were alerted and able to arrest him before he could press the detonator he was carrying when apprehended.

Tomas Tuhy, the regional police director who supervised the arrest in the Czech Republic, told reporters: "We are working with the idea that the suspect probably sympathizes with known murderer Anders Breivik from Norway."

On November 20, 2012, Polish authorities announced the arrest of a 45-year-old lecturer of the Agricultural University of Cracow, under suspicion of preparation for a terrorist attack. According to the authorities, Brunon K, as he was called, was an admirer of Breivik and was further inspired by the Oklahoma City bombing in 1995.

The Polish domestic intelligence service ABW first found out about Brunon K after it launched an investigation into Breivik's Polish contacts, when it became known that Breivik had ordered some of the chemicals for his bomb from Poland via the Internet. According to ABW, Brunon K was preparing an attack against Sejm (the lower house of the Polish parliament). He planned to detonate four tons of explosives in a car bomb parked at the building during deliberation of the following year's budget. It is at such a time that all the members of Parliament, the prime minister, and the president are present in the building. Breivik had similar plans, only he sabotaged his own efforts by planning his attack for a Friday afternoon in the middle of summer.

Brunon K intensified his preparations after Breivik's conviction. He conducted—and filmed—an experimental explosion of a 250-kilogram bomb in the Polish countryside in the municipality of Przeginia. He had also recruited other people for his cause.

He told investigators, "Breivik and McVeigh made mistakes. I will be better."

∞

On July 26, 1764, near present-day Greencastle, Pennsylvania, four Lenape Native Americans entered the schoolhouse and shot and killed the schoolmaster and all but three children. Known as the Pontiac's Rebellion massacre, it was the first U.S. school shooting.

In February 1997, over two centuries later, a sixteen-year-old boy in Bethel, Alaska brought a shotgun to school and opened fire, killing the principal and a student. In October of the same year, in Pearl, Mississippi, two students died. In December, in West Paducah, Kentucky and Stamps, Arkansas, seven died and sixteen were wounded. In 1998, ten people were killed, thirty-five wounded, in five separate school shootings.

Over the years, on the unlikely battlefield of school grounds, crazed professors have killed themselves and each other. Parents have killed because they didn't like the way their children were treated, and students have killed, as at the University of Central Florida, on March 18, 2013, when James Oliver Seevakumaran, age thirty-one, planned to destroy his world with an assault weapon, a couple of hundred rounds of ammunition, and four homemade bombs inside his backpack.

After pulling a fire alarm at the Tower 1 dormitory, Seevakumaran, according to his written plans, intended to attract a large number of people inside the building so that he could murder them. He then pointed a handgun at his roommate and threatened to shoot him inside their dormitory room. His roommate ran into a bathroom and called 911. Seevakumaran then shot himself in the head.

According to the *New York Times*, the FBI study of 160 shooting sprees in the United States since 2000 showed that 486 people were killed—366 of them in the past seven years—and 557 others were wounded, many of them gravely incapacitated for years afterward. Sixty percent of the sprees ended before police could arrive, and forty percent of the shooters committed suicide. FBI analysts also found that many of the gunmen had studied earlier gun massacres and were attracted to the attention mass killers received.

Jack Hobson, a former high school School Resource Officer (SRO), currently a college instructor in Boston, is the author of *Drifters*, a book examining the drift theory of juvenile delinquency. "There seem to be common attributes that drive a shooter," Hobson explained in an interview. "The most prolific of these are revenge fantasies, the need to get even for some wrong, real or imagined. Some school shooters go after their bullies, others their sexual or academic rivals. Many of their mental issues stem from an unfulfilled attachment with parents in pre-adolescence."

According to Hobson, paternal disappointment often breeds a convoluted sense of self-esteem and shame. "And that festers into a fantasy that, *if I do something horrific, maybe Dad will love me and be proud.*"

Maternal attachment, or lack thereof, breeds either a safe comfort zone or a relationship that smothers the child and stymies strong interpersonal relationships with peers. "And within the confines of school, these kids cannot adapt to the normal nuances of the social jungle, and they are preyed upon in hurtful ways," Hobson said.

Breivik's unstable mother and distant father impaired his interpersonal relationships as a young man. He was the weird kid who just didn't fit in and became an easy target for bullying. The lone wolf has that in common with many rampage killers. However, most of these school shooters were not lone wolf killers, but depressed and suicidal young men who fed off lone wolves and other rampage killers for a sick sort of inspiration.

ISLA VISTA, SANTA BARBARA, CALIFORNIA

Hobson's description applies well to Elliot Rodger, the 22-year-old college student who murdered six people in Santa Barbara, California, on May 23, 2014. Although never formally diagnosed with mental illness, Rodger struggled with depression and had seen multiple therapists since he was eight years old. In his YouTube manifesto, Rodger complained that, being of mixed race, he wasn't accepted and girls weren't attracted to him.

"How could an inferior, ugly black boy be able to get a white girl and not me?" he wrote. "I am beautiful, and I am half white myself. I am descended from British aristocracy. He is descended from slaves."

Rodger once said to his father that he wished he wasn't Asian. "I had no idea he was so racist," Peter Rodger said.

Born in London to British filmmaker Peter Rodger and Malaysian Li-Chin, a research assistant for a film company, Rodger was raised in Los Angeles. His parents divorced when he was young. Rodger never adjusted. He also had a hard time trying to live up to his successful father, who had married a beautiful actress a year after he left Rodger's mother.

According to his father, Elliot was a quiet and invisible kid growing up. "I lived just down the road from him," one of the survivors said. "I went to the same school as him, and I never saw him."

His killing spree was revenge for the rejections and all the bullying he had been subjected to over the years. It was a super-suicide.

"On the day before the Day of Retribution," he wrote, "I will start the First Phase of my vengeance: Silently killing as many people as I can around Isla Vista by luring them into my apartment through some form of trickery."

The second part of the manifesto was dedicated to his "War on Women." "I will attack the very girls who represent everything I hate in the female gender: The hottest sorority of UCSB," he wrote.

According to a May 27, 2014 article in the *Washington Post*, Rodger was an adherent of the so-called "manosphere" on the Internet. Notably, he was linked to an account on the pickup site PUAhate.com, where he promoted an overthrow of "this oppressive feminist system" and envisioned "a world where WOMEN FEAR YOU." On YouTube, he followed a number of accounts that claimed to teach pickup artistry—a skill that's equal parts pseudoscience, manipulation, and objectification. In his last YouTube video, in which he announced the start of his killing spree, Rodger stole some classic pickup lingo: "You will finally see that I am, in truth, the superior one. The true alpha male."

His father described in an interview with Barbara Walters on ABC's *2020* his son's fear of other people, which led him to isolation. "He was obsessed with finding a girlfriend," Peter Rodger said, and tormented by the fact that no girls were attracted to him, and jealous of couples around him.

"If I can't have it," Rodger wrote, "I will destroy it." Too terrified to make connections with women, he decided to hate them.

"He was unable to engage," a friend of his father said to Barbara Walters. "He couldn't communicate."

Several incidents prior to May 23 indicated his violent behavior and mental instability. In July 2011, Rodger stalked and threw coffee on a couple outside of Starbucks at the Camino Real Marketplace in Goleta. In a later incident, he threw coffee on two girls sitting at a bus stop in Isla Vista for not paying attention to him.

In the summer of 2013, he tried to shove some girls off a ledge at a college party. His father told Walters that Rodger had been beaten up by boys at the party after the incident, and that his son never told him what had really happened.

"He was a very good liar," Peter Rodger said.

His mother saw some of his YouTube videos and, terrified over her son's threats and behavior, contacted the police. Six officers made a visit to Rodger's apartment, but the well-spoken, intelligent, and polite young man convinced them that it had all been a misunderstanding. The police left without entering his place.

"Had they demanded to search my room," Rodger later wrote, "that would have ended everything. For a few horrible seconds, I thought it was all over." The police neither watched the YouTube videos, nor ran a background check for purchasing guns.

Three years of planning led to the "Day of Retribution" in which he stabbed to death his roommate and two friends at his apartment before going off on his shooting spree, killing three more and injuring thirteen others. In his journal, Rodger wrote down every detail of what he would do, and how. He had even planned to kill his younger half-brother, in fear that the young child would one day "surpass him."

After driving erratically around Isla Vista, shooting from inside his car, Rodger crashed it and pointed the trigger at his own head. Depressed and suicidal, Rodger was a rampage killer much like the Columbine killers and Adam Lanza.

SANDY HOOK, CONNECTICUT

On December 14, 2012, Adam Lanza, a twenty-year-old male, killed his mother in their Sandy Hook, Connecticut home. Then, after having shot the locking device off the door of a nearby elementary school, Lanza started firing his weapon at the children and staff. Before taking his own life moments later, he managed to slaughter twenty first-grade children and six adult members of the faculty.

Almost immediately, it was reported that Lanza, a young man who had always remained on the fringe of society, "wanted to kill more people than Norwegian mass murderer Anders Breivik, and he picked Sandy Hook because it had the most potential targets" (MAIL On Line, July 23, 2013).

Both Lanza and Breivik shared a love of *Call of Duty* and other violent computer games. Detectives found thousands of dollars worth of these games in a darkened den in Lanza's home. Both killers used American-made assault rifles and similar handguns. There were other similarities, but Lanza had smashed his hard drive and left no manifesto or notes. After a more thorough comparison, we are left with how the two killers differed rather than how alike they might have appeared to be at first glance.

Perhaps there is more reason to study the comparison between Adam Lanza and the Columbine killings committed by students Eric Harris and Dylan Klebold at their own high school on April 19, 1999.

Before taking their own lives, Harris and Klebold shot and killed twelve of their fellow students and one teacher, in addition to wounding many others. The Columbine massacre was the first one that America witnessed fragments of on live television. Students called media from their cell phones, and were interviewed on live TV from the school during the massacre.

Harris and Klebold, who had met in the seventh grade, were best friends. They attended football games, school dances, and a variety of shows, and worked together on a school video production. Dylan worked backstage at the sound board at school plays, and he was good at it. Neither of them was particularly athletic, but they both loved watching sports. "His life was baseball," a friend said about Dylan.

"Eric fancied himself a nonconformist," Dave Cullen wrote in *Columbine*, "but he craved approval and fumed over the slightest disrespect. His hand was always shooting up in class, and he always had the right answer."

Both were heavy drinkers, but Eric was better at hiding it from his parents. Eric always seemed the obedient one. Like Breivik, he was also a control freak.

"He gauged his moves and determined just how much he could get away with. He could suck up like crazy and make things go his way," according to Cullen.

They were both intelligent, but Eric was the leader. He knew when to play and when to get serious. If they got into trouble, Eric would do the talking. He knew how to read people and how to tailor his responses. Apologies, evasions, claims of innocence, whatever the subject was susceptible of. "He was like a robot under pressure. Nothing could faze him, not when he cared about the outcome," Cullen wrote.

The boys were gifted analytically, as was Breivik. They loved math and technology and spent hours on new gadgets, computers, and video games. Unlike Breivik, the Columbine killers didn't intend to make any political demands, nor did they have a mission. They committed suicide in the library, forty-nine minutes after beginning the attack.

Unlike Breivik and other lone wolves, Harris and Klebold left a paper trail of criminal behavior. In their junior year, they'd been caught breaking into a van to steal electronic equipment. Arrested, they entered a twelve-month juvenile diversion program, which included community service and counseling, and had finished the program with excellent reviews ten weeks prior to the massacre.

The police had also received numerous complaints from the parents of Brooks Brown, a classmate and childhood friend of Harris and Klebold's. The Browns told the *New York Times* that Harris had made death threats—ten pages of murderous rants on his web page—toward Brooks. In addition, thirteen months before the massacre, Sheriff's Investigators

John Hicks and Mike Guerra had investigated one of the Browns' complaints and discovered that Eric was building pipe bombs. Guerra drafted a search warrant to search the Harris home, but for some unknown reason the warrant was never presented before a judge.

It's possible that Klebold was clinically depressed and just did whatever Harris directed him to, but it is also plausible that he craved the attention of a super-suicide. Harris had clear sociopathic tendencies. Both wanted to top McVeigh's bombing in Oklahoma, and by choosing the same date as the Oklahoma City bombing, perhaps they were commemorating their hero. Had their bombs not failed, they would have succeeded.

On November 7, 2007, at Jokela High School in Jokela, Tuusula, Finland, eighteen-year-old Pekka-Eric Auvinen came to school with a semiautomatic pistol, shot eight people to death, wounded one other, and then shot himself in the head. Auvinen died later that evening in a Helsinki hospital.

His was the second school shooting in Finland's history. Angry and suicidal, Auvinen had been inspired by the Columbine killers, but he had also studied other mass murderers. The typical white male, intelligent, and using his hatred for humanity as justification, he wanted to take as many people to the grave with him as possible.

VIRGINIA POLYTECHNIC INSTITUTE AND STATE UNIVERSITY, BLACKSBURG, VIRGINIA

The deadliest shooting in the United States by a lone gunman occurred on the Virginia Tech campus on April 16, 2006. The killer, a South Korean student, Seung-Hui Cho, killed twenty-seven fellow students and five faculty members and wounded seventeen others, during a two-hour rampage. Able to avoid being stopped after the first phase in his attacks, he visited his dorm room, cleaned up, destroyed the hard drive of his computer, and then continued his massacre. Also during this pause in his killing spree, he went to the post office and mailed forty-three still photos and twenty-seven video clips, including ten minutes of his own rantings, to NBC TV.

Using both his Walther .22-caliber pistol and 9-mm Glock, Cho fired 174 rounds, shooting each victim at least three times. When no longer free to roam the campus without facing the police's firepower, he shot himself in the head with one of his own handguns.

Occurring about five years before Breivik, the Virginia Tech killer could have been stopped. A special review panel organized by the college detailed numerous incidents of Cho's aberrant behavior, going back to his high school experiences. His package to NBC included an 1800-word clip, similar to a letter he left in his dorm room. In both, he expressed hatred for the rich. In the video, he proclaimed his admiration for Klebold and Harris, the Columbine killers.

Like Breivik, he had become isolated and spoke of being ostracized. Unlike Breivik, Cho had a history of mental illness. He was sent to a psychiatrist after writing in a school paper, in the eighth grade, that he wanted to "repeat Columbine." Doctors had labeled him as a danger to himself and others. In college, various instructors were concerned about him but were told there was nothing that could be done. Professor and poet Nikki Giovanni felt that Cho's writing was "intimidating" and asked to have him removed from her fall 2005 poetry-writing class approximately six weeks into the course.

Cho's rampage prompted Virginia to close loopholes that had previously allowed him, despite his long history of mental illness, to purchase the weapons he used to kill and maim so many innocent victims. Based on his troubled background, he shouldn't have been able to legally purchase the guns; but because of the laws at the time, his history of mental illness was protected by confidentiality legislation, and he wasn't about to reveal that history when he went to purchase his weapons.

BOSTON MARATHON

The Boston Marathon bombings on April 15, 2013 presented an eerie mirror image to Breivik's act of terror. Tamerlan Tsarnaev, age twenty-six, and his brother, Dzhokhar, age nineteen, were Muslim immigrants from Chechnya, near the Russian border. The older brother, Tamerlan, had gotten himself listed on a database aimed at ferreting out opponents of the government. In his case, it was his outspoken rants against the United States' invasions of Iraq and Afghanistan. Breivik was flagged by the Norwegian government for buying large amounts of fertilizer and other chemicals suitable for bomb-making.

The carnage at the finish line of the Boston Marathon was caused by two homemade kettle bombs. The bombs killed three, including an eight-year-old boy, and sent 264 others to three Boston hospitals. Most victims were treated for severe trauma and terrible wounds, while some required amputation.

The cooperation of the Boston Police and the FBI was commendable. Within four days after the attacks, an unprecedented manhunt had located the brothers, but not before they had killed Officer Sean Collier of the Massachusetts Institute of Technology Police Department. The elder brother, Tamerlan, was killed hours later. That night, after the residents of Watertown, a city near Boston, were ordered by the FBI to stay in their homes, the younger brother, Dzhokhar, was apprehended. Covered in his own blood and exhausted, he surrendered after being found hiding in a boat parked in a Watertown resident's back yard.

Dzhokhar Tsarnaev, at the time of his capture, was a student at the University of Massachusetts, Dartmouth, with a major in marine biology. According to those who knew him, Dzhokhar greatly admired his older brother, Tamerlan, who had, in the three years before his death, become more devout and religious. A YouTube channel in Tamerlan's name linked to Islamic supporter videos. The FBI was informed by the Russian Federal Security Service in 2011 that he was a "follower of radical Islam." In response, the FBI interviewed Tamerlan and his family and searched databases, but they found no evidence of terrorist activity, domestic or foreign.

Here were two brothers living apparently normal lives in a country that had accepted their parents with open arms. What had happened to them?

Some experts believe they were motivated by an anti-American, radical version of Islam acquired in the United States. Others believe their turn to radicalism happened in Dagestan, a republic of Russia. Tamerlan had visited Dagestan, known for its violent militant Islamic gangs, not long before he decided to employ his brother in making the bombs they placed near the finish line of the Boston Marathon. Police found evidence of other bomb construction and uncovered their plans to strike again in New York's Central Park.

Dzhokhar, while recovering from gunshot wounds he had suffered during his manhunt and capture, claimed he and his brother were self-motivated and not connected to any terrorist group. Through Facebook and

Twitter, he is referred to as "Jahar," and the very young and very ignorant have already begun the process of projecting him as a martyr.

In the August 2013 issue of *Rolling Stone*, the editors of the magazine elected to put a frontal portrait of Dzhokhar, looking like a Jim Morrison–type young rocker, with the bold headline THE BOMBER on its cover. Featuring this killer in the place reserved for music icons and popular legends caused immediate outrage, enough that many newsstands refused to sell the issue. *Rolling Stone* had won a national magazine award for its exclusive 1970 prison interview with Charles Manson, and that interview caused no national boycott. So, what made this cover so outrageous?

Fear of copycats, of course, might be one answer, but the magazine wasn't concerned about that. However, this isn't the place to debate whether the cover was a wise decision. More important is what it says about our culture.

"Where's the definitive line between what's acceptable and what takes it too far?" asked Marla Moore, who had designed that cover. "In this particular case, the article about 'Jahar' is insightful, informative, and a relevant piece of journalism, helping to lend background information on how a young, seemingly sweet and good-natured student could become a monster. Something that all concerned over the Boston bombings should read."

The article, written by contributing editor Janet Reitman and titled "Jahar's World," is a well-crafted piece that takes the reader into Jahar's family and how they began as assisted immigrants, father, mother, two sons, and two daughters, living in a small apartment at 410 Norfolk Street in Cambridge.

Early on, it seems the brothers, especially Jahar, had found a real home.

Reitman wrote at the end of her article how different the family unit had become. "It's hard to understand how there could be such disassociation in that child," said Larry Aaronson, a former teacher at Cambridge Rindge high school, who had taken pictures of Dzhokhar wrestling. He was stunned when he learned about what had really been going on. "They supposedly had an arsenal in that fucking house! In the house! I mean, he could have blown up my whole block, for God's sakes."

According to the indictment, the brothers went to a firing range on March 20, 2013 where Jahar rented two 9-mm handguns, purchased two hundred rounds of ammunition, and engaged in target practice with Tamerlan. On April 5, Tamerlan went online to order electronic components that could be used in making Improvised Explosive Devices (IEDs). Jahar's friends would later tell the FBI that he had once mentioned that he knew how to build bombs. But no one seemed to really take his claims all that seriously.

"People come into your life to help you, hurt you, love you and leave you and that shapes your character and the person you were meant to be," Jahar tweeted on March 18.

Two days later: "Evil triumphs when good men do nothing."

April 7: "If you have the knowledge and the inspiration all that's left is to take action."

April 11: "Most of you are conditioned by the media."

Four days later, the bombs went off.

Dr. Puckett indicated a post on Tamerlan Tsarnaev's Facebook page: "I do not have a single American friend."

He didn't say that in triumph, Dr. Puckett pointed out. "No, he said it in the ongoing consternation he was feeling. The extremist ideology gave him something he wasn't getting any other place. What you see are repeated attempts at connection. McVeigh repeatedly tried. He was known as a weirdo, as was Breivik."

"A DANGEROUS EXAMPLE"

Shortly after the Boston Marathon bombings, former White House counterterrorism adviser Richard Clarke gave a warning, in which he pointed out how the most dangerous impact of the Boston bombings could be repeated by radical copycats. "Now that people have seen what two men can do with easily obtainable materials—close down a city, get the President of the United States to show up," Clarke said on ABC's *This Week* with George Stephanopoulos, "other people around the country who have been radicalized have watched this, and they're going to wonder, is there a way now that I can do this?"

Clarke said the events in Boston provided a dangerous example for "self-radicalized" extremists, who may have previously thought carrying out such an act was too difficult to attempt alone.

We are now dealing with a different type of copycat than ever before. Clarke and other advisers on radical racism point to some facts that changed the dynamics in the Tsarnaev family before the brothers changed drastically from being fairly well assimilated with their American peers. Their father, a former bookstore owner, had become disenchanted with his auto-mechanic job. Blaming customer prejudice and the bad economy in the United States, he left for his home country to stockpile some money. Their mother lost her job as a hairdresser and was arrested for shoplifting. The two sisters had entered into disastrous arranged marriages. Tamerlan had married an American woman, had a child, but he was starting to fall apart. His dream of becoming a U.S. Olympic boxing champion would never be realized due to a new Olympic committee rule stating that he must be an American citizen to compete. He became immersed in the Koran and tried to get his mother, sisters, and brother to join him in praying at the local mosque.

Then the family's government funding ran out. No more cash vouchers, and no more food stamps. The mother left to join her husband across the Atlantic. Dzhokhar had used up his $2,500 college scholarship and was selling marijuana on campus to make ends meet. His close friends began to wonder what had happened to their "cool" buddy. Many remarked to investigators later how much he had latched on to his brother, the "intense" one. The metamorphosis was then complete. Left alone to serve his older brother, he set out to blow up as much of his world as possible. The question now remains, how many more Jahars are out there?

Poverty is a strong motivator, and so is feeling powerless. Indeed, that helpless feeling of having no way out, no way to change one's circumstances, is a major ingredient in the lethal cocktail that can lead to the creation of a mass murderer or a lone wolf killer. That is why Anders Breivik is such a perfect example. Being raised in Norway, land of the Law of Jante, he was taught from an early age that he didn't matter. Yet, unlike other Norwegian children who accepted their fate, or fewer children who left it and their country of birth behind, Breivik raged in silence, unable to find an outlet or anyone he felt would listen. So he turned to an extremist ideology. And then he struck.

How many more, in how many other countries, will follow his path or a similar path? And how can we detect them before they do?

CHAPTER FIFTEEN

GUN LEGISLATION:
AN INADEQUATE PREVENTIVE

*You can't really allow yourself to be stopped by any of them as it will
lead to your collective death. You will do anything to put out that
fire despite of [sic] the fact that they are trying to stop you. Anything
else would be illogical.*

—ANDERS BREIVIK MANIFESTO

The murders of July 22, 2011 would not have been prevented with stricter
gun legislation. The heavily emotional and financed gun-control debate
distracts focus from the real issues. When many people are murdered and
injured in one day by one perpetrator, citizens naturally seek something to
blame, and the weapon is the first suspect. Yet there is no logical connection
between removing access to guns and removing the problem.

These tragedies sadly cannot be prevented that easily. The lone wolf will find any way to unleash his wrath; with new technology, the possibilities for disaster are endless.

Both sides of the debate, however, share one goal. They want to save lives. They can accomplish that only when they understand the killers and look at the true elements contributing to their crimes. Gun legislation would not have stopped the Boston bombers. Nor will it stop the next McVeigh, regardless of where he lives. More than a problem of laws and control, it is a problem of visibility, a question of paying attention to that odd young man who can't seem to fit in anywhere. While there are many issues pertaining to gun control in the United States that could doubtless be improved upon, it will not specifically prevent men like McVeigh or Breivik from attacking.

Norway has one of the toughest firearm laws in the world. Traditionally a country of farmers and hunters, it allows shotguns and rifles to be purchased with a license. Storage and transportation of guns are strictly regulated, and no one—even police officers, unless they're on a specific mission—is allowed to carry handguns, concealed or not. Some types of guns, such as automatic weapons and big handguns, are outlawed. Norway, along with most European countries, is the ideal society that many in the United States and elsewhere long for.

This did not prevent Breivik from legally obtaining the weapons for his attack in 2011. With his hunting license and by his membership in a pistol club, he easily got the necessary approval. The new type of mass murderer does not have a criminal record. He is intelligent and appears as normal as everybody else, and even small warning signs slip by until it is too late. He can speak for himself and even appears sympathetic and trustworthy. He is meticulous and takes his time to plan.

This type of killer is not restricted to one type of weapon. Breivik managed to produce a powerful car bomb similar to McVeigh's that could have killed hundreds more had he been able to park where he had planned to, or if he had exploded it earlier that day when more people were at work. With his farm as cover, he ordered huge amounts of fertilizer and chemicals used in agriculture or, in his case, to produce a bomb.

The Columbine killers had planned to bomb the school and take out more than five hundred people. The Columbine High School massacre is still the deadliest mass murder committed on an American high school campus, and it is noted as one of the first and most serious of a series of high school shootings. Both Eric Harris and Dylan Klebold wanted to commit suicide and top McVeigh's bombing in Oklahoma. Had their bombs not failed, they would have succeeded. Their attack with guns was Plan B.

When something as tragic as the shootings in December 2012 at Sandy Hook Elementary School occurs, it is easy to blame the weapon that caused so many deaths, especially as Adam Lanza had stolen his mother's weapons. Most Europeans believe that American culture and attachment to guns are part of the problem. If Lanza hadn't had access to guns, some people reason, the lives of the twenty children between the ages of six and seven would have been spared. This argument is only partly correct. Lanza's psychology was so warped, he would likely have turned to a bomb, like Breivik did, someone Lanza admired.

Study these different killers, and patterns begin to emerge, regardless of culture or country. Mass shootings in Europe usually have many more victims than in the United States. In countries such as Norway with strict gun control, killers like Breivik still easily obtained guns legally. Because the targets were unprotected and vulnerable, and because none of the bystanders carried guns, the ramifications of the massacre were much greater. Anders Breivik would not have been allowed to walk around, in a calm and systematic manner, and shoot sixty-nine young adults on the island for approximately ninety minutes if someone on that island other than the killer had had a gun. In the United States, a mass shooter is usually shot down or apprehended after a few seconds or minutes. In Europe, the killer has more time to accomplish his mission before he is stopped.

Criminals with guns, even mass murderers, are deterred from killing if a policeman or a bystander also brandishes a gun. If they are insane (or suicidal) enough not to be deterred, they are shot down quickly.

Killers act rationally: they will go for the easy targets, those who cannot defend themselves. As soon as they are confronted by armed law enforcement or armed citizens, they usually try to escape, surrender, or commit suicide.

Most gun owners are law-abiding citizens, and statistics prove that their guns will rarely be used to harm anyone. Allowing them to carry concealed guns has a deterring effect on criminals. Some believe it actually reduces crime, and that they and not the killers will be the ones affected by gun control. This may be true, but when it comes to mental illness, the legislation could be improved to prevent disturbed citizens from buying weapons.

However, mass murderers such as the lone wolves are not typical criminals. They are the exception to the rule. They do not have previous criminal records, nor do they have significant documented mental issues that would prevent them from legally obtaining guns.

The legislation debate has escalated, along with outrageous tactics on both sides. President Obama had the families of the Sandy Hook victims flown in the Presidential Air Force One jet to Washington as a strategy to help push the gun bill on background checks. In April 2013, a 225-page report on school safety funded by the National Rifle Association recommended properly trained armed employees to provide "an important layer of security in schools." The task force recommended that schools designate willing staff to be armed and trained, and it proposed a model training program of forty to sixty hours per person. The American Federation of Teachers called the report "a cruel hoax."

Whether to arm schoolteachers is not a debate for this book. However, compelling research supports the theory that stricter gun laws, which disarm law-abiding citizens only, will not prevent mass killings, or even reduce crime.

In a 2001 study of homicide rates across forty-four countries, Jeffrey Miron of Harvard University found that the differences in violence rates cannot—as previous analysis might have concluded—be attributed to the differences in gun control or availability.

Miron takes diverse factors into consideration that have not previously been accounted for in cross-country comparisons, and he uses data for a large set of countries rather than subjectively selecting a half-dozen or a dozen as is normally done. According to his findings, each year there is roughly one homicide per 100,000 people in England or Japan, countries with relatively strict gun legislation, but nine per 100,000 in the United States. Several countries, including Israel, Switzerland, and New Zealand, have relatively lax gun-control laws and high firearms availability, just like the United States, yet have homicide rates that differ little from those in England or Japan. The difference in the rates of violence might then be attributed to differences in culture, as well as economic and social factors. Miron's paper also suggests that differences in the enforcement of drug prohibition can explain the different violent rates across countries, and that the elevated rate of violence in the United States compared with Europe is perhaps due to greater drug prohibition enforcement.

Others agree with Miron that stricter gun legislation does not reduce violence. Joyce Lee Malcolm, professor of law at George Mason University Law School, in an op-ed in the *Wall Street Journal* in December 26, 2012, wrote that "Great Britain and Australia, for example, suffered mass shootings in the 1980s and 1990s. Both countries had very stringent gun laws when they occurred. Nevertheless, both decided that even stricter control of guns was the answer."

The homicide rates, however, did not go down in either country. Malcolm claims the results have not been what advocates of the stricter legislation wanted. "Within a decade of the handgun ban and the confiscation of handguns from registered owners, crime with handguns had doubled according to British government crime reports. Gun crime, not a serious problem in the past, now is." Neither has the new gun legislation had a favorable impact on mass murder, she states. In June 2010, Derrick Bird, a taxi driver in Cumbria, shot his brother and a colleague, and then drove off through rural villages, killing twelve people and injuring eleven more before killing himself.

After the Dunblane massacre in Australia in 1996, where thirty-five people were killed, the Australian government banned most guns and made it a crime to use a gun defensively. According to the Australian Bureau of Statistics, in the next four years, armed robbery increased by 51 percent, unarmed robbery by 37 percent, assaults by 24 percent, and kidnappings by 43 percent. Murder fell by 3 percent, but manslaughter rose by 16 percent. In Sydney, handgun crime rose by 44 percent from 1995 to 2001. "Strict gun laws in Great Britain and Australia haven't made their people noticeably safer, nor have they prevented massacres. The two major countries held up as models for the U.S. don't provide much evidence that strict gun laws will solve our problems," Malcolm concludes.

On April 13, 2013, the *Daily Mail* reported that crime had soared in Great Britain between the 1950s and today. Homicide rates are more constant, but violent crime has increased the most. At the same time, the number of legally owned handguns has decreased. Since 2006, violent crime has declined, but this might be due to the fact that more resources were injected into law enforcement and more criminals are in prison.

Great Britain and Australia are ideal places for gun control as they are surrounded by water, making gun smuggling relatively difficult. However, stricter gun laws did not deliver the promised reductions in crime.

In the United States, crime has decreased while the number of handguns has increased. Total violent crime from 1973 to 2009 in the United States decreased by 65 percent, or is only about a third as high, according to the Bureau of Justice Statistics, based on FBI data. The U.S. murder rate has fallen every year since 2006, and decreased 8.1 percent between 2008 and 2009.

Luxembourg, according to the Canadian Center for Justice Statistics, Homicide in Canada, Juristat—having banned handguns—has nine times the murder rate of Germany, where handguns are restricted but allowed.

Adam Lanza, along with most of these killers, chose a "soft" target, a place where they knew no one would be armed and able to stop them before they had finished what they came for. James Eagan Holmes, the Aurora shooter who killed twelve people in 2012, had a choice of seven movie theaters that were showing the Batman movie he was obsessed with. All were within a twenty-minute drive of his home. "The Cinemark Theater the killer ultimately chose wasn't the closest, but it was the only one that posted signs saying it banned concealed handguns carried by law-abiding individuals," John Fund wrote as online national-affairs columnist for *National Review*. "All of the other theaters allowed the approximately 4 percent of Colorado adults who have a concealed-handgun permit to enter with their weapons."

According to Don Kates and Gary Mauser, in the *Harvard Journal of Law & Public Policy*, "The political causation is that nations which have violence problems tend to adopt severe gun controls, but these do not reduce violence, which is determined by basic sociocultural and economic factors."

Kates and Mauser maintain that "International evidence and comparisons have long been offered as proof of the mantra that guns mean more deaths, and that fewer guns, therefore, mean fewer deaths. There is a compound assertion that (a) guns are uniquely available in the United States compared with other modern developed nations, which is why (b) the United States has by far the highest murder rate. Though these assertions have been endlessly repeated, statement (b) is, in fact, false and statement (a) is subsequently so." This is not to say that tougher gun legislation "*causes* nations to have much higher murder rates than neighboring nations that permit handgun ownership," Kates and Mauser emphasize. Instead, as they show on the table below, nations with stringent gun controls tend to have much higher murder rates than nations that allow guns.

NATION	HANDGUN POLICY	MURDER RATE	YEAR
A. Belarus	Banned	10.40	late 1990s
[Neighboring countries with gun law and murder rate data available]			
Poland	Allowed	01.98	2003
Russia	Banned	20.54	2002
B. Luxembourg	Banned	09.01	2002
[Neighboring countries with gun law and murder rate data available]			
Belgium	Allowed	01.70	late 1990s
France	Allowed	01.65	2003
Germany	Allowed	00.93	2003
C. Russia	Banned	20.54	2002
[Neighboring countries with gun law and murder rate data available]			
Belarus	Allowed	10.40	late 1990s
Finland	Allowed	01.98	2004
Norway	Allowed	00.81	2001

Murder Rates of European Nations that Ban Handguns as Compared to Their Neighbors that Allow Handguns (rates are per 100,000 persons)

The worst mass shootings in the last few years, besides Sandy Hook in 2012, have been outside of the United States in countries with strict gun legislation. In 1996, thirty-five victims were killed in Australia. In 2002, a school shooting in Germany left sixteen dead. In 2008, a mass murderer at a Finnish high school killed ten students. In 2010, a shooter in the United Kingdom left twelve dead. And in 2011, Breivik killed seventy-seven people in Norway. In these and other cases of mass murder worldwide, the massacre might not have been prevented with stricter gun legislation, certainly not a lone wolf killer like Breivik. Nevertheless, this doesn't mean that regulation of guns is not necessary, particularly with regard to mentally disturbed citizens.

TOMOSHIRO KATO: MASS STABBING IN AKHIABARA, JAPAN

On Sunday, June 8, 2008, at a commercial area of Akhiabara, in the district of Chiyoda, Tokyo, Tomoshiro Kato, aged twenty-five, drives a truck at full speed into the crowd and stops. He gets out of the truck armed with a knife and begins stabbing the people around him. Only two minutes later, the police apprehend him, but not before he kills seven people and injures twelve more.

Born and raised in the wealthy area of Aomori, Kato was extremely intelligent. His severe parents demanded that he must be the best and inflicted humiliating punishments when he was anything less. Isolated, he suffered from not having a girlfriend and not fitting in. Kato saw himself as a failure, and when his employment contract came to an end, he unraveled.

Right before his mayhem, he wrote on a website: "I will kill people in Akhiabara. . . . If only I had a girlfriend, I wouldn't have quit work . . . I wouldn't have become addicted to my cell phone. Anybody with hope couldn't possibly understand how I feel . . . I don't have a single friend and won't have in the future. I'll be ignored because I'm ugly. I'm lower than trash because at least trash gets recycled."

Although he also suffered from isolation, Kato was no lone wolf killer like Breivik. Kato is an example of a depressed rampage mass murderer who didn't use a handgun, but a truck and a knife. He was only stopped when the police arrived, pointing a gun at him, at which point he surrendered. In 2011 he was sentenced to death.

This example shows us that the defensive use of a gun is—in many cases—the only way to stop a killer.

JARED LEE LOUGHNER: DEMOCRATIC PARTY MEETING MASSACRE, TUCSON, ARIZONA

On January 8, 2011, at 10:10 A.M., Jared Lee Loughner, age twenty-two, opens fire on a crowd at a Safeway supermarket location in Casas Adobes, Tucson, where U.S. Representative Gabrielle Giffords is holding a constituents' meeting. Giffords, along with numerous bystanders, is shot from close range. Six people die, and fourteen are injured by gunfire. Giffords, the apparent target of the attack, is shot in the head, critically injured, and barely survives.

Earlier that morning, Loughner went to a Walmart store in the Foothills Mall to purchase ammunition, but he left that store and completed his purchase at a Walmart on North Cortaro Road at 7:28 A.M. He was stopped by Arizona Fish and Game Department officer Alen Edward Forney at 7:34 A.M. for running a red light, but once the officer determined that there were no outstanding warrants for Loughner, he was allowed to proceed to his destination with a warning to drive carefully.

Loughner is a rare case where the mass murderer was tackled by bystanders not using guns to stop him. It was a heroic group effort, while the shooter was trying to reload his gun. Although it was successful in this case, several people were injured in the process.

In the minutes after the shooting, while many of the victims were still being treated, Jared Lee Loughner calmly told the police "I just want you to know that I'm the only person that knew about this." He refused to answer questions and pled "the Fifth." In searching Loughner, officers found he was wearing earplugs and carrying two loaded ammunition magazines in his left front pocket. Arrested on site, he was later sentenced to life in prison without parole.

CBS News, on March 27, 2013, reported details from more than 2,700 pages of released police files, which include pictures of Loughner's weapon, a 9-mm Glock, witness statements, and transcripts of 911 calls.

His mother, Amy Loughner, said he no longer used alcohol and had tested negative for drugs. "My concern was like, meth or something . . . because his behavior and his, was, um, odd," she said in one of the interviews.

Randy Loughner, his father, said he was so concerned, he took away Jared's shotgun and often disabled his son's car at night to prevent him from leaving the house. Just hours before the shooting, Randy Loughner said he had tried to confront his son. "He came in and I wanted to talk to him. And he took off," he said. He was carrying a backpack.

One of the most chilling pieces of evidence is a voicemail, first played by *60 Minutes* in January 2011. At 2 A.M., eight hours before the shooting, Loughner left this message for a friend he had not spoken to in nearly a year: "Hey. Hey, it's Jared. I just want to tell you good times. Peace out. Later." He also left several rants against the government on MySpace.

The papers also revealed that Loughner did not seek mental-health treatment. When he was expelled from college, his parents were urged to have him evaluated, but they never followed up. Perhaps when he bought his gun, Loughner had no record of mental illness; however, his parents could have removed the shotgun permanently and gotten help for their son.

Loughner is no lone wolf like Breivik, but a rampage killer. He had no ideology other than his own misery due to mental illness. After the shooting, he was diagnosed with schizophrenia and underwent forcible psychotropic drug treatments. He was sentenced to life in prison in November 2012.

JAMES EAGAN HOLMES: MOVIE THEATER SHOOTING, AURORA, COLORADO

James Holmes is twenty-four on July 20, 2012, the day of the massacre. Depressed, he wants to go down with a "bang" and take as many people with him as possible. He decides to attack—during a late-night show of *Batman*—a cinema that has a "no-arms" policy, to make sure no one will prevent him from completing his massacre. The gunman throws two canisters emitting gas or smoke, partially obscuring the audience members' vision, making their throats and skin itch, and causing eye irritation. He then fires a 12-gauge Remington 870 Express Tactical shotgun, first at the ceiling and then at the audience. He also fires a Smith & Wesson M&P15 semiautomatic rifle with a 100-round drum magazine, which malfunctions after reportedly firing about 30 rounds. He finishes the job with a Glock 22 40-caliber handgun.

Born on December 13, 1987, in San Diego, Holmes was raised in Castroville and San Diego, California, with his sister. His mother is a registered nurse and his father a mathematician and scientist with degrees from Stanford, UCLA, and Berkeley. A seemingly normal child, Holmes played soccer and ran cross-country in high school, and attended a local Lutheran church with his family. Graduating from Westview High School in San Diego in 2006, Holmes attended the University of California, Riverside (UCR) and, in 2010, received his undergraduate degree in neuroscience with the highest honors.

Intelligent, he was a member of several honor societies, including Phi Beta Kappa and Golden Key. According to a UCR recommendation letter submitted to the University of Illinois at Urbana-Champaign (UIUC), Holmes graduated in the top one percentile of his class with a 3.949 GPA. The UCR letter also described Holmes as "a very effective group leader" and a person who "takes an active role in his education, and brings a great amount of intellectual and emotional maturity into the classroom."

In 2008, Holmes worked as a counselor at a residential summer camp in Glendale, California, that catered to disadvantaged children aged seven to fourteen. There he was responsible for ten children and had no disciplinary problems. In June 2011, Holmes enrolled as a Ph.D. student in neuroscience at the University of Colorado Anschutz Medical Campus in Aurora. He received a $21,600 grant from the National Institute of Health, according to agency records, which was disbursed in installments from July 2011 to June 2012. Holmes also received a $5,000 stipend from the University of Colorado, Denver.

In 2012, his academic performance declined, and he scored poorly on his exams in the spring. Although the university didn't plan to expel him, Holmes was in the process of withdrawing from the university. Three days after failing a key oral exam at the university in early June 2012, Holmes dropped out of his studies without further explanation. At the time of his arrest, he gave his occupation as "laborer."

He killed twelve people and injured fifty-eight, and the police arrived after only ninety seconds. Chances are that he could have been stopped by a civilian carrying a concealed handgun, which certainly would have limited the number of victims. When the police arrived, Holmes had already left the building. He was apprehended without any resistance in the parking lot. Two weeks prior to the shooting, Holmes sent a text message asking a graduate student if they had heard of the disorder dysphoric mania, and warning the student to stay away from him "because I am bad news."

All the weapons Holmes used in the massacre were bought legally in May and June 2012, and background checks were performed. With no criminal record, Holmes had no trouble buying 3,000 rounds of ammunition for the pistols, 3,000 rounds for the M&P15, and 350 shells for the shotgun over the Internet. On July 2, he placed an order for a Blackhawk Urban Assault Vest, two magazine holders, and a knife at an online retailer. Also in this case, a required mental checkup might have prevented the rampage.

On June 25, less than a month before the shooting, Holmes e-mailed an application to join a gun club in Byers, Colorado. The owner, Glenn Rotkovich, called him several times throughout the following days to invite him to a mandatory orientation, but could only reach his answering machine. Due to the nature of Holmes's voicemail, which he described as "bizarre, freaky . . . guttural, spoken with a deep voice, incoherent and rambling," Rotkovich instructed his staff to inform him if Holmes showed up, though Holmes never appeared at the gun range, nor did he call again.

"In hindsight, looking back—and if I'd seen the movies—maybe I'd say it was like the Joker—I would have gotten the Joker out of it. . . . It was like somebody was trying to be as weird as possible," Rotkovich said. Holmes was a big fan of superheroes, including Batman, and his apartment was decorated with Batman paraphernalia.

Because of disputes over Holmes's mental state, the trial was postponed until January 2015. In May 2015, two court-appointed psychiatrists deemed Holmes mentally ill but legally sane. Both experts diagnosed him with schizotypal personality disorder. On June 9, three of the jurors were dismissed for leaking reports to the press and the trial came to a standstill. Holmes's childhood and teen years differ from Breivik's in that he seemed to function well. His problems and mental issues began later. A depressed and mentally ill rampage killer, Holmes had more in common with Loughner and Lanza than with Breivik.

ADAM LANZA: SANDY HOOK ELEMENTARY SCHOOL SHOOTING

On the day of the Sandy Hook massacre, Adam Lanza, dressed in black clothing and olive green utility vest, wearing earplugs, and carrying ammunition for his rifle, heads out to his old elementary school. Lanza shoots his way through a glass door and enters the school at 9:35 A.M. He stops shooting between 9:46 and 9:49 A.M. after firing 154 rounds with his mother's Bushmaster XM15-E2S rifle. The shooting lasts less than fifteen minutes.

Born on April 22, 1992, Lanza lived with his mother in Sandy Hook, Newtown, five miles from the elementary school he himself had attended as a child and where the massacre took place on December 14, 2012. He did not have a criminal record; however, he did have mental issues and was described by his father as a "weird" child. Students and teachers who knew him in high school described Lanza as "intelligent, but nervous and fidgety." He avoided attracting attention and was uncomfortable socializing, and therefore had no close friends in school.

According to an article by Andrew Solomon in the *New Yorker* on March 17, 2014, Lanza was diagnosed with sensory-integration disorder as a child, and also underwent speech therapy and occupational therapy in kindergarten and first grade. Teachers were told to watch for seizures. Later, Lanza would be diagnosed with Asperger's syndrome, a form of autism. In 2001, his parents separated, and Lanza was left in the care of his mother.

According to his father, Lanza was a fan of Ron Paul and liked to argue economic theory. He became fascinated with guns and with World War II, and showed an interest in joining the military. But he never talked about mass murder, his father said, and he wasn't violent at school. He seldom revealed his emotions, but had a sharp sense of humor.

When Lanza started middle school, his parents' worry increased. "It was crystal clear something was wrong," his father told Solomon. "The social awkwardness, the uncomfortable anxiety, unable to sleep, stress, unable to concentrate, having a hard time learning, the awkward walk, reduced eye contact. You could see the changes occurring."

Although Breivik didn't have the mental issues Lanza had, there are still similarities. Michael Stone, a psychiatrist who studies mass murder, said that, as children grow up and tasks become more difficult, what seems like a minor impairment becomes major. "They're a little weird in school. They don't have friends. They do not get picked for the baseball team," he said. "But, as they get to the age when kids begin to date and find partners, they can't. So the sense of deficit, which was minor in grade school, and getting to be a little bit more in junior high, now becomes very acute." He added that, without the brain getting worse, "life challenges nudge them in the direction of being sicker."

After realizing he had been spotted by a pair of police officers who had entered the building, Lanza fled from their sight, then shot himself in the head with a Glock 10-mm handgun. He died immediately. In addition to these guns, the police found a 9-mm SIG Sauer P226 handgun, and an Izhmash Saiga-12 combat shotgun in Lanza's car outside the school.

He was fascinated by Breivik and other mass murderers, according to the police investigations. His mother, Nancy Lanza, was described by her sister-in-law as a "gun enthusiast who owned at least a dozen firearms." She often took her two sons to a local shooting range and taught them how to shoot.

Lanza's super-suicide took the war on guns to a new level. The most devastating massacre yet, involving twenty children, it could have been stopped sooner had there been an armed security officer inside the school building or his mother had been more responsible with her weapons, given that she had a documented mentally ill child at home.

SEUNG-HUI CHO: THE VIRGINIA TECH MASSACRE

On March 22, 2007, Seung-Hui Cho purchases two 10-round magazines for the Walther P22 pistol through eBay from Elk Ridge Shooting Supplies in Idaho. Based on a preliminary computer forensics examination of Cho's eBay purchase records, investigators suspected that Cho may have purchased an additional 10-round magazine on March 23, 2007 from another eBay seller of gun accessories. Cho also buys jacketed hollow-point bullets—the same type Breivik used—which result in more tissue damage than full metal jacket bullets against unarmored targets by expanding upon entering soft tissue.

Thirty-two people died on that day, and seventeen were injured.

Born on January 18, 1984, Seung-Hui Cho was twenty-three years old when he went out on his rampage mission on April 16, 2007. His family had immigrated to the United States in September 1992 from South Korea. Cho was eight years old at the time. The family first lived in Detroit, then moved to the Washington metropolitan area, which had one of the largest Korean communities in the country. Cho's parents opened a dry-cleaning business in Centreville and became members of a local Christian church. Later, Cho railed against his parents' strong Christian faith, and in a note he left in his dormitory he raged against Christianity and "rich kids." "Thanks to you," he wrote, "I died like Jesus Christ, to inspire generations of the weak and defenseless people."

Unlike Breivik, Cho had a history of mental issues. Some members of his family, who remained in South Korea, had concerns about his behavior during his early childhood. According to Cho's uncle, Cho "didn't say much and did not mix with other children." Cho's maternal great-aunt, Kim Yang-Soon, described Cho as "cold" and a cause of family concern from as young as eight years old. He was otherwise considered "well-behaved," readily obeying verbal commands and cues.

Influenced by the Columbine massacre, Seung-Hui Cho wanted to commit a super-suicide. There are obvious signs of attachment issues, blaming others for his misery, and wanting to leave a message of justification.

During February and March 2007, Cho began purchasing the weapons he later used during the killings. His first handgun, a .22-caliber Walther P22 semiautomatic pistol, he bought online from TGSCOM Inc., a federally licensed firearms dealer based in Green Bay, Wisconsin. TGSCOM shipped the Walther P22 to JND Pawnbrokers in Blacksburg, Virginia, where Cho completed the legally required background check for the purchase transaction and took possession of the handgun. Cho bought a second handgun, a 9-mm Glock semiautomatic pistol, on March 13, 2007 from Roanoke Firearms, a licensed gun dealer located in Roanoke, Virginia.

Cho was able to pass both background checks and successfully complete both handgun purchases after he presented to the gun dealers his U.S. permanent residency card, his Virginia driver's license to prove legal age and length of Virginia residence, and a checkbook showing his Virginia address, in addition to waiting the required thirty-day period between each gun purchase. He did not disclose on the background questionnaire that a Virginia court had ordered him to undergo outpatient treatment at a mental-health facility, as there was no requirement to do so.

The package Cho sent the day of the killings included a photograph of the hollow-point bullets with the caption "All the [shit] you've given me, right back at you with hollow points." During the investigation, the police found a note in Cho's room in which he criticized "rich kids," "debauchery," and "deceitful charlatans." In the note, Cho continued by saying that "you caused me to do this." In one video, he mentioned "martyrs like Eric and Dylan," referring to Eric Harris and Dylan Klebold, the perpetrators of the Columbine High School massacre. Cho committed suicide after law-enforcement officers breached the doors of the building where the majority of the shooting had taken place.

The Virginia Tech Massacre is one case of mass murder where gun legislation might have made a difference. Indeed, after the killings, Virginia modified the current legislation so that one's background information, including mental health history, must be revealed before purchasing a gun. Granted, had Cho not been able to get guns legally, he might have built a bomb or bought the guns on the black market. But stricter gun legislation would have made this sick person's task harder, and might also have raised a red flag for law enforcement to follow up on. However, Cho was not a lone wolf like Breivik and McVeigh. He left a paper trail, and following that trail might have stopped him.

All these cases point out a simple fact: gun legislation is not going to stop the next Breivik or McVeigh, because it can never prevent killers who don't leave a paper trail, not even in countries where gun legislation is extremely strict and citizens believe they are safe. Until we find other solutions, the lone wolf will continue to evade detection.

CHAPTER SIXTEEN

NEW METHODS, NEW HOPE

Still, such apathy is the root cause of both U.S. and especially, Western Europe's problems.

—ANDERS BREIVIK MANIFESTO

There will be more Anders Breiviks. Unless law enforcement focuses on psychology more than criminal history, men like Breivik will escape detection until it is too late. Identifying these killers before they strike requires investigating their personalities and watching for subtle warning signs, like when Breivik was flagged for stockpiling fertilizer, instead of their police records, because their police records won't exist until after they have struck.

Somebody like Dr. Puckett might have been able to evaluate Kaczynski's mental state based on his narcissistic behavior, his high intelligence, and his inability to connect on any level with others. She might have noticed McVeigh's constant attempts to participate in militant extremist groups, or his sacrificing a promising career as the perfect soldier because of foot blisters, or his paranoia regarding the U.S. government. Breivik's constant attempts to join right-wing political groups and his subsequent rebuffs would also have come under scrutiny. These men had no criminal records to lead the authorities to them in a traditional manner. They did, however, share the characteristics that define the lone wolf. A trained professional with sources in fringe groups might have better luck than law-enforcement personnel with no trail to follow.

No one bothered to investigate Breivik's stockpiling of bomb-making materials. Nobody reported his retreat to the isolated, violent world of the kind of computer games he chose. No one paid attention to his ranting and failed attempts to participate in extreme political groups. The only way Breivik could get anyone to acknowledge his existence was to murder his government symbolically that day in Oslo and on the island of Utøya.

The way Kaczynski murdered his government. The way McVeigh murdered his. All of them were so detached that they saw only one way to get the recognition on which they believed their very survival depended. Yet nobody felt they mattered enough to be dangerous.

NORWAY: A COUNTRY IN DENIAL

Who do you think you are? What makes you think you matter? Breivik received the message time after time, by way of the Law of Jante. The individual in Norway is suppressed and repressed. In a way, Norwegian society has become the ultimate bully, and the individual the victim. You should not raise questions about the group's rules or disagree with the majority in any serious way.

Most people, regardless of their country of origin, don't ask questions about their society. They take it at face value and accept it as is. They may not be particularly happy, but at least they're not a threat to others. Luckily, most do not have the psychological makeup of a lone wolf, and they learn early on how to adjust to a group and to fit in, more or less, and find their own ways of expressing themselves and making meaningful connections. As children, we are told that we must go out and be like the other children on the playground. We learn and adapt to the social rules in order to belong and be accepted. In Norway, this means not standing out or asking critical questions.

That is why, in Norway, no one has even questioned if there is anything in society that may have helped form Breivik. Instead, the discussions have focused on mental issues and right-wing opponents of the government.

Neither of these is the real issue. First, because, if Dr. Puckett is correct, Breivik isn't psychotic; and second, because Breivik would have taken upon himself almost any cause or ideology. Multiculturalism was simply the most obvious one.

In the meantime, Breivik is manipulating the public from within his prison cell and will probably attain his goals and continue working for his cause while being behind bars. As of September 2015, he was admitted to the University of Oslo to study political science from his prison cell.

Only Breivik is responsible for his actions, but he was not a born killer. Neither were Kaczynski, McVeigh, nor Rudolph. All of them had been bullied and isolated. Because they were highly sensitive children, and because they couldn't achieve the seemingly simple act of human connection, the damages caused by their surroundings were beyond repair.

No matter how gruesome Breivik's acts were, he raised some important points about Norwegian society. Dr. Puckett believes the court's final sanity ruling is correct. Narcissistic and egotistical? Yes. Attachment issues from childhood? Definitely. And like other lone wolf killers, such as Kaczynski and McVeigh, Breivik is highly intelligent and calculating.

One may not agree with his politics. Disagreeing with one's government does not make one a bad person. Instead of debating the political and sociological issues raised by Breivik, Norwegians blame the extreme right-wing blogs and groups for giving Breivik the idea to kill. They quote Fjordman's essays as examples. Simen Sætre, a Norwegian journalist, even wrote *Fjordman: Portrait of an Anti-Islamist*, a book that attempts to discredit and ostracize Fjordman.

Many are concerned that the Internet is being used for communities with extreme right-wing views, and that bloggers such as Fjordman, who are hiding their identities, are allowed to flourish. Had they not been cast away in their home environments, they might not have needed their pseudo identities. Norway and its Law of Jante have taught its citizens to hide their true feelings, opinions, and identities in order to blend in. If we really wish to deal with the new growing extremism, we must start by daring to be ourselves and tolerating different opinions. It is not by simply accepting what we are told about other cultures. As discussed in chapters three and seven, the anger stems from having to accept newcomers when, as a native, one isn't truly accepted or allowed to be oneself.

Breivik would have taken on any cause or ideology and used it for his acts of violence. He needed to make a difference, to become visible, be recognized as a savior. Just as important, he needed to break free from the homogeneity of Jante culture and feel like he mattered. All he had to do was find a cause to fuel his rage against society, much as McVeigh's rage at his government for how he thought they were bullying him and other American citizens fueled his rampage.

The life of a lone wolf is not a life anyone would choose. It is one of the loneliest and most desperate of existences. The lone wolf suffers from not being able to make meaningful connections. Very few radicals, even in terrorist groups, actually turn to violence, and even fewer to murder. That is because extremist groups are also social groups. No matter how strongly one may believe in the group's ideology, most people join purely for social reasons.

"Their social needs are met, and they feel they have a place in the world that defines them as part of something important, something that *matters*," Dr. Puckett wrote. "For most of them, just being part of the group is enough. Although they may posture and spout extremist rhetoric, and they may cheer loudly when others commit violent acts in service of the cause, most are happy to let someone else do the dangerous and bloody work of terrorism."

They are, however, frequently paranoid, which leads them to suspect that unconnected events may well be plots. They then seek out extremist groups that share their paranoia. But the lone wolf is unable to connect to a group, at least not for long. All that is left for him is a direct connection with the ideology.

"The isolation he has felt all his life is replaced by a sense of strong belonging to the cause, the ideology itself, and he can focus all his energy and attention on action in its service," Dr. Puckett said. A warning flag for identifying a prospective lone wolf would be watching for a particular person who keeps trying to join various extremist groups but seems to keep bouncing around.

The rest of the world has the misconception of Norway as a nearly perfect society, but Norway has its own societal flaws. Bruce Bawer has referred to Breivik as the Inner Viking. "Not only because he managed to do so much harm, but because his very existence seemed to [illustrate] the lie [within] the myth of distinctive Norwegian goodness." Though Norway definitely projects an image of a perfect country, a culture of goodness, fairness, and solidarity for all, there is resentment lingering beneath the surface. *Norwegian exceptionalism*, as it has been called, suggests that there is something better, nobler, and wiser about the Norwegian people than those from other parts of the world. They award the Nobel Peace Prize, after all.

This has become the only acceptable way of standing out in Norway: not as an individual, but as a country, as a superior ethnic group. The individual has no value in Norwegian society. Yet the Norwegian people ironically celebrate their country as the ultimate humane society.

Because of Breivik's deluded "war on Islam," innocent people died. Yet it was neither Islam nor the Muslims that drove him to murder; it was his inability to openly protest and try to change, in a democratic way, what he saw as an inequitable system. His extreme need to matter and be recognized went unmet again and again. This resulted in a rage so strong that it finally culminated in violence on a societal level that the world witnessed on July 22, 2011. He had a ready-made enemy: his own government.

By its extensive global humanitarian work, and by claiming that it takes care of those who cannot take care of themselves, Norway has been viewed by many as Utopia. By trying to point out its humanitarian legal system through Breivik's travesty of a trial and much-too-lax punishment, the country took its exceptionalism too far. In contrast, the twelve jurors in the Boston Marathon bombing case condemned Dzhokhar "Jahar" Tsarnaev to death by lethal injection on May 15, 2015. Tsarnaev is expected to be executed at the U.S. Penitentiary Terre Haute, known by some as "Guantanamo North." In the meanwhile, he may be transferred to the ADX "Supermax" prison in Colorado, where McVeigh stayed before he was executed and where Kaczynski and Rudolph are serving their life sentences.

One cause behind facilitating a lone wolf like Breivik lies in the structure of modern Norwegian society and its culture. Bullying is indirectly tolerated and basic individual expression is suppressed, and concepts such as sacrificing "for the common good" have installed a hatred of the good, for the sake of *being* good. Altruism has branded the pursuit of self-interest as evil. Multiculturalism can lead to positive discrimination, which in turn can deny equal opportunity to those who are more qualified and/or more driven to succeed. The line between black and white, of good versus evil, has been blended into something less recognizable. Repressing and de-powering the individual make it easy for someone like Breivik to turn to extreme violence.

By branding Breivik's crime as a one-time event, and by living in denial, Norway is making itself even more vulnerable to other people with similar psychologies. If we are to believe Dr. Puckett, this type of killer is an increasing phenomenon and threat to all of us, just as Breivik himself may continue to be a threat to Norway and beyond.

Breivik's defense attorney, Geir Lippestad, published *What We Stand For* in April 2013, in an attempt to justify his choice of defending the indefensible Breivik. By taking on Breivik's defense, he became the devil's advocate in the view of many. His goal in writing a book was obvious: create a distance between himself and his client and make it clear that he does not share his client's political views.

In that book, Lippestad writes about the values of the Norwegian legal system and about "value-based communication," as he calls it. He says that "Instead of discussing cultural *differences* that separate us into different categories, as people such as Breivik, Fjordman, and other like-minded people know how to exploit," we should instead discuss our common basic values and what unites us. "We must not tolerate intolerance," he declares. By this logic, should we then not tolerate Fjordman and all those who do not agree with the majority's opinion?

The essential question in Lippestad's book is (literally translated): "How can we deal with the growth of extreme political weather, whether it comes from East or West, from religious extremists or egotistical individuals and fanatics?" Further, he wonders, how do we deal with the anger that surfaces because our societies are changing more radically and many cannot keep up and often turn to destructive outlets?

Telling survivors like Adrian Pracon not to write a book about his experiences on that Friday afternoon is not the answer. Neither is suppressing opposing political opinions by ignoring them, excluding people from society, or threatening their lives.

That is what happened to Christian Tybring-Gjedde, a Member of Parliament. In the aftermath of July 22, 2011, Tybring-Gjedde's skepticism and concerns about immigration were ridiculed. He suffered a breakdown, which caused him to miss work for several weeks. He received many death threats, was harassed, followed, condemned by other politicians, media, and even blamed for Breivik's massacre. He and his family had to move and get a secret address and phone number. For a period of time, he even escaped with his family to Denmark in search of a sense of peace that no doubt still escapes him.

Fjordman, and those of like minds, have every right to, and should, be taken seriously. Lippestad and his family, who were obliged to have police protection during the trial, should be the first to understand this. Someone even cut off the brakes from Lippestad's bicycle in an attempt to seriously injure him or worse. His children were also threatened. But Lippestad, in his attempt to appease and repair burned bridges in Norwegian society, doesn't want to discuss that tragic footnote to the case that has brought him more recognition than any other in his career.

MORE HYPOCRISY

Ironically, Breivik had to commit mass murder before he was finally taken seriously and treated as an individual. In his mind, he was not punished. He was rewarded by the trial, the media attention, and his sentence. It finally gave him the attention he craved.

His trial was a circus of confusion, suppressed anger and grief, and injustice for the victims. As previously discussed, his mental state had not been determined before the trial began, even though that is the custom in Norway. No one in attendance seemed to understand, or care, what kind of person Breivik was, not to mention the peculiar psychological makeup that led to his violent actions.

He had never before experienced having a voice, never felt the power of having influence. Maybe just as important, he had never experienced respect. In his inability to connect with others and have meaningful relationships, Breivik has never been closer to having such relationships than he is now. A lot of societies are flawed, and they act as facilitators for killers, but not all of them reward their killers as Norway rewarded Breivik. It is remarkable that Norwegian society gives more individual deference to this mass murderer than to the victims of his crime, as well as to its citizens in general.

Not only did Breivik come out as a winner from the trial, but Lippestad has also managed to turn his life around, in terms of his career and by the way the Norwegian population views him. Because of his book and the speeches he gives at conferences about his "value-based communication," he has gone from being the second most hated man in Norway to a national hero. Lippestad was awarded the "Name of the Year" prize by several newspapers, among them *Verdens Gang*, in 2012. The Press Photographers Association awarded him the "Good Boy" prize in early 2013, and he has received other honors as well.

Maybe what the press and the citizens really appreciated about Lippestad is that he pulled off something astonishing in Norway: namely, to use the Breivik case to his own advantage, while at the same time staying within the Law of Jante and insisting that he was only doing his job, that defending Breivik was strictly his part of a communal benevolent service.

Although many claim that the system can keep Breivik locked up for life, he will probably be released at a relatively young age. Most people tend to view perpetrators differently over time, and the political will to keep him in jail might be different twenty years from now. Furthermore, this forgiveness factor is the way the legal system in Norway is supposed to work. If Breivik is rehabilitated and no longer considered a danger to society, he must be set free after having served his sentence. With Breivik's intelligence and proven capability to manipulate the trial proceedings and expert psychiatrists, he will probably manage to convince the court one day that he regrets his crimes and has learned his lesson. In the meantime, he has the freedom—although somewhat limited—to communicate with kindred spirits all over the world. In 2014, he went on a hunger strike because prison authorities refused to provide him with the video games he requested. Life has never been this satisfying for Anders Breivik.

Pracon and AUF (the Labor Party's Youth League) were very clear that they didn't want to let Breivik win. They were never going to stop believing in their politics and in the democratic system in Norway. Yet Breivik won anyway, not in the sense of changing the government and its politics, although the Labor Party and the socialist coalition lost the most recent parliamentary election in 2013. Instead, he attained something close to what he had always longed for: to be heard, to connect to someone at some level, and to matter.

According to Dr. Puckett, law enforcement can't follow a paper trail to these killers, which makes it difficult to find them. "We must have local awareness by local law enforcement," she said. "They come from the same town, the same school, and the same PTA meetings as people of these extremist groups."

These killers can be spotted, but they can't be spotted in traditional ways because they aren't traditional killers.

CHAPTER SEVENTEEN

OUT OF HIDING

Cornered prey will often mount a final desperate attack.

—ANDERS BREIVIK MANIFESTO

We do not have to sit back and wait for the next Breivik, the next Kaczynski, or the next McVeigh. We need to track these lone wolves in a new way, a way that will reveal them before they are able to assassinate young people on an island or set off a bomb. We cannot do it with a tidy list of how-to bullet points either. According to Dr. Puckett, tracking these lone wolves is not a matter of profiling; it's a matter of analysis.

"Paper trails don't exist," she said, "but the behavior trail does exist. How do we see it? By citizen involvement. That is critical."

No one else but the neighbors and community members who observe this killer can identify him. Unlike the sociopath, the lone wolf is not stripped of empathetic feelings. Psychopaths exhibit few emotions; lone wolves have a lot of them. They over-care about themselves because no one in their lives wants to deal with them. They are all they have.

"McVeigh was a pretty normal kid in a pretty normal house," Dr. Puckett said. "When his parents divorced, his social world was crumbling. If someone had recognized that he was moving toward isolation more than connection, he might have been stopped."

The same is true of Anders Breivik at a much younger age. Child Protective Services in Norway was already aware that this child was not in a good environment. His mother herself alerted the institution that she couldn't handle him. CPS did actually step in to analyze the child's behavior, but the court decided against CPS's recommendation and let young Breivik stay with his mother. Had the court given custody to the father and his new wife, he might have been a different person. He wasn't a killer when he was four. He wasn't invisible. He was, as are all children that age, emotionally oriented to his parents and peers. Could there have been a different outcome? Perhaps.

CPS established early that Breivik had behavioral problems. He was withdrawn and lacked a sense of security and joy. In the sixth grade, he helped found a boy-only gang he named the Skøyen Killers. Although the group was not violent, Breivik wanted it to appear threatening. He already had an attraction to extremist groups with hateful ideologies. In junior high, young Breivik tried to be a part of the illegal taggers and hip-hop groups. In high school, he attempted to belong to a white-boys-only gang with a racial agenda. Then he dropped out of high school a couple of months before graduation and entered politics. The obvious lack of connection, the repeated attempts at meaningful relationships, combined with isolation, violent computer games, and anabolic steroids, must be looked at as a whole. In Breivik's case, it turned out to be a lethal cocktail. The signs were there, red flags from childhood. None of the signs alone was enough to trigger an alarm. But if one were to look at all of them as a whole, they point to the development of something much more sinister.

When Breivik moved back in with his mother and isolated himself completely from his friends and acquaintances, his transformation was probably complete. Was it too late to stop the massacre at this point? Possibly not. Friends and family noticed how he turned to extreme ideologies, and they could have warned local police. Law enforcement could and should have checked out and verified the appropriateness of someone without any experience in farming using his investment company to order chemicals suitable for bomb-making.

Stopping the development of such a killer before it starts—the earlier, the better—is difficult, and it involves the old balance between individual freedom and national security. To accuse someone of a crime they have not yet committed raises difficult moral questions.

"In the U.S. we teeter constantly between the two because liberty is so important," Dr. Puckett said. "In Norway, the norm is conformity, and that can provide a false sense of security, as was the case before the Breivik killings."

Norwegian culture, where the individual has no place or worth outside of the group, strongly influenced Breivik's need to matter. Dr. Puckett believes that a "social cripple"—as Kaczynski described himself, and as all the other lone wolves might also be described—"would be under even greater interpersonal stress" in a culture that values the group over the individual.

"In many other cultures," Puckett wrote, "to live outside the group is literally a matter of life and death psychologically as well as physically." Norway is such a country.

The Norwegians are so used to being cared for by the state and institutions that they no longer notice one another. The state has removed individual responsibility, and people don't think it's up to them to meddle in someone else's life in any way. The July 22 massacre has not changed their behavior.

In the United States and most countries, matters must escalate to a breaking point before they are addressed. A withdrawn child can mean a lot of things. But if a rare and particularly withdrawn child is a Breivik in the making, those closest to him may see him trying and failing to be part of a group. They may notice that he doesn't feel normal in the usual social setting. Ultimately, his alienation will become the engine for his development. He will fail to even navigate and make connections within a fringe group. Yet he will never stop trying to connect with something. He must be stopped before that connection proves deadly.

Breivik's killings were an astonishing experience for Norwegians because they had no idea anything like that could happen in their country. That's not so different from what happened in Connecticut with Adam Lanza, Boston bombers Tamerlan and Dzhokhar Tsarnaev, or Elliot Rodger in Santa Barbara. Many times we hear "I never would have guessed that kid could have done this." It is the tragic echo of our times. These people are rejected by society because they are odd, but they do not behave in a menacing way or cause those around them to worry or do anything but dismiss them until it is too late.

At this time, analyzing behavior and activities is proving successful in both identifying the lone wolf and others with a paper trail before they strike. Even though Adam Lanza had not broken the law, there were tremendous indicators of danger because of his total alienation from others. Lanza had a long history of mental issues and was obsessed with guns. He spent considerable time on violent computer games and studying the Columbine killers and Breivik. Obsessive studying of past mass murders should be another red flag. All of the killers have studied and taken inspiration from others before them, whether it was Breivik studying McVeigh or Seung-Hui Cho of the Virginia Tech massacre studying the Columbine killers. If anyone had noticed, the outcome might have been different. In Elliot Rodger's case, his mother actually did notify the police, but the local authorities didn't follow up. Involved citizens and local law enforcement must work together as a team.

After the Unabomber was caught, the FBI asked Dr. Puckett to do a study investigating what the lone wolves have in common. The FBI realized they could not track murderers with no tracks. Dr. Puckett traveled extensively and investigated for eight months, and what she learned may change the way lone wolves are being identified today. They were all intelligent. They shared attachment to a violent ideology and an attraction to weapons. Dr. Puckett also discovered something just as important.

"If law enforcement does not have contact with the guy, the people he attempts to connect with, the people he expresses himself to, are the only ones who can identify him."

Because of her report and the input of others in similar roles, the FBI helped to disrupt or prevent nearly 150 shootings and violent attacks in 2013 alone, in part by steering potential gunmen toward mental-health professionals. As unbelievable as that sounds, potential killers were identified before they struck.

According to an Associated Press interview with Andre Simmons, chief of the Behavioral Threat Assessment Center, a division of the FBI's Behavioral Analysis Unit, the FBI has for years been working with state and local authorities to profile potential offenders with the goal of preventing violent crimes like mass shootings. The prevented shootings and violent attacks from January through November 2013 represent 148 cases that the Behavioral Threat Assessment Center has conferred on during 2013—up thirty-three percent from 2012.

In that year, the unit received about three new cases a week referred by federal, state, local, and campus law enforcement, schools, businesses, and houses of worship. This center becomes involved only after someone notifies law enforcement about some troubling behavior.

Dr. Puckett believes this is what must happen. The spotting of these killers comes from the communities themselves—and that does include schools, businesses, houses of worship, PTA meetings, and, in some cases, fringe groups.

"Awareness needs to be brought to the FBI by law enforcement, and the public needs to be the observers," she said. "Law enforcement can't do it, because no crimes have been committed yet."

Most people, even the Breiviks of the world, are involved in some sort of social participation in their own communities, or at least are trying to break in. Dr. Puckett is quick to point out that not all mentally ill people are violent, and lone wolves are as rare as they are deadly.

"If altruism and dedication to a cause were enough," she wrote, "there would be no end to the supply of selfless and dedicated terrorists who were ready to surrender their lives and even die for their ideological causes."

But when they do strike, the damage is massive. The community must play an important part in assessing the threat.

Adam Lanza killed twenty children and six women with a semiautomatic rifle at Sandy Hook Elementary School. Before driving to the school, he killed his mother. After the shooting, Lanza has been described as "troubled." Investigators said his fascination with violence was apparent to teachers and other acquaintances.

In the case of the Boston bombers, the signs were there as red flags, just as they had been in Breivik's case. Tamerlan's radicalization to extreme ideology had nothing to do with possible connections to al Qaeda or other terrorist groups. He turned to radical Islam just as Breivik turned to his hateful ideology. The change in the two brothers' behavior as well as their fascination and stockpiling of weapons should have been enough for their friends and family to take notice.

All these killers, according to Dr. Puckett, had experienced something in their childhood that made them feel isolated and insignificant. Lanza is the one outlier, with his documented history of signs of mental illness. Breivik, as well as McVeigh, had parents who divorced during their child-hoods. McVeigh considered that his mother had abandoned him. Kaczynski was convinced that his parents had mistreated him emotionally. Most of these lone wolves had above-average intelligence. All of them had few friends and were quiet and withdrawn as children. In appearance, McVeigh seemed different than the others in that he was a social child; but as he grew past boyhood, McVeigh too was increasingly described as a loner. None of them managed to establish or keep a relationship with a woman. The lack of physical relationship, or even connecting with another person, is important to creating a lone wolf. All the offenders in Puckett's study were heterosexual and interested in women, and most of them were tortured by the fact that they couldn't establish a lasting relationship.

Dr. Puckett also pointed out that the more intelligent a person is, "the more he is able to look to his own ideas as authority for his actions, rather than to the direction of others (such as a government or an extremist group)." This means that although they had trouble affiliating with other people, these killers were not directionless.

"They were able to form their own ideological variants of the agendas of an extremist group and adapt them to their own uses." Most important, Breivik, McVeigh, and Kaczynski all used their intellectual capacity to compensate for being unsuccessful in their social lives.

"They needed to matter in the world," Puckett said, "and if they couldn't do it socially, they needed to make their mark in another way, a way that would be noticed."

Kaczynski wrote in his journals that he wished to start an anti-technology organization, but he added that he couldn't because of his social disability. Kaczynski was the only one of these killers who didn't repeatedly try to con-nect with an extremist group, perhaps because of his high IQ and capacity to replace human connection with his ideology even more easily than someone of a more average IQ. Blaming his parents for making him "a social cripple," he spent nearly twenty years seeking revenge on "the technological society" he couldn't live in by sending increasingly sophisticated bombs to complete strangers he had read about in newspapers or looked up in *Who's Who in America* who seemed connected to everything he hated in society.

"To make an impression on society with words is almost impossible for most individuals and small groups," Kaczynski wrote to the *New York Times*. "Take us (FC) for example. If we had never done anything violent and had submitted the present writings to a publisher, they probably would not have been accepted. If they had been accepted and published, they probably would not have attracted many readers . . . in order to get our message before the public with some chance of making a lasting impression, we've had to kill people."

Kaczynski operated under a group identity. Breivik claimed he was part of the Knights Templar, an organization that probably does not exist. Both Breivik and McVeigh saw themselves as starting a revolution against their governments.

The Behavioral Threat Assessment Center operates with the knowledge that mass shootings like Newtown are uncommon; and that's important, affirmed Ronald Schouten, a psychiatrist at Massachusetts General Hospital and expert on threat assessments. "These occur very rarely, and there's no consistent profile," Schouten said of those who carry out the shootings.

Dr. Puckett, who has worked with Schouten, concurs. When investigating a case and a potential killer, she tells her sources: "Throw everything at me. I can't have too much stuff to look at."

She's looking not just for past behavior but for something still more amorphous. Although past behavior in most people is the best prediction of future behavior, in the lone wolf it is not.

"We study environment," Dr. Puckett said. "What they're thinking. Who they're with and not with. Who they've *tried* to be with. What successes, what failures. What's happened in their lives. The development is complex. When they act, it's after a long period of alienation."

The Threat Assessment Center—staffed by agents and analysts of the FBI, the U.S. Capitol Police, the Bureau of Alcohol, Tobacco, Firearms and Explosives, and a psychiatrist—helps the local officials assess the threat posed by the person of concern.

A certain university student (not one who has been mentioned in this book), as an example, began to display bizarre behaviors and an increasing interest in firearms. Although he had roommates, he now uses their photos as bull's-eye targets in the shooting range he created in their basement.

None of this was illegal activity, but the roommates looked at the behavior and contacted university authorities, who contacted local police. With the FBI behavioral analysts, the university arranged an interview with the disturbed student, who agreed to be admitted to a psychiatric facility.

Although the center was launched in the fall of 2010, the unit's existence is not yet common knowledge around the country. But awareness is growing, as the FBI has recently been sponsoring two-day conferences about the threat of active shooters, Simmons said.

"In the same way that these American Lone Wolves were compelled to take up their solitary campaigns," Dr. Puckett wrote, "it's logical to assume that extremist ideologies from abroad will be adopted by one or more new Lone Wolves who decide to commit acts of societal-level violence as a result." They may be homegrown like Breivik, McVeigh, and Kaczynski, or they may be immigrants like the Boston bombers. But their motivation is the same, no matter where they live or come from.

"A world where domestic and international terrorism collide will be an increasingly dangerous one," according to Dr. Puckett. "Since 9/11, the primary U.S. response to attacks from international terrorists has been from the military." Civilian law enforcement, she continued, has been overwhelmed by the challenge of preventing terrorist acts on American soil. The Patriot Act and executive orders from the White House attempt to monitor the vast number of terrorist targets in the country but are inefficient when it comes to a lone wolf.

Dr. Puckett believes, after having worked the most difficult homegrown terrorism cases, that it is possible to free our citizens from the threat of terrorism without depriving them of their personal freedoms. A strong law enforcement and an aware public who know what to look for are crucial.

Again, assessment comes back to community. Identifying the lone wolf is not a job for profilers. The huge amount of money being poured into NSA and the increasing manpower used to collect intelligence from citizens is not going to stop these killers. They are too subtle.

"The analysis will not be done unless someone in the community realizes what's going on," Dr. Puckett said. "Bring it to the community level. Don't expect institutions to take care of your society and yourself."

Government is not responsible for our lives. We are responsible for our lives and for each other.

SOURCES & SUGGESTED READING

CHAPTER 1

Breivik, Anders B. *2083: A European Declaration of Independence.* http://fas.org/
programs/tap/_docs/2083_-_A_European_Declaration_of_Independence.pdf;
https://publicintelligence.net/anders-behring-breiviks-complete-manifesto-2083-a-
european-declaration-of-independence/

CHAPTER 2

Sorrano, Richard A. *One of Ours: Timothy McVeigh and the Oklahoma City Bombing.* New
York: W. W. Norton, 1998.

Michel, Lou, and Dan Herbeck. *American Terrorist: Timothy McVeigh & The Oklahoma
City Bombing.* New York: Regan, 2001.

Chase, Alston. *A Mind For Murder. The Education of the Unabomber and the Origins of
Modern Terrorism.* New York/London: W.W. Norton, 2003.

Stickney, Brandon M. *All-American Monster: The Unauthorized Biography of Timothy
McVeigh.* New York: Prometheus, 1996.

Johnson, Sally. "Psychiatric Competency report of Dr. Sally C. Johnson. September
1998. In The United States district court for the Eastern district of California.
United States of America, plaintiff, v. Theodore John Kaczynski, defendant."
CR. NO. S-96-259 GEB ORDER. http://www.chicagotribune.com/media/
acrobat/2008-04/37849352.pdf.

Christensen, Marit. *Moren: Historien om Wenche Behring Breivik.* (Aschehoug, 2015),
EBOK.NO Kindle edition.

Seiersted, Åsne. *En Av Oss: En fortelling on Norge* (Kagge Forlag, 2015), EBOK.NO,
Kindle edition.

CHAPTER 3

Michel and Herbeck. *American Terrorist.*

Borchgrevink, Aage Storm. *En Norsk tragedie: Anders Behring Breivik og veiene til Utøya.* Gyldendal, 2012.

Sandemose, Aksel. *En flyktning krysser sitt spor.* Oslo: Aschehoug, 1988.

Johnson. "Psychiatric Competency report."

Chase. *A Mind For Murder.*

CHAPTER 4

Michel and Herbeck. *American Terrorist.*

Stormark, Kjetil. *Massemorderens Private E-poster.* Oslo: Spartacus, 2012.

Stormark, Kjetil. *Da terroren rammet Norge: 189 minutter som rystet verden.* Oslo: Kagge Forlag, 2011.

NRK Brennpunkt. "Fedrene." December 21, 2011. https://tv.nrk.no/serie/brennpunkt/MDUP11002111/21-12-2011.

Borchgrevink. *En Norsk tragedie.*

CHAPTER 5

Breivik. *2083: A European Declaration of Independence.*

Stormark. *Da terroren rammet Norge.*

CHAPTER 6

Stormark. *Da terroren rammet Norge.*

Michel and Herbeck. *American Terrorist.*

Seiersted. *En Av Oss.*

Obertone, Laurent. *Utøya: Norvège, 22 juillet 2011, 77 morts.* Ring Editions, 2013.

CHAPTER 7

Breivik. *2083: A European Declaration of Independence.*

Michel and Herbeck. *American Terrorist.*

"The Failure of Multiculturalism: Community Versus Society in Europe." *Foreign Affairs,* March/April 2015 Issue. https://www.foreignaffairs.com/articles/western-europe/2015-03-01/failure-multiculturalism

CHAPTER 8

The July 22nd Commission Report, NOU 2012: https://www.regjeringen.no/no/dokumenter/nou-2012-14/id697260/; http://www.norway-nato.org/eng/News/22-July-Commissions-report/#.VYFCyGC_aS0

CHAPTER 9

Michel and Herbeck. *American Terrorist.*

Christensen. *Moren.*

Seiersted. *En Av Oss.*

Lippestad, Geir. *Det kan vi stå for.* Oslo: Aschehoug, 2013.

Finnøy, Ellen Kolsrud, and Pelle Finnøy. *Den misunnelige morderen.* Frognerforlaget, 2012.

CHAPTER 10

Breivik. *2083: A European Declaration of Independence.*
Michel and Herbeck. *American Terrorist.*

CHAPTER 11

Breivik, Jens. *Min skyld? En fars historie.* Oslo: Juritzen forlag, 2014.

CHAPTER 12

McFadden, Robert D. "PRISONER OF RAGE—A special report: From a Child
of Promise to the Unabom Suspect." *New York Times*, May 26, 1996. http://www.
nytimes.com/1996/05/26/us/prisoner-of-rage-a-special-report-from-a-child-of-
promise-to-the-unabom-suspect.html
Turchie, Terry D., and Kathleen M. Puckett, Ph.D. *Hunting The American Terrorist: The
FBI's War On Homegrown Terror.* (History Publishing Company, 2007), Kindle edition.
Pracon, Adrian. *Hjertet mot steinen: En overlevendes beretning fra.* Cappelen Damm 2013.
Bawer, Bruce. *The New Quislings: How the International Left Used the Oslo Massacre to
Silence Debate About Islam.* (Broadside e-books, 2012), Kindle edition.

CHAPTER 13

Turchie and Puckett. *Hunting The American Terrorist.*
Spaaij, Ramón. *Understanding Lone Wolf Terrorism: Global Patterns, Motivations and
Prevention.* (Springer Netherlands, 2011), Kindle edition.
Stickney. *All-American Monster.*
Michel and Herbeck. *American Terrorist.*

CHAPTER 14

Lavergne, Gary M. *A Sniper In The Tower: The Charles Whitman Murders.* Denton:
University of North Texas Press, 1997.
Cullen, Dave. *Columbine.* Twelve, Paperback Edition, 2010.
Hobson, Jack. *Drifters: Stories from the Dark Side of Delinquency.* Black Opal, 2013.
"Jahar's World." *Rolling Stone*, August 2013 issue. http://www.rollingstone.com/
culture/news/jahars-world-20130717

CHAPTER 15

Miron, Jeffrey A. *"Violence, Guns, and Drugs: A Cross-Country Analysis."* The University
of Chicago Press, 2001. http://www.jstor.org/stable/10.1086/340507?seq=1#pag
e_scan_tab_contents
Kates, Don B., and Gary Mauser. "Would Banning Firearms Reduce Murder And
Suicide? A Review Of International And Some Domestic Evidence." *Harvard Journal
of Law and Public Policy.* http://www.law.harvard.edu/students/orgs/jlpp/Vol30_
No2_KatesMauseronline.pdf
Malcolm, Joyce Lee. *Guns And Violence: The English Experience.* Harvard University
Press, 2002.

Lott, John R., Jr. *More Guns, Less Crime: Understanding Crime and Gun-Control Laws.* Third Edition. Chicago and London: University of Chicago Press, 2010.

Lott, John R., Jr. *The Bias Against Guns: Why Almost Everything You've Heard About Gun Control Is Wrong.* (Regnery), Kindle edition.

CHAPTER 16

Sætre, Simen. *Fjordman: Portrett av en antiislamist.* Oslo: Cappelen Damm, 2013.

Turchie and Puckett. *Hunting The American Terrorist.*

Lippestad. *Det kan vi stå for.*

CHAPTER 17

"FBI disrupted nearly 150 mass shootings, violent acts in 2013: Attorney General Eric Holder." The Associated Press, *Daily News.* December 16, 2013. http://www. nydailynews.com/news/politics/fbi-disrupted-150-mass-shootings-violent-acts-attorney-general-eric-holder-article-1.1549473

"The Reckoning: The father of the Sandy Hook killer searches for answers." The New Yorker, March 17, 2014 Issue. http://www.newyorker.com/magazine/2014/03/17/the-reckoning

ACKNOWLEDGMENTS

When I woke up from the numbness I felt after the July 22, 2011, massacre, I knew I had to write this book. I've always been a ferocious reader and loved writing, but I didn't know how to write an actual book. The Universe must have known that I was on the right path, because some wonderful people all of a sudden appeared in my life to help me do just that. Without them, this book would not be what it is today.

Bonnie Hearn Hill not only taught me how to write, she helped me discover my voice. She showed me it is okay to speak and write the truth. She taught me to believe in myself and to dream big. She is an amazing mentor and friend. I could not have done this without her. Bonnie, you are the true Rock Star and I am forever grateful.

My agent, Peter Riva, helped me shape this book into something infinitely better. Your guidance is always spot on. Thank you for taking me under your wing and for not giving up.

A huge thanks to Jessica Case and her team at Pegasus Books. Jessica's vision, edits, and clarity about how and what to change was remarkable.

A special thanks to Kathleen Puckett for helping me understand the psyche of the lone wolf killer, for your extraordinary insight, and for sharing your knowledge with me. You are not only brilliant, you are a wonderful human being, and I am honored to know you.

My research led me to Steven Kleinman and Ali Soufan at the Soufan Group. Thank you, Steven, for your thorough and intelligent answers to all my questions. The world needs more people like you.

Thank you, Jack Hobson, for sharing your experience and knowledge about the psychology behind juvenile delinquents and school shooters.

Cristina Buffon has accompanied me through this whole process and helped me attain a better understanding of humanity, myself including. Violence comes from a place of deep suffering. Wounded children do not stop loving their parents; they stop loving themselves. With your guidance, I'm learning to feel compassion and be less judgmental. You taught me how to write from my heart. Thank you.

Finally, I express gratitude to my husband, Samuel, for believing in me and for your encouragement despite all the late nights, weekends, and holidays spent writing and re-writing. Thank you for being such a wonderful husband and father, and for accepting me as the free spirit I am. Thank you for your edits and valuable input in every aspect of my new career. Without you, this journey would not have been possible. I love you.

APPENDICES

1. Anders Behring Breivik's résumé
2. Diagram of the center of Oslo in relation to where Breivik parked and where the bomb exploded
3. Map of Breivik's route on Utøya
4. Timeline of events, July 22, 2011
5. Breivik's private e-mails
6. In Memoriam: The Human Price

APPENDIX ONE

ANDERS BEHRING BREIVIK'S RÉSUMÉ

"I was considering pasting in my complete and updated CV," Breivik wrote in his manifesto. "However, I don't want to make my past network public and I don't think it would be that relevant."

He then must feel that the nine-page CV included in his manifesto is relevant. Contrary to what he states, it is extensive. A resume is a normal tool normal people use to find employment. Breivik uses this form to balance out the crazy-sounding rants in his manifesto. It is another tool he uses to attract followers by attempting to appear reasonable, a leader. I've included it in its entirety because it shows how potentially dangerous Breivik is, even behind bars.

- 6 years Primary School
- 3 years Secondary School
- 2.5 years High School (last 6 months underwent complete curriculum).

- An informal education, consisting of the equivalent of eight university years (or equivalent to two bachelor's degrees and one master's degree), consisting of the following: Approximately 16,320 hours of study (one year at the University = 2,040 hours of study per year: 8 hours per day, 5 days per week, 51 weeks per year) on various fields:

Approximately 8,000 of these hours were dedicated to the study of fields relating to Small Business Management, Business, Marketing/Sales, Economical/Financial Analysis (including stock/commodity/currency analysis), Business Logistics. The rest was dedicated to Political Science, World History, and Language: English/Norwegian and various other subjects (everything from cryptography to biochemistry).

Not included: daily reading/reviewing/watching: Newspapers, Scientific/Cultural/Economical—magazines/papers/articles: Approx. 10,000 hours +

Not included: 12 years work experience, Project Management, practical work experience, project analysis, stock/commodity analysis/trading. Approx. 10,000 hours +

Not included: Relevant social experience/interaction related to business/culture/science/economy (3 specific mentors), various forum discussions/exchange of knowledge, travelling to 25 countries + interaction with thousands of experienced professionals or other individuals with vast knowledge on multiple fields.

PERSONAL FACTS

Name: Andrew Berwick [his name in English]
Nationality: Norwegian
Born: February 1979
Height: 183 cm
Weight: 80 kg
Ethnicity: Nordic/Norwegian
Address: Oslo, Norway
Personality: Optimistic, pragmatic, ambitious, creative, hard-working

Political view: Cultural conservative, revolutionary conservative, Vienna school of thought, economically liberal

Religion: Christian, Protestant but I support a reformation of Protestantism leading to it being absorbed by Catholicism. The typical "Protestant Labor Church" has to be deconstructed, as its creation was an attempt to abolish the Church.

Religious: I went from moderately to agnostic to moderately religious

Education: Non-formal equivalent to 7 years + at university level

Professions: Investor, Director, Manager—founder of several companies, small business management (including organizational development), political analyst, author, stock analyst/trader. I'm unsure whether resistance fighter (Justiciar Knight Commander) and martyr counts as a profession. :)

Nicotine: Yes

Alcohol: Occasionally

Drugs: No

Tattoos: No

Sports: Snowboarding, fitness (body building/spinning), running

Watch sport: Only women's sand volley ball. :P Perhaps I would if Norway didn't suck so hard in football

Name of your primary weapon: Mjöllnir

Name of your sidearm: Gungnir

Hobbies: Political analysis, studying new topics, Freemasonry, Heraldry, Genealogy, gaming (MMO or Modern Warfare 2), traveling—learning about new cultures, music, friends. I have had the privilege of experiencing the following countries:

Sweden, Denmark, UK, Germany, Poland, Belarus, France, Austria, Hungary, Austria [*sic*], Croatia, Lithuania, Estonia, Latvia, Spain, Cyprus, Malta, US, Turkey, Mexico, China, Nigeria, Cote d'Ivoire, Liberia.

KEY POINTS—CURRICULUM VITAE

Key qualifications:

Organizational/business development—Experience with the establishment, development, and management of smaller businesses related to the fields; organizational/business development, small business management, marketing and sales. Financial analysis—stock/currency analysis relating to the fields/indicators; candlesticks, RSI, stochastic, MACD, Bollinger bands, DMI, momentum.

2005–2007: Managing director of E-Commerce Group AS (part investment company—50%, part sales/outsourcing company—50%). I converted ABB ENK to a corporation (AS). Total of 7 employees: 3 in Norway, 1 in Russia, 1 in Indonesia, 1 in Romania, 1 in the US. Distribution of outsourcing services to foreign companies, sold software/programming solutions. Worked part time with day trading (stocks/options/currency/commodities). This was a front (milk cow) with the purpose of financing resistance/liberation-related military operations. The company was successful although most of the funds were channeled through a Caribbean subsidiary (with base in Antigua, a location where European countries do not have access): Brentwood Solutions Limited with bank accounts in other Caribbean nations and Eastern Europe. E-Commerce Group was terminated in 2007 while most of the funds were channeled in an "unorthodox manner" to Norway available to the coming intellectual and subsequent operations phase.

2002–2004: Director of Anders Behring Breivik ENK (part time from May 02, shortly after my inclusion in PCCTS)—Dec. 02, full time from March 03. Same emphasis as E-Commerce Group. This was a front (milk cow) I established and focused on shortly after my inclusion in PCCTS, Knights Templar with the purpose of financing resistance/liberation-related military operations.

2002–2003: Supervisor/internal adviser for Bankia Bank ASA (Apr. 02–March 03).

2001–2002: Customer service representative for Bankia Bank ASA (Nov. 01–Apr. 02).

2000–2001: Managing director of Media Group AS. Development and sales of outdoor media solutions (primarily billboards). My company was partially acquired/bought by Mediamax Norway AS after I (and my employee, Kristoffer Andresen) had built a billboard portfolio from scratch in the Oslo area which was then sold to Mediamax Norge AS (which was later bought by JC Decaux Norway) and Clear Channel (July 00–July 01).

1999–2000: Team leader for the customer service rep. dept. for Enitel Telephony/mobile/internet/support division (March 99–July 00).

1998–1999: Director for Behring & Kerner Marketing DA. Implementation and sales of telephonic services (part time from Aug. 98–Feb. 99).

1997–1999: Corporate customer care rep. for customer care/internet support for Telia Norway AS (Nov 97–Feb 99).

1996–1997: Part time as a sales rep. for ACTA Economical Counseling (Feb 96–97).

Education: Non-formal studies/degrees: Bachelor of Business Administration (major: small business management), part time studies using the curriculum/online study courses from AIU, American InterContinental University (98–02), Bachelor of Political Science (major: political science and history) part time studies (00–05), Master of Political Science, full/part time studies (05–10). See other chapter for specification.

Other professional activities:

2005: Was coached by my friend, former mentor and independent stock analyst, Xun Dai over a 6 month period on the areas: technical stock analysis: candlesticks, RSI, stochastic, MACD, Bollinger bands, DMI, momentum.

2000–2001: Was coached by my former mentor—and managing director of Hypertec AS, Richard Steenfeldt-Berg over a 12 month period on the areas: management, administration, corporate/business/organization development (May 00–May 01).

1995–1998: Oslo Handelsgymnasium/Hartvig Nissen High School

Board positions, professional activities, responsibilities

2003: Candidate for the Oslo City Council election on behalf of the Oslo Progress Party. This was during the "crossroad" when I was in the process of deciding whether I would fully abandon conventional politics (and a career within conventional politics) as a solution/source to acquire funds for the future operation or if I would rather leave conventional politics altogether and rather focus on entrepreneurship/business as the source for financing my future and clandestine participation in the pan-European Conservative Revolutionary Movement/pan-European Resistance Movement. As you already know, I became one of the founding members of the PCCTS, Knights Templar in 2002 and among the very first Justiciar Knight Commanders. However, regardless of this choice, I was not completely convinced I was done with conventional politics. I actually decided to do a last push (after my pledge to the PCCTS) as I was already nominated on behalf of the Oslo Progress Party for the City Council election in 2003/2004. I came relatively close to being elected but was not among the final contestants due to the fact that the Progress Party Youth (lead by my rival Jøran Kallmyr) refused, for strategic reasons, to support my candidature. At the time I was more popular than Jøran but needed the support of the youth organization (an organization I had been a part of for a few years). I don't blame him for backstabbing me like that, though. After all, he had invested so much more of his time in the organization than I had. He deserved it while I didn't, and I would probably have done the same thing if I was him.

Also, during the "crossroad phase" I had lost all faith in the Progress Party as a solution to Norway's rapid disintegration due to multiculturalism and Islamization. A moderate cultural conservative political party like the Progress Party is incapable of solving any of our primary problems as they are systematically ridiculed and isolated by all other political parties and a united media sector. This, even despite of [sic] the fact that they have taken measures and gotten rid of all true nationalists ending up with only opportunistic career cynics unwilling to take any political risks.

The Progress Party is now a part of the problem as they continuously give the Norwegian people false hope and thus contributes to pacifying them. They should rather be honest and admit that all hopes for the democratic change of the society is futile and rather encourage all patriotic Norwegians to resist the multiculturalist regime through armed resistance. Their unwillingness to do this makes them a central part of the problem and in fact an obstacle to the liberation of and the reconquista of Norway.

I anticipate that the Norwegian media will persecute and undermine the Progress Party for my earlier involvement in the organization. This is not a negative thing as an increasing amount of Norwegians will then have their "illusions of democratic change" crushed (if the Progress Party is annihilated by the multiculturalist media) and rather resort to armed resistance. From a tactical and pragmatic viewpoint, the PC Media's defeat of the Progress Party will benefit the armed National Resistance Movement in Norway. The more moderate alternatives are persecuted, the more likely it is that the average nationalist's illusions of peaceful reform will be crushed, which will lead to him seeking "other means." Because at this point, armed resistance and the violent overthrow of our regime is the only thing that can save us.

2002: Founding member (national representative) of the PCCTS, Knights Templar, in London (April).

2002: Member of the board of directors of the control authority for Majorstuen Eldresenter (Majorstuen Retirement home), political position for the Norwegian Progress Party.

2002: Member of the board of directors for Uranienborg Elementary and Secondary School, political position for the Norwegian Progress Party.

2001: Development of the financial prospectus for Hypertec AS in cooperation with NB Partner AS and PriceWaterhouseCoopers DA (Jan 01–May 01).

2000–2003: Board member in Progress Party Frogner and Vice Chairman in the Progress Party Youth–Oslo West.

DIAGRAM OF THE CENTER OF OSLO IN RELATION TO WHERE BREIVIK PARKED AND WHERE THE BOMB EXPLODED

H-BUILDING = HOUSING THE PRIME MINSTER, JUSTICE DEPARTMENT, AND POLICE DEPARTMENT

R4 = THE MINISTRY OF TRADE, INDUSTRY AND FISHERIES

R5 = HOUSING DIFFERENT DEPARTMENTS INCLUDING THE MINISTRY OF TRANSPORT AND COMMUNICATION, LOCAL GOVERNMENT AND REGIONAL DEVELOPMENT, DEPARTMENT OF CULTURE, DEPARTMENT OF CHILDREN AND EQUALITY, AND THE DEPARTMENT OF LABOR.

Y-BUILDING = DEPARTMENT OF EDUCATION

G-BUILDING = DEPARTMENT OF FINANCE

S-BUILDING = HEALTH DEPARTMENT

M17 = SERVICE CENTER FOR THE DEPARTMENTS

GRUBBE STREET 1 = FISHING AND COASTAL AFFAIRS

R6 = DEPARTMENT OF HEALTH AND CARE

VG = VERDENS GANG (NATIONAL NEWSPAPER)

RING 1 = ONE OF THREE MAJOR STREETS GOING AROUND OSLO CITY CENTER TO AVOID TOO MUCH TRAFFIC THROUGH THE INNER CITY STREETS.

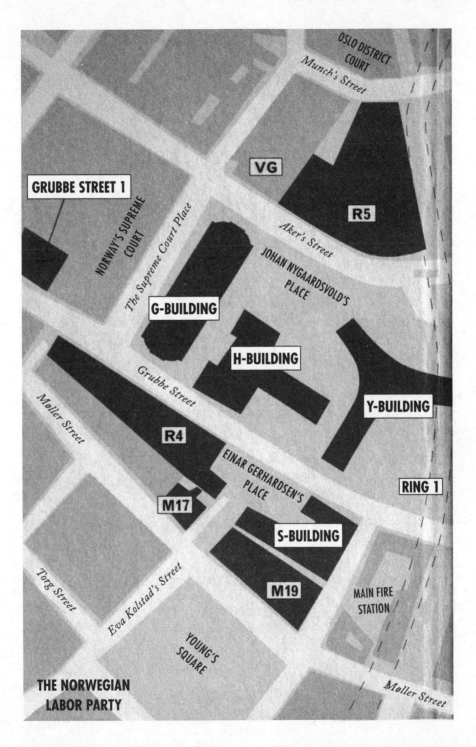

MAP OF BREIVIK'S ROUTE ON UTØYA

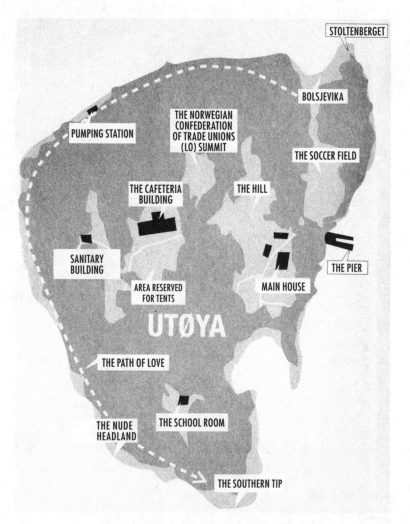

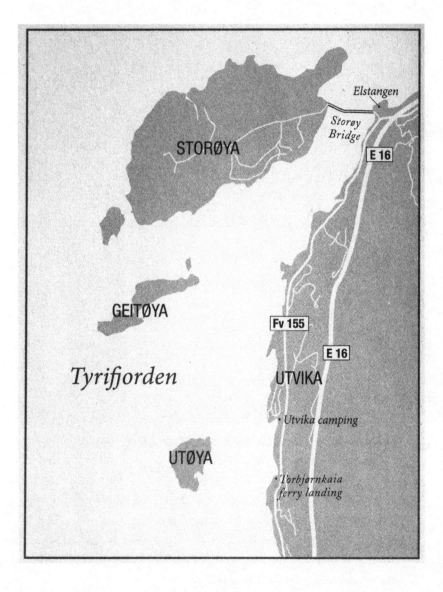

Elstangen

Storøy Bridge

E 16

STORØYA

GEITØYA

Fv 155

E 16

Tyrifjorden

UTVIKA

· *Utvika camping*

UTØYA

· *Torbjørnkaia ferry landing*

TIMELINE OF EVENTS
JULY 22, 2011

15:00 HOUR

15:16:30: Anders Behring Breivik drives a white Volkswagen Crafter and parks it in front of the main entrance of government building H, ignoring the NO ENTRY sign. Building H houses the Prime Minister and the Justice Department. Inside the car is a 950-kilogram bomb made from a mixture of fertilizer and fuel oil, inspired by Timothy McVeigh's bomb in Oklahoma City.

Breivik is angry when he discovers a car already parked where he had planned to park his van. In this location, the impact of the explosion would make the building collapse.

15:16:46: Breivik opens the front door of the car.

15:17:02: Breivik steps out of the car. He stands outside it for seven seconds.

One of the guards takes note of the van parked illegally and of the man dressed like someone working in private security.

15:17:09: Breivik quickly walks away toward Hammersborg Square, where he has a silver-gray Fiat Doblo waiting.

15:18:30: A witness spots what he describes as a suspicious-looking man in the government quarter in downtown Oslo. Seconds later he hears the man unlock a car at Hammersborg Square and gets a glimpse of Breivik's face as he drives down a one-way street in the wrong direction. He takes note of the car's registration number and calls the police to report it.

15:25:22: The bomb placed in the Volkswagen Crafter explodes, killing eight and injuring several hundred.

15:26: The police receive the first reports of the explosion from witnesses.

15:28: The first police patrol arrives at the scene of the explosion.

15:58: The press confirms that Prime Minister Jens Stoltenberg is not among the victims of the attack. Shortly later, the press announces that no government ministers have been injured.

The police emergency phone line has been jammed with calls from witnesses. Witnesses provide police with the description and license plate number of Breivik's getaway car. However, in the confusion, the police take too long to react on the information, and Breivik gets away.

16:00 HOUR

16:22: Breivik's rented Fiat Doblo passes a traffic camera at Næss Camping. It takes three minutes to drive the distance from Næss Camping to the Utøya ferry landing.

The police have still not sent out an alarm to try to find the suspicious silver-gray Fiat Doblo with the license plate VH 24605 after the tip they received following the explosion.

16:30: The participants at the summer camp of the Labor Party's youth division on Utøya gather in the camp's main house to be informed about the explosion in Oslo.

16:55: Breivik, disguised as a police officer, arrives at the ferry landing in Tyrifjorden, a lake some 40 kilometers northwest of Oslo.

He identifies himself as Martin Nilsen from the Police Intelligence Unit. He gets help to carry a big black case containing weapons and ammunition onto the ferry. A witness describes Breivik carrying a handgun and a rifle and wearing some sort of police uniform and an ID card around his neck. From there he is transported by the Labor Party Youth League's ferry MS *Torbjørn* to Utøya.

17:00 HOUR

17:18: Breivik arrives at Utøya.

17:22: Breivik fires the first shot.

17:24: The Emergency Medical Services (AMK) in Drammen is informed of the shooting.

17:25: The police in Oslo are informed of the shooting.

17:26: The local police in Hønefoss learn about the shooting.

17:30: The Emergency Response Unit, a counter-terrorist police unit situated in Oslo, is dispatched from Oslo to Utøya. No helicopter is available, and they are obliged to take a car and get through rush-hour traffic as they are driving out of Oslo.

17:33: The first police patrol leaves Hønefoss.

17:38: The local police officially ask the Oslo police district for assistance.

17:50: The police patrol from Hønefoss arrives at the Utøya ferry landing, but the officers have to wait for a suitable craft before they can cross the 600 yards over to Utøya.

18:00 HOUR

18:01: Breivik calls 112 (emergency telephone number) to surrender, hangs up, and continues to kill.

(Breivik later claimed he had dialed the number several times but had trouble getting through. And when he finally did, he introduced himself and said he wished to surrender.)

18:09: The Delta Emergency Response Unit from Oslo arrives at a landing north of the Utøya ferry landing, unable to find the nearest landing. They have to wait for a boat to take them to the island. The boat that is finally provided is too small for the number of personnel and their equipment, and the engine stops during the crossing. The team transfers over into two privately owned open leisure boats.

18:25: The Delta Emergency Response Unit arrives on Utøya and goes ashore.

18:26: Breivik calls 112 again to surrender and hangs up.

18:34: Breivik is apprehended, without resistance, by the police.

Eight people died in the bombing attack in the center of Oslo, and at least 209 people were physically injured from the bombing, twelve of them seriously.

In total, seventy-seven people were murdered that day.

Sixty-nine people died in the Utøya massacre, and at least 110 people more were injured, fifty-five of them seriously. Thirty-two of those killed were under 18 years old; the two youngest were 14 years old. The average age of those killed at Utøya was 19.7 years old.

BREIVIK'S PRIVATE E-MAILS

In 2012, after the trial, Kjetil Stormark, a Norwegian journalist and author, published part of Anders Breivik's email correspondence prior to the attacks on July 22, 2011. Stormark had received—six days after the massacre—more than seven thousand e-mails from numerous accounts Breivik used from Norwegian hackers who were just as appalled by the bloodshed as the rest of the world. He was told to deliver the material to the police in order to help the investigation, and he did.

The information in these e-mails, which Breivik never meant to publish, indicates what this Lone Wolf was thinking, and how he was functioning in the years before he committed mass murder. The e-mails show that Breivik was an intelligent and balanced person in most ways, and that he seemed to function normally. He even showed compassion for others. Like other lone wolves, Breivik knew how to pretend to function in social situations when necessary. Extremely calculating and protective of himself and his cause, he was able to hide his true motives, and there is no reason to believe that the people he corresponded with had any idea what Breivik was planning.

The following is a translation of a selection of the e-mails Stormark published in *The Mass Murderer's Private Emails*.

COMPUTER GAMES

On June 6, 2012, *Verdens Gang* published a letter Breivik's sister wrote to their mother about her concern for her brother isolating himself and playing computer games:

Anders is going nowhere, Mom. He wants nothing in life, apart from what he has done in the last few years plus what he is doing now. When you gave him the phone after you and I had spoken, he asked if he could call me back later, because he was in the middle of a "discussion." I asked him what kind of discussion, and he didn't want to answer. When he called me back, he told me he was playing. So evidently he is still doing that! It's not normal you know, Mom! He is 30 years old!! There are no normal human beings that keep on like this.

∞

Date: Saturday, May 17, 2008 13:32:38
From: xxxxx
To: andersbehring@hotmail.com
Subject: Hey

Hey mate,

bored in IF (Ironforge, a city in WoW) on my mage and thought i'd say hi. Things are going ok in the guild but new mage sucks compared to you and xxxx's missing you so much he's losing hair even faster than before! Soon he'll be bald like Andersugly . . . i mean Andersnords :P

anyway, we miss you a lot in the guild and i hope you're (not :P) having fun in AoC and that you'll come back to us soon :(

Regards,

Xxxx

∞

Date: Friday, May 23, 2008 09:59:14
From: andersbehring@hotmail.com
To: xxxxxxx
Subject: RE: Hey

Haha, hope he get's bald:D Miss you as well mate. Ill stop by forum as often as I can;p I wish Nevermore could just roll AoC, would make it easier for everyone!

:D

∞

Date: Sunday, May 18, 2008 04:19:00
From: xxxxxx
To: andersbehring@hotmail.com
Subject:

Can you join the ventrilo server or be on msn when you play to talk about stuff'; . . . ;' tomorrow I might only be on late, I might blag an hour out of the raid though.

∞

Date: Tuesday, May 20, 2008 17:25:04
From: andersbehring@hotmail.com
To: xxxxxx
Subject: RE:

hey mate,
I added you on friends list. My nick name is Anderson btw:)

∞

Date: Tuesday, July 22, 2008 01:00:01
From: xxxxxx
To: andersbehring@hotmail.com
Subject: '; . . . ;'

So what now? Any games goin on or just Work Work.

∞

Date: Saturday, July 26, 2008 04:20:24
From: andersbehring@hotmail.com
To: xxxxxxx
Subject: RE: '; . . . ;'
   Just finished Bioshock, playing Mass Effect atm. Pretty cool:) What you up to?

∞

Date: Friday August 1, 2008 15:27:57
From: xxxxx
To: andersbehring@hotmail.com
Subject: I pity The Fools
   hehe, alot of people leaving are there?:D
   Would love to check out a game like Starcraft or something like that. Atm, not really sure about what kind of game to chose:D
   Hope to play with you again soon though mate, :)

∞

Correspondence with his sister
Date: Monday May 5, 2008 23:14:59
Subject: :))
   Hello Elisabeth:))
   Greetings. Hope you guys are doing well:))
   I'm quitting WoW, but checking out AoC for a time. We'll see what happens after. I'm possibly starting a masters degree in the fall.
   Anders

∞

Date: Friday June 13, 2008 11:53:51
Subject: RE: :))
   Hi Anders!!!

How are you? Is everything all right with you and Mom? Haven't heard anything from Mom in several months.

How do you like the new game? (AoC??) And how is your summer otherwise?

Missing my brother :).

Hugs from Elisabeth

∞

Date: Thursday June 19, 2008 08:36:19
Subject: RE: RE: :))

All is well. Do you have any plans for the summer?

I'm not on facebook. AoC is ok for now.

∞

Elisabeth sent the following email to her brother after having given birth:
Date: March 2, 2010
From: Elisabeth

Hi,

Sending some pictures. Hope you guys are doing well. We're doing ok.

∞

From: andersbehring@hotmail.com
To: Elisabeth

Hi Elisabeth!

A THOUSAND thanks for the great pictures, I will show them to Mom!:D

Will try to call you tomorrow, sis.

Hope you're feeling a little better!

Annis<3

∞

Date: June 30, 2010
From: andersbehring@hotmail.com
To: Elisabeth
Subject: Wedding movie
Hey sis:)
Compressed the movie to 172 MB so I'm sending it on CD;) Mailing it tomorrow.
Annis<3

∞

Date: July 2, 2010 07:42:39
From: Elisabeth
Subject: RE: Wedding movie
Thank you so much, Anders :). Looking forward to watching it.
Sis

∞

Date: January 13, 2011 03:17:17
From: anders.behring@hotmail.com
To: Elisabeth
Subject: Changing email address
Hi sis!
Just wanted to inform you that the old email address: andersbehring@hotmail.com is changed to anders.behring@hotmail.com. The first one I no longer have access to because it has been hacked due to a security breach on Facebook.
Kind regards.
Annis

∞

Date: Monday January 17, 2011 14:52:34
From: Elisabeth

Subject: RE: Changing email address

Ok, Annis :). Is everything all right with you? Are you coming to visit soon?

Hugs

∞

Date: Friday, January 21, 2011 15:33:54
From: anders.behring@hotmail.com
To: Elisabeth

All is well. Will give you further notice.
Annis

∞

Date: Tuesday January 25, 2011 15:33:54
From: Elisabeth

Hey! What do you mean? :) Further notice . . .

∞

Date: Wednesday January 26, 2011 11:30:56

Hi!:D

I'm in a acquisition phase, have been for quite a while, where I'm more or less on stand-by waiting for delivery from up to 5 suppliers (in connection to the research phase of the 4 projects I'm considering). This will continue in an unspecified period up until launch of my new company in august.

Many of the suppliers are unfortunately slackers of unknown proportions and are in addition often located in China so scheduled time of delivery is often changed and/or delayed. <3 It's very difficult to plan trips abroad in such a phase but I recon I will get a window next spring for the planned West Europe trip and also a possibility to visit you for a long weekend, for example:))

Hope everything is well with you guys!:) Greetings to xxxx, xxxx, and xxxx!:D

Annis

∞

Date: Saturday April 23, 2011 21:19:11
From: Elisabeth

Hi Anders,

Sorry I haven't called you back, it's been so busy lately. I will try to call you this week. We're going on holiday to Hawaii on Friday April 29. Staying there until May 7. Really looking forward!

Haven't spoken to you in a long while. How are you and what are you up to?? I don't even know what you're doing these days:). I read your email one more time, and I don't think I have ever read anything as "general" . . . haha . . . ;)

Hope you are well. Haven't spoken to Mom in a long while either. Hope she's well too.

Hugs

∞

The following is the last e-mail Breivik wrote to his half-sister, on April 25, 2011, and it appears to be a "good-bye."

Hi Elisabeth!:D

So nice to hear from you! That holiday in Hawaii sounds fantastic!:D You've been there 5-10 times by now? If so it has got to be great there, as you are a demanding person;)) <3 I'm more of a culture freak, as you know . . . LOVE European history, architecture and other similar cultural aspects, the less known the better.

As you know, I've been a Free Mason for 6 years so I have the possibility to visit Free Masons brothers all over the world, including Los Angeles. Los Angeles has a HUGE Free Masons organization with grand locations! The Free Masons protect old European traditions and rituals that have been forgotten for hundreds of years.

Last fall, in Prague, I spent most of my time camping at all historical places:D Am really keen on traveling to Israel to visit the most sacred of the Christian places, in the southern part of the country. But I probably won't have time to travel much the next six months, possibly with the exception of the trip to Western Europe. Visiting you would have been a priority though before these things. If I were to go, it would be best for me before May, but that would probably not work for you. Generally speaking, it's not a good time, but I would have set things aside for a couple of days with you.

I have not decided 100% yet if I'm going to go for the security-equipment project, forest and hunting project, or the farming project (become a farmer), but these are the ones I've work the most on. The launch date is getting closer so the establishment will most likely happen quickly once I've made my decision. Would be great if you don't discuss these projects with Mom as it will only result in her stressing me in an unconstructive way . . . <3 My financial budget is fine, so there are no problems there. I've always been great at financial management and I've lived in a pretty ascetic way the last 5 years.

By the way, I've worked out a lot the last six months. I now weigh 94 kg (overweight by 19 kg)!:D Normally, that would mean that I've become a real fatty, haha!:D However, approximately 80% of the overweight is muscle!:D So in other words, I've never been as fit and muscular as I am at this moment. I take a bit of supplements; 100% Gold Whey Protein (short periods, 3 shakes per day), 100% Gold Whey Protein Casein (long, 1 shake before going to bed), creatine-capsules—best brand on the market (6 per day), no-Explode (pre-workout shake).

Xxxx is working in the fire brigade and has become a real fitness freak, we are working out together. He's tattooed half his body . . . xxxx is a lawyer in the Defense Department, his girlfriend is pregnant. Xxxx just moved in with xxxx (she has a kid from another relationship), but the relationship went to hell a couple of days ago. We're still a close group (including some others), with the exception of xxxx, who's isolated himself in Drammen with the new girlfriend.

Concerning the financial and political outlook for Western Europe as well as the United States, it looks as if a lot will happen over the next two years. Groruddalen (Oslo East) has unofficially been declared an area of cultural catastrophy (Muslim enclave with part Sharia laws) and there is a mass fleeing of Norwegians from this area. The situation is the same in most European big cities (especially in France but also in Sweden, UK, Germany). As an example there are now more than 800 no-go zones in France . . . double of what it was only 10 years ago. As an example there were Muslim riots outside of Göteborg a few days ago where they set fire to cars, buildings, etc. This is now happening on a weekly basis all over Western Europe (with the exception of Norway due to the fact that the state is managing the 3000 billion oil fund). This is called;

low-intensity Jihad. There has been an extreme evolution in this area the last 10 years and a lot is pointing at a possible civil war long term in and around the European capitals. Some claim it's already started, but it will escalate gradually in line with the Muslim demographic expansion (the mass immigration is continuing since 80% of the political parties still support multiculturalism (cultural Marxism), combined with the Muslim birthrate of +3). Oh well. Ignorance is a bliss and 90% don't even want to think of this at the moment . . . :D

The U.S. situation is not directly comparable as most Asian/Africans over there are non–Muslim, so that will likely limit the potential conflict. In any case, I would make sure I settle down in a heavily European enclave in Los Angeles (with many NRA members<3), faaar away from the nearest African or Asian enclave . . . Because WHEN the U.S. goes bankrupt (officially), the government will have no choice but to cut all social welfare, resulting in extremely violent riots (up to 10 times as violent as what you experienced in the 90s). I'm stressing the fact that this may possibly take longer than 24 months, but it's better to be safe than sorry:)) I do not at all mean to stress you guys, there is no necessity to think of such things all the time, but keep the information in the back of your mind.

No matter what, I'm proud of how well you guys are doing!:) Keep at it, we'll speak soon, Elisabeth!

Anders

And it's correct, that email was very generic, haha!:D

ACQUIRING WEAPONS AND AMMUNITION

On February 19, 2011, Oslo Pistol Club wrote:

Hi Anders,

We've received feedback from the police that you have applied for (permission to buy) a 9mm weapon on the background of the "NAIS" program. They are skeptical to this justification. If you had specified "Military field," or heavy pistol it would unproblematic. NAIS, even NAIS in heavy caliber is probably too new for them. It's only this year that NAIS has become a recognized training. Do you have weapons of heavy caliber already? Everything from caliber 38 and above is allowed to use in NAIS, so if you already possess a weapon of this category you're unlikely to get permission for another, unless you have participated in enough

*competitions (10) with the weapon of subject. In that case, you will get permission
to buy an extra weapon. Did we sign the additional declaration from the club?*

   Kind regards,

   Xxxxx, Oslo Pistol Club

∞

To: <contact@aseutra.fi>
Sent: Wednesday, March 30, 2011 11:28 PM
Subject: Palautelomake
Name: Anders Breivik E-mail: breivikanders@hotmail.com

   *Hello, After discussing with your supplier of supressors [sic] in Norway I
have purchased a jet-Z CQB-BL cal. 5.56 mm supressor (with BL mounting
collar). They said this would fit my Ruger Mini 14 Ranch rifle. In this context
I have just had the gunsmith remove the ruger front sight. However; as the BL
mounting collar does not fit I googled for possible solutions and found out that I
would need a mil spec A1 or A2 flash hider. So my question is; do you have any
idea where I can order this online and are there any available for Ruger Mini
14 Ranch rifle? I assume there is no other way to get your supressor to attach
to the rifle. It would be a real shame if I was unable to attach it as I waited 5
months for the supressor and it cost 700 Euro. Hope to hear from you soon. Best
regards, Anders Breivik Oslo Norway*

∞

From: contact@aseutra.fi
To: breivikanders@hotmail.com
Subject: Re: Palautelomake
Date: Thu, 31 Mar 2011 10:47:10 +0300

   *Mr. Breivik, Is your Mini 14 Ranch rifle now threaded for the 1/2»x28
UNEF thread? As if I recall correctly, it does not have a thread from the fac-
tory. The BoreLock mounting collar is intended for rifles with the 1/2»x28
UNEF thread. Primarily the intended weapons are AR15, M16, M4 and
HK416 rifles and carbines. The reason for the BL-mounting collar is if an end
user has for example a Vortex flash hider, he can still use that flash hider and*

be able to mount our BL-equipped suppressors. I can look which Finnish shops might have the A1/A2 bird carge flash hiders and I would suggest you to contact Norwegian shops that sell for example AR15 type rifles. Please send me an e mail if you can not locate one there. Best Regards! xxxxxxxxxxxxx

∞

From: Anders Breivik <breivikanders@hotmail.com>
Date: Thu, 31 Mar 2011 14:49:10 +0200
To: <contact@aseutra.fi>
Subject: RE: Locate a European supplier of an A1/A2 flash hider or alternatively a thread adapter?

Dear Mr. xxxxxxxx AR-15s are not readily available for civilians in Norway (and most European countries) so many people select the "poor-mans AR-15" (Ruger Mini 14) :-). And you are correct; it does not have a 1/2»x28 UNEF thread. Here is a diameter illustration of the Ruger Mini 14 Ranch barrel: (link has been removed) I have done extensive research online and with Norwegian accessory suppliers and I have not managed to locate a A1/A2 bird carge flash hider that fits a Ruger Mini 14 (and most flash hiders do not contain A1/A2 in product description) nor a thread adapter. There are a couple of flash hiders for Ruger but I do not know if they are A1/A2 or if they are adaptible with your supressor. I did find something that may prove to become a solution; a thread adapter for .223, but the US store does not sell to Europeans; Steel Muzzle Thread Adapter For .223 Caliber Rifles http://www.m1surplus.com/index.php?main_page=index&cPath=68 69&ze nid=03vj4312vfe4dcrt59bq4gde26 The following only works for pre-2005 rifles (and I have the newest—version 581 series (2010). http://www.midwaynorge.com/apps/eproductpage.exe/showproduct?SaleItem1D=415123 http://www.midwaynorge.com/apps/eproductpage.exe/showproduct?SaleItemID=423746 Theoretically, it shouldnt be very complicated to create a universal .223 thread adapter (tightened with 4-8 screws) that is designed to fit your supressor but I havent managed to locate one. I would imagine that creating such an adapter (and making it available) would contribute to help your company penetrate new markets and as such, would be a very positive factor. In any case; I would be really grateful if you could help me find a solution (by finding a supplier of a A1/A2 flash hider or a thread adapter that fits the Ruger Mini 14 Ranch rifle). Alternatively, I would also welcome an improvised solution if no commercial solutions are available (I assume that duct tape or any other material would perhaps be to risky to work as an improvised adapter if the diameter was equivalent to that of a A1/A2 flash hider?). Hope to hear from you soon. Thanks and best regards,

Anders Breivik

∞

From: contact@aseutra.fi
To: breivikanders@hotmail.com
Subject: Re: Locate a European supplier of an A1/A2 flash hider or alternatively a thread adapter?
Date: Thu, 31 Mar 2011 16:22:19 +0300

Mr. Breivik, I am sorry for your situation, but then you have been sold a product to a weapon that it is not intended for. With regards to possible adapters, when you start putting more parts in between the barrel and the suppressor, the chances of the suppressor not aligning correctly can increase. How is the Ruger barrel fixed to the receiver? If a gunsmith can easily remove it, the easiest solution is to thread the barrel to 1/2»x28 UNEF. Then the only thing you need is an A1 or A2 flash hider for example. I can help you out with regards to the flash hider, if necessary I can send one of ours.

Take Care! xxxxxxxxxxxx [. . .]

∞

Fra: Anders Breivik <breivikanders@hotmail.com>
Dato: Fri, 1 Apr 2011 23:17:02 +0200
Til: <contact@aseutra.fi>
Emne: RE: Locate a European supplier of an Al/A2 flash hider or alternatively a thread adapter?

Mr. xxxxxx Thanks for the feedback, I appreciate it. I returned the suppressor to the supplier today as a 14 mm diameter A1 flash hider won't be able to fit my 16 diameter Ruger Mini 14 Ranch.Perhaps it would be possible to fix by a gunsmith if the diameter measurements were reversed. Regardless; you should consider manufacturing flashhiders (as a Primary fastening/adapter system perhaps) in different sizes (12-20 mm), f example for the 10-15 most popular civilian semi-rifles in the future It would be a great way to penetrate new markets and contribute to create a new universal standard for suppressor fastening systems, which would then contribute to marked your "easy-fit" suppressors.

Thanks and best regards,
Anders Breivik Oslo, Norway

∞

Breivik used the affiliation with the pistol club to be able to purchase the guns he needed for his massacre. Although he wrote numerous e-mails to organize a shooting competition, he wasn't interested in participating. So he wrote this message:

From: Anders Behring <anders.behring@hotmail.com>
Date: Fri, 8 Apr 2011 13:56:09 +0200
To: xxxxxxxxxxxxx
Subject: RE: SV: SV: Distribution of shooting places/stands (standplasser) + miscellaneous

Hi, I caught a bug from a family member a couple of days ago and as a result I'm feeling weak and unable to do anything. I really hope I'll be better by Sat/ Sun but I've gotten worse today, Friday. Unfortunately, I won't be able to make it to the shooting competition this weekend as I don't expect I will be well enough in two days:-(I do hope you guys will have a fantastic time!

Kind regards,
Anders Behring Breivik

ATTEMPTING TO CONNECT

Breivik wrote numerous e-mails to his idol Fjordman—using the name Andreas Borg—trying to make a connection. Breivik did not know Fjordman's identity until it was revealed during the trial. To my knowledge, and according to Fjordman himself, Fjordman only responded three times to Breivik's e-mails. Breivik also contacted others who he thought shared his ideology, such as Hans Rustad (owner of Dokument.no) and English Defence League.

Fjordman, I've now worked fulltime more than three years on a solution based creation (the compendium written in English). I've focused on contribution on areas on the sideline of your main area. Much of the information is unknown for most people, even you. If you send me an email to year2083@gmail.com I will email you an electronic version once I'm done. Norway has, for me, been completely uninteresting until now. The main focus should be on an intellectual platform consolidation of European conservative cultural organizations/individuals. This alliance should have a main focus of de-legitimize multiculturalism (cultural Marxism) to the "European hate-ideology" it really is. Its goal (or indirect result) is as known to completely destroy Western civilization, sovereign states, Western culture/traditions, Christianity—European/Norwegian identity. If this main work is finalized it will facilitate a Marxist super-state (EUSSR) without the necessary culturally conservative/nationalistic components, which could have prevented Islam from dominating this new ethnicity.

∞

On Fri, Sep 11, 2009 at 1:48 AM, Fjordman Blogger <fjordman555@ gmail.com> wrote:

Hey from Fjordman, You wanted to reach me?

∞

From: Andreas Borg <year2083@gmail.com>
Date: 2009/9/11
Subject: Re: Hei
To: Fjordman Blogger <fjordman555@gmail.com>

Hey:)) Already have the email address to Gates of Vienna, but now I can also use this one. The book is ready but it will take a few months to prepare some practical issues before publishing. Will send it electronically to a few. Defeating Eurabia is great, but it'll take time before books like this one will be able to overcome censorship in an efficient way. I've chosen free distribution as a counter strategy, I've been farming email addresses for a couple of weeks (everything from

culturally conservative members of parliament in Armenia to New Zealand),
haha, the truth must come out;p Let me know and I will send you my email
database;)

AB

∞

From Breivik in 2009:

LOL@ your tourettes comment, insanely good :O

Hoping you come on Thursday (you should jump in your car from trondheimi:D)

By the way, I chatted a lot with a FB friend, xxxxx, it turns out she was
dating your best friend, xxxxx. Small world . . .

Add me on FB you slacker:D andersbehring@hotmail.com

∞

Response from Fjordman:

I would appreciate if you say as little as possible about me publicly. I might
go public one day with my full name, but I would like to wait a bit until I have
finished what I'm writing on now.

F.

∞

On September 15, 2009 12:54, Breivik wrote to Hans Rustad (editor of
Dokument.no):

Hello:) Don't know if you have followed the discussion http://www.document.
no/2009/09/en_streng_som_dirrer.

Where do you stand with regards to becoming the editor of a new national
culturally conservative media company with possible investors from the Progres-
sive Party and other strategic investors? This election show that we cannot live
with today's one-sided media coverage (full war on the Progressive Party (FrP)).
They managed to reduce FrP with 6-7% in four weeks.

Kind regards,
Anders Behring

∞

From: xxxxxxxxxx
To: andersbehring@hotmail.com
Subject: Re: The new Aftenposten
Date: Tue, 15 Sep 2009 14:12 +0200

Anders Behring oh yes! I did follow the debate and my position is that I'm non-committal but open. With non-committal I mean that there has been previously speculations and dreams that have turned to be just that, dreams. However, if you have something more concrete I'm open. There is no doubt that your analysis is correct. If we're going to win in 2013 we must have powerful press. That's really the disadvantage for FrP. They are being harassed and they have no third party to back them up. It's not enough to have their own website. Even with limited means it should be possible to accomplish much.

What do you have in mind? Please use (email address removed) in the future.

hans

∞

From: Anders Behring ‹andersbehring@hotmail.com›
Date: 2009/9/15
Subject: RE: The new Aftenposten

Hi, It's great that you are open to this. My thought was to arrange a meeting with myself and Geir Mo to discuss FrP's view with regards to this alternative. I know that they have wanted this for several years and I think they will be enthusiastic about this alternative. I will keep you updated as soon as I have discussed this with him. I have many contacts in FrP as I was an active member and officer for several task groups. I became a member when I was 16, so 14 years ago:) This has given me an oversight of political background for central editors in Norwegian press (such as the chief editor of Aftenposten). Do you have information regarding political background of others? I am sure you have an idea, but a more certain overview would be better.

Anders

∞

On October 28, 2009, at 19:00, Anders Behring wrote:

Hi:)

I feel that I have to call out to you about something. You can with simple steps double (maybe even triple) dokument's penetration capacity. By adding a standard script to each article (share on facebook/twitter icon) many will surely spread the articles more than 30-100 facebook networks depending on the article. When the articles have been shared, others will spread them as they will appear on each person's network page (Norwegian articles will find they're way to Sweden and Denmanrk). I estimate with high likelihood that the current readers of 3000 will become 9000 without increasing your costs. You can find the script here: http:// addthis.com/bookmark.php

You can also find it at the bottom of this page: http://shine.yahoo.com/channel/ life/5-simple-ways-to-share-articles-online-508419/

If you have any problems doing this you can easily hire a programmer on http:// www.scriptlance.com who can do it for you. I've often used this service (to hire programmers for a low price) and you can get tasks like this done for >50USD.

Kind regards,

Anders Behring

∞

From: xxxxxxxxxxxxx
To: andersbehring@hotmail.com
Date: Thu, 29 Oct 2009 06:52:41 +0100
Subject: Re: Document Fra 3000 til <9000

thanks so much for the tip, I've forwarded this to the it-man, we're in the process of transferring to wordpress, but it's possible we can already do this. thanks. hans r

∞

From: andersbehring@hotmail.com
Date: Thu, 29 Oct 2009 22:06:35 +0100

To: xxxxxxxxxxxxx
Subject: RE: Document Fra 3000 til <9000

That was quick!:D Great! The most important subjects can now be circulated in a much more efficient way. :))

∞

From: Anders Behring <andersbehrIng@hotmail.com>
To: fjordman555@gmail.com
Date: Fri, Dec 11, 2009 at 10:07 AM

Hey, I might as well give you a summary. Not much happened at the meeting, but more people came than expected (About 20, of these 18 men, 2 women:D). Hans and a couple of the others are afraid to consolidate in an efficient way. They're afraid that they're participating in creating a "monster" they will lose control over later on. They do not wish to support FrP to make a national newspaper and also do not wish any connection to other established culturally conservative organizations. Still thinking of helping them get financial solutions but will never write there, just going to be censored lol. I'm expecting feedback from FrP soon, I know they have been wanting an alterantive for several years (they have been wanting to develop Progress, the party's newspaper) and I'm exciting to hear what they answer. In January I'm going on a trip around Europe to speak about my book—2083. The book is very strategy-oriented, among other about how to consolidate modern culturally conservative movements/parties, which retorick/political doctrines are tactical and that will be in tune with future development, etc. Other parts of the book project future scenarios based on pre-defined demographic development (conflict vs. elements relating to historical examples as Lebanon's demographic development, civil war when the Muslims reach 50-60%). Which plan of action future culturally conservative movements must have in given hypothetical situations. For instance, when the first regime breaks free from the dominance in about 20-70 years. What consequenses they must expect and which counter-actions they can implement based on different scenarious. A lot will appear as science fiction for most people today:). Many of the basic methods are in principal a copy of the Marxists work from 50-68 up until today, very efficient if presented correctly. Have been working on the compendium full-time for almost three years, and it's now 1150 pages. At the moment, I'm working on email farming via facebook (have accomplished a database of several *thousand). The strategy is really to invite several thousand expedient conservative leads (from targeted FB groups) who will receive an electronic edition of the book for free, in order to improve the penetration rate in the appropriate audience—targeted marketing (political involved culturally conservative around Europe). It's exciting with your new book:)) There is a big awakening happening right now and we should especially watch Marseilles (38% atm) that will be a Muslim city within 20 years. I think the development in the UK, or France will be decisive in Europe's fate. But the consolidation will no matter what be important in all regions and the most important task for Norwegians/Swedes will be to create a culturally conservative national newspaper that can contribute to get the truth out. Have you mapped and actively tried to contact minority publishers in Europe/the United States? As far as I know, Defeating Eurabia is within legal limits so it should be possible to publish it in a more efficient way? By the way, never have someone culturally conservative in Northern Europe done so much as you for so many for so little in return;) You're goind to have to be recognized at some point. But it's perhaps not strategically right to focus on etno-centrism at this time. It will of course be essential in a conflict situation, but will give too much ammunition to your critics if you focus too much on that. Keep up the good work:) If you're ever in Oslo, let me know and we can go out for a couple of beers. All my friends are a-political and there are few culturally conservative intellectuals, to say the least, lol:D I've worked several years for FrP and to be honest I have to say that I've not met one person who impressed me< 3*

There are of course "beasts" such as Siv, Geir Mo, and some others, but they would never dare to speak out about real politically incorrect problems. People do not want unnecessary risks (including me, really) and they remain therefore to a great extent in the closet;)

∞

From: Anders Behring <andersbehring@hotmail.com>
Date: January 22, 2010 07.13.57 GMT +01:00
To: xxxxxxxxxxxxxxx
Subject: Response from FrP—further regarding independent investors

Hi Hans:)

I've now received feedback from Geir (finally;p). I only introduced you/document as a general consept based on certain factors. I registered that you, as a starting point, are uninterested in any contact with political parties, however, I feel that it won't hurt to collect potential partners' thoughts around the establishment of a culturally conservative publication.

What remains now is to contact independent investors and existing groups of owners of related editorials/publications. I'm considering contacting Hegnar and a couple of others to try to sell the concept. Will keep you posted if I chose to make a move. Do you have any updates on your end that you would like to share? I hope you haven't lost respect for me with regards to earlier possibly "lightely considered) comments from my part? ;o You have to remember that I have no other wish than that Dokument is successful:) Anyhow, I'm leaving for my book-promo within the end of February, and will possibly be away for 6 months.

Kind regards,

Anders

∞

From: Breivik
Date: Thursday, February 11, 2010 at 9:35AM:

Hey again Fjordman:-)

Thought I would send you a couple of suggestions. I have approximately 5000 contacts on Facebook now, absolutely all the best (well connected) patriotically oriented in Europe (East/West), US, Canada, New Zealand, and Aussie, etc. (even South Africa). You will loose terrain if you do not use FB as all other European intellectuals do. I will happily share my two networks with you (I have two profiles). I could, for instance, give you the 200 absolutely best connected FB patriots in Europe and in the US. Many of these would, by the way, let you post your articles on their pages, myself included. You would hence reach up to 30,000 to 50,000 by simply posting on a few high quality profiles. In addition there are twenty-something FB groups that are worth mentioning.

Many of the contacts I know reasonably well are running many of these groups and would with pleasure let you contribute. Just let me know :-)

My compendium will be finished within a couple of weeks after three years of work. Will send you an electronic version when it's done. You are going to like it;-)

Have given up on dokument.no. Hans is censoring even the most moderate contributions that share your ideology:P Anders

∞

Response from Fjordman, Thursday, February 11 at 10:41PM:

Thanks for the offer. But I am not planning on using FB directly at the moment. I will be writing on dokument.no for now, but so many of my comments have been censored that I might not bother for long. F.

∞

On March 9, 2011, Breivik reached out to English Defence League (EDL). He posted the following on their forum, using the pseudonym "Sigurd":

Hello. To you all good English men and women, just wanted to say that you're a blessing to all in Europe, in these dark times all of Europe are looking to you in surch of inspiration, courage and even hope that we might turn this evil trend with islamisation all across our continent. Well, just wanted to say keep up the good work, it's good to see others that care about their country and heritage.

All the best to you all

Sigurd

∞

"Sigurd" receives a response asking if he's a member of the Norwegian Defence League.

I was, but the site has been put down now. There was to be a demo in Oslo on the 26 of February but after the police security service put us on the "danger-list" the internet site was sadly shut down.

The biggest problem in norway is that there is no real free press, there is a left-wing angle on all the political topics so most people are going around like idiots. And ofcourse with our norwegian labour party beeing in power for most of the last 50 years dont help. but i i think there is an awakening now, at least I hope so. Do some of you know the truth about what happened to the ndl, there was some clames that neo-nazis had hijacked the organisation, but on the ndl site I cant really say I noticed anything like that. So my guess is that there were some kind of police pressure to stop the movement. Anyone here heard anything?

I've seen with my own eyes what has happened to england, I was in bradford some years ago, me and a friend walked down to the football stadium of bradford, real «nice» neighborhood, same thing in the suburbs of london. Well thinking about taking a little trip over the sea and join you in a demo, would be nice with a norwegian flag alongside with union jack or the english flag, that is if a norwegian would be welcome of course?

∞

He receives a message saying that he's welcome to join them, to which he responds:

I hoped so:) it's our common struggle against the islamofacists.

∞

One of the members of EDL, with user name "Concerned," says the following:

Bravo sigurd admire your views and courage. no surrender and welcome.

BREIVIK'S LAST EMAIL CONTAINING THE MANIFESTO

At 14:08 PM, just one hour before the explosion in Oslo, Breivik receives his own e-mail with his manifesto. It reads as follows:

From: Andrew Berwick <behbreiv@online.no>
Reply to: noreply <noreply@facebookmail.com>
Dato: Fri, 22 Jul 2011 14:08:50 +0200
Subject: The Islamisation of Western Europe and the status of the resistance Movements.

Western European patriot,

I'm hereby sending you my new compendium (3 books); «2083—A European Declaration of Independence», in Word 97 format, which includes the following main topics: 1. The ongoing Islamisation of Western Europe 2.The current state of the Western European Resistance Movements (anti-Marxist/anti-Jihad movements) 3. Solutions for Western Europe and how we, the cultural conservative resistance, should move forward in the coming decades 4. And covering all, *highly relevant topics including solutions and strategies for all of the 8 different political fronts The compendium/book presents advanced ideological, practical, tactical, organisational and rhetorical solutions and strategies for all patriotic minded individuals/movements. The book will be of great interest to you whether you are a moderate or a more dedicated cultural conservative/ nationalist. After years of work the first edition of the compendium «2083» is completed. If you have received this e-mail and book, you are either a former Facebook friend or you are the friend of my Facebook friend. If you are concerned for the future of Western Europe you will definitely find the information both interesting and highly relevant. I have spent several years researching and compiling the information and I have spent most of my hard earned funds in this process (in excess of 300 000 Euros). I do not want any compensation for the work as it is a gift to you, as a fellow patriot. The content of the compendium truly belongs to everyone and is available to be distributed non-commercially in any way or form. In fact, I ask only one favour of you; I ask that you distribute this book to everyone you know. Please do not think that others will take care of it. Sorry to be blunt, but it does not work out that way. If we, the Western European Resistance, fall or become apathetic, then Western Europe will fall, and your liberties with it. It is essential and very important that everyone is at least presented with the truth before our systems come crashing down within 2 to 7 decades. So again, I humbly ask you to re-distribute the book to as many patriotic minded individuals you can. I am 100% certain that the distribution of this compendium to a large portion of European patriots will contribute to ensure our victory in the end. Because within these three books lies the tools required to win the ongoing Western European cultural war, the war against the anti-European hate ideology known as multiculturalism. Multiculturalism (cultural Marxism/political correctness), as you might know, is the root cause of the ongoing islamisation of Europe which has resulted in the ongoing oloniz olonization of Europe through demographic warfare and conquest. This compendium presents the solutions and explains exactly what is required of each and every one of us in the coming decades. Everyone can and should contribute in one way or another, it's just a matter of will.<*

I hope you enjoy this compendium, It currently offers the most comprehensive database of solution oriented subjects. As mentioned, I only ask one thing from you; that you distribute this book to your friends and ask them to forward it to «their» friends, especially to individuals who have a patriot mindset. Please help us and help yourself, your family and friends by contributing to spread the tools which will ensure our victory; for the truth must be known. . . . It is not only our right but also our duty to contribute to preserve our identity, our culture and our national overeignty by preventing the ongoing Islamisation. There is no Resistance Movement if individuals like us refuse to contribute. . . . Time is of the essence. We have only a few decades to consolidate a sufficient level of resistance before our major cities are completely demographically overwhelmed by Muslims. Ensuring the successful distribution of this compendium to as many Europeans as humanly possible will significantly contribute to our success. It may be the only way to avoid our present and future dhimmitude (enslavement) under Islamic majority in our own countries. I have been unable to send this compendium to many people, for various reasons, so I truly hope you will be willing to contribute.

This compendium is sent to you in the word 2007—docx format. If you do not have MS Word 2007 or newer you May get a "2007 Word Viewer" at no cost at the main Microsoft site or just get a trial version. (. . .) For translation from English to another language I would recommend Google translation engine as a short term solution.

Sincere and patriotic regards,

Andrew Berwick, London, England—2011

Justiciar Knight Commander for Knights Templar Europe and one of several leaders of the National and pan-European Patriotic Resistance Movement. With the assistance from brothers and sisters in England, France, Germany, Sweden, Austria, Italy, Spain, Finland, Belgium, the Netherlands, Denmark, the US etc.

IN MEMORIAM: THE HUMAN PRICE

Every crime is about more than the perpetrator. One can debate endlessly what causes lone wolves like Anders Breivik to strike. However, until these killers are identified and stopped before they plan, carry out, and attack, the price of human life will escalate. In Breivik's case, the cost was high—seventy-seven lives—human beings who have not received the same attention their murderer has.

VICTIMS OF THE BOMBING IN OSLO CENTER

Hanna M. Orvik Endresen, 61 years old, female, Oslo.

Kai Hauge, 32 years old, male, Oslo.

Ida Marie Hill, 34 years old, female, Oslo.

Anne Lise Holter, 51 years old, female, Våler Østfold.

Tove Åshill Knutsen, 56 years old, female, Oslo.

Jon Vegard Lervåg, 32 years old, male, Oslo.

Hanne Ekroll Løvlie, 30 years old, female, Oslo.

Kjersti Berg Sand, 26 years old, female, Nord-Odal.

SLAUGHTER AT UTØYA

17:21: On arrival at the dock on Utøya

1. Trond Berntsen, male, 51 years old. Shot five times, two bullets in the head and neck; third bullet in the right arm, fourth and fifth in the back. Immediate death from the injuries to the head and chest.

2. Monica Elisabeth Bøsei, female, 45 years old. Shot three times. Two bullets entered the head and brain, one in the back. Immediate death from the injuries to the head.

3. Rune Halvdal, male, 43 years old, shot five times. First bullet hit the right side of the back, the second hit the stomach and right lung; third bullet hit chest and right lung. Fourth and fifth bullets to the head. Immediate death from the injuries to the head.

17:23: In front of the main building

4. Hanne Anette Balch Fjalestad, female, 43 years old. Shot three times, one time in the back hitting both lungs; two times in the head. Immediate death from the injuries to the head and chest.

5. Snorre Haller, male, 30 years old. Shot three times, one in the back and two to the head. Immediate death from the injuries to the head.

6. Rolf Christopher Johansen Perreau, male, 25 years old. Shot three times, one in the back, and two shots to the head. Immediate death from the injuries to the head.

17:25: The camp surrounding the cafeteria

7. Lejla Selaci, female, 17 years old. Shot twice in the head. Immediate death from injuries to the head.

8. Steinar Jessen, male, 16 years old. Shot twice. First bullet entered left arm before entering the chest. Second bullet to the head. Immediate death from injuries to the head and chest.

9. Brigitte Smetbak, female, 15 years old. Shot three times, one bullet entering the back of the right knee, one hitting the right calf, and the third bullet hitting the left shoulder. Death from external bleeding after hours of agony.

10. Gunnar Linaker, male, 23 years old. Shot twice, with one bullet to the back and one to the head. Died the following day in the hospital from the injuries to the head.

    In addition, six boys and girls were wounded by gunshots in the camp.

17:26: Cafeteria building

11. Margrethe Bøyum Kløven, female, 16 years old. Shot three times, with first bullet to the right arm, the second in the right thigh, and the last in the head. Immediate death from the injuries to the head.

12. Silje Merete Fjellbu, female, 17 years old. Shot six times, died quickly from injuries to the head.

13. Guro Vartdal Håvoll, female, 18 years old. Shot four times, once behind the left knee, once in the right hip, once in the right flank, and the last bullet in the head. Quick death following the damage to the head.

14. Ronja Søttar Johansen, female, 17 years old. Shot four times, once in the left shoulder, once in the back, twice in the head. Immediate death from injuries to the head and stomach.

15. Mona Abdinur, female, 18 years old. Shot three times, once in the right arm, in the thorax, and once in the head. Quick death from the injuries to the head.

16. Sondre Kjøren, male, 17 years old. Shot six times after having thrown himself at Breivik, trying to disarm him. Died quickly from injuries to the head.

17. Bendik Rosnæs Ellingsen, male, 18 years old. Shot eight times, in the left thigh, left leg, the thorax, twice in the left arm, the left hand, and twice in the head. Quick death from injuries to the head.

    In the small room, three additional girls and two boys were injured from bullets.

18. Eivind Hovden, male, 15 years old. Shot three times, once in the thorax, twice in the head. Immediate death from injuries to the head.

19. Lene Maria Bergum, female, 19 years old. Shot four times, in the stomach, shoulder, throat, and in the mouth. Quick death from injuries to the head.

20. Elisabeth Trønnes Lie, female, 16 years old. Shot three times, in the right shoulder, twice in the head. Died quickly from injuries to the head.

    In addition, in the big room, one girl was injured from a gunshot.

21. Henrik André Pedersen, male, 27 years old. Shot three times, the first bullet hit left jaw, the second hit the nose, and the third the right eye. Quick death from injuries to the head.

22. Ida Beathe Rogne, female, 17 years old. Shot twice. The first bullet went through the right hand, hitting the side of the head. The second entered the right side of the head. Immediate death due to the injuries to the head.

23. Aleksander Aas Eriksen, male, 16 years old. Shot six times in different areas, once in the head. Quick death from the injuries to the head.

    Breivik leaves the cafeteria, starts walking around the island.

17:30: The Love Trail

24. Eva Kathinka Lütken, female, 17 years old. Shot twice, in the shoulder and throat. Died quickly from her injuries.

25. Tore Eikeland, male, 21 years old. Shot once in the head, bullet entering the right temple. Immediate death from injuries to the head.

26. Tarald Kuven Mjelde, male, 18 years old. Shot five times, once in the left thigh, once in the back, hitting the heart, once in the throat, twice in the head. Quick death from injuries to the heart and head.

27. Maria Maagerø Johannesen, female, 17 years old. Shot three times, in the right thigh, in the back, and in the head. Quick death from injuries to the head.

28. Monica Iselin Didriksen, female, 18 years old. Shot three times, once in the right hand, once in the back, and once to the head. Died quickly from injuries to the head.

29. Åsta Sofie Helland Dahl, female, 16 years old. Shot three times, in the left ankle, in the back, and in the head. Immediate death due to the injuries to the head.

30. Anders Kristiansen, male, 18 years old. Shot twice, once in the right ankle and once in the head. Died quickly from injuries to the head.

31. Bano Abobakar Rashid, female, 18 years old. Died quickly from two gunshot wounds to the head.
32. Andreas Edvardsen, male, 18 years old. Shot three times, once in the head, and twice in the neck. Died quickly from injuries to the head.
33. Silje Stamneshagen, female, 18 years old. Shot five times, once in the left thigh, in the back, in the throat, and twice in the head. Died quickly from injuries to the head.

The hill below the trail

34. Sondre Furuseth Dale, male, 17 years old. Shot four times, once in the back, once in the stomach, and twice in the right flank under the armpit. Died quickly, following hemorrhaging from wounds in the chest. His body was found in the water, thirty meters from the beach.
35. Simon Sæbø, male, 18 years old. Shot twice, once in the right knee, once in the back. Died quickly from injuries to the torso.
36. Modupe Ellen Awoyemi, female, 15 years old. Shot four times, in the neck, back, and flanks. Died quickly from injuries to the neck and back.
37. Sharidyn Meegan Svebakk-Bøhn, female, 14 years old. Shot twice in the left shoulder. Death caused by external and internal bleeding.
38. Marianne Sandvik, female, 16 years old. Shot once in the left groin. Bled to death.

    In addition, five girls and three boys were wounded on this part of the trail.

17:40-17:45

39. Gizem Dogan, female, 17 years old. Shot twice in the head. Immediate death from injuries to the head.
40. Johannes Buø, male, 14 years old. Shot three times, twice in the head, once in the throat. Died quickly from injuries to the head.

17:59: Breivik calls the police emergency line to give himself up
18:01 Breivik continues his massacre

41. Even Flugstad Malmedal, male, 18 years old. Died quickly from one shot to the head.

42. Syvert Knudsen, male, 17 years old. Shot three times, twice in the head, once in the back. Died quickly from injuries to the head and torso.

43. Synne Røyneland, female, 18 years old. Shot three times in the head. Died quickly due to injuries to the head.

18:08 Bolsjevika

44. Torjus Jacobsen Blattmann, male, 17 years old. Died immediately from one bullet to the head.

45. Ingrid Berg Heggelund, female, 18 years old. Shot three times, in the left hand, in the back, and in the head. Immediate death from injuries to the head, throat, stomach, and torso.

46. Isabel Victoria Green Sogn, female, 17 years old. Shot three times, in the left shoulder, in the left breast, and in the head. Immediate death from injuries to the head.

47. Karar Mustafa Qasim, male, 19 years old. Shot four times, one bullet hit the left buttock, one the left hand, and two bullets hit the back. Died quickly from injuries to the torso.

48. Carina Borgund, female, 18 years old. Shot three times, twice in the head and once in the back. Died quickly from injuries to the head.

18:13 Pompehuset (Pumping station)

49. Tina Sukuvara, female, 18 years old. Immediate death from one gunshot wound to the head.

50. Ruth Benedichte Vatndal Nilsen, female, 15 years old. Shot once in the stomach. Died in one minute from injuries to the stomach.

51. Henrik Rasmussen, male, 18 years old. Shot three times, in the back and head. Died quickly from injuries to the head and torso.

52. Espen Jørgensen, male, 17 years old. Shot four times, in the left hand, left shoulder, lower back, and left flank. Died quickly from injuries to the torso and stomach.

53. Porntip (Pamela) Ardam, female, 21 years old. Shot three times, to the right leg, in the left hand, and in the head. Immediate death from injuries to the head.

54. Thomas Margido Antonsen, male, 16 years old. Shot twice, in the back and head. Died quickly from injuries to the head.

55. Ismail Haji Ahmed, male, 19 years old. Immediate death from one gunshot wound to the head.

56. Fredrik Lund Schetne, male, 18 years old. Shot in the left eye, causing massive injuries to the brain. Died immediately.

57. Hanne Kristine Fridtun, female, 19 years old. Shot three times, in the left elbow, in the chest, and in the head. Died quickly from injuries to the head.

58. Emil Okkenhaug, male, 15 years old. Shot three times, in the upper part of the arm and twice in the head. Immediate death from injuries to the head.

59. Håvard Vederhus, male, 21 years old. Shot four times, in the head, in the back, and twice in the neck. Died quickly from injuries to the neck.

60. Victoria Stenberg, female, 17 years old. Shot three times, in the buttocks, in the throat, and in the back. Died quickly from injuries in the throat and torso.

61. Sverre Flåte Bjørkavåg, male, 28 years old. Immediate death from two gunshot wounds to the head.

62. Diderik Aamodt Olsen, male, 19 years old. Shot once in the head, rendering him unconscious. Death by drowning.

One additional girl and two boys were injured from bullets at the pumping station.

18:19 Breivik makes a call to the police
The South Tip of the Island

63. Tamta Lipartelliani, female, 23 years old. Shot twice in the back. Died after a few minutes following injuries to the back.

64. Kevin Daae Berland, male, 15 years old. Shot four times, in the right arm, the right hand, the throat, and in the head. Immediate death from injuries to the head and throat.

65. Karin Elena Holst, female, 15 years old. Died quickly from gunshot wound to the head.

66. Jamil Rafal Mohamad Jamil, female, 20 years old. Shot twice, in the right hand and shoulder. Died quickly from injuries to the head and throat.

67. Andrine Bakkene Espeland, female, 16 years old. Shot three times, in the left buttocks, in the chest, and in the neck. Died quickly from injuries to the head and chest.

Four more girls and one boy were injured at the South Tip.

68.

and

69. Andreas Dalby, male, 17 years old, and Birgitte Smetbak, female, 15 years old, died from a fall and/or drowning between 17:37 and 18:01.

∞

Any man's death diminishes me,
Because I am involved in mankind,
And therefore never send to know for whom the bell tolls;
It tolls for thee.

John Donne
"No Man Is An Island"